199 **EDITION**

The Zondervan
Church and Nonprofit Organization

Tax & Financial
Guide

Daniel D. Busby, CPA

ZondervanPublishingHouse
Grand Rapids, Michigan

A Division of HarperCollinsPublishers

THE ZONDERVAN CHURCH AND NONPROFIT ORGANIZATION TAX AND
FINANCIAL GUIDE: 1996 EDITION

For information write to:
Zondervan Publishing House
Grand Rapids, Michigan 49530

Publisher's note: This guide is published in recognition of the need for clarification of tax and other laws for churches and nonprofit organizations. Every effort has been made to publish a timely, accurate, and authoritative guide. The publisher, author, and the reviewers do not assume any legal responsibility for the accuracy of the text or any other contents.

Readers are cautioned that this book is sold with the understanding that the publisher is not rendering legal, accounting, or other professional service. Organizations with specific tax problems should seek the professional advice of a tax accountant or lawyer.

References to IRS forms and tax rates are derived from preliminary proofs of 1995 forms or 1994 forms. Some adaptation for changes may be necessary. These materials should be used solely as a guide in filling out 1995 tax and information returns. To obtain the final forms, schedules, and tables for filing returns and forms, contact the IRS or a public library.

ISBN 0-310-49701-9

Printed in the United States of America

95 96 97 98 99 / DH / 10 9 8 7 6 5 4 3 2 1

Contents . . .

1995 Tax Highlights 1

Financial Accountability 13
- Organizations promoting accountability 14
- Accountability to an independent board 14
- Accountability to donors 20
- Accountability to government 24

Tax Exemption 25
- Tax exemption for churches 26
- Advantages and limitations of tax exemption 27
- Starting a nonprofit 28
- Unrelated business income 32
- Private benefit and private inurement 39
- Filing federal returns 41
- Filing state returns 43
- Political activity 44

Compensation Planning 47
- Reasonable compensation 47
- Organization-provided housing 48
- Maximizing fringe benefits 51
- Nondiscrimination rules 60
- Paying employee expenses 61

Employer Reporting 65
- The classification of workers 65
- Reporting compensation 70
- Payroll tax withholding 70
- Depositing withheld payroll taxes 73
- Filing the quarterly payroll tax forms 74
- Filing the annual payroll tax forms 78
- Refunds and abatements 86

Information Reporting 87
- General filing requirements................................. 87
- Reporting on the receipt of funds........................ 89
- Reporting on the payment of funds...................... 91
- Summary of payment reporting requirements 97

Your Financial Records 99
- Budgeting... 99
- The money comes in 100
- The money goes out 107
- Accounting records 115
- Financial reports.. 118
- Audit guidelines 124
- Church internal audit guidelines 125

Charitable Gifts 129
- Percentage limitations 130
- Gift options 131
- What gifts are not tax-deductible? 134
- When is a gift tax-deductible? 135
- Gift reporting requirements............................. 137
- Receipting charitable contributions.................... 142
- Special charitable contribution issues 158

Insuring Your Organization 167
- Abuse or molestation insurance 168
- Automobile insurance 168
- COBRA 168
- Crime insurance 169
- Dental insurance 169
- Director's and officer's liability insurance 169
- Disability insurance...................................... 170
- General liability insurance 170
- Group life insurance...................................... 171
- Health insurance.. 171
- Key employee insurance 174
- Long-term care insurance................................ 174
- Professional liability insurance 174
- Property insurance.. 174

- Travel and accident insurance 175
- Umbrella liability insurance 175
- Workers' Compensation 175

Laws for Nonprofits 177
- Age discrimination 178
- Americans With Disabilities Act 178
- Canadian Goods and Services Tax 179
- Charitable solicitation 179
- Church-operated child care facilities 179
- Equal pay.. 180
- Environmental issues 180
- Fair Labor Standards Act 180
- Family and Medical Leave Act 182
- Immigration control 182
- Mailing at third-class rates 182
- National Child Care Act... 185
- Occupational Safety and Health Act 185
- Pregnancy discrimination... 185
- Racial discrimination 185
- Religious discrimination 186
- Sexual harassment.. 186
- State taxes and fees 186

Citations 189

Index.. 194

Ten Biggest Tax Mistakes 198

SPECIAL INDEX
FOR CHURCH TREASURERS
A guide within a guide

Employer identification numbers
        (Every church needs one)... **29**

Tax-exempt status
        Applying for tax-exempt status *(Not required but it may be
        appropriate)*.. **29**

Unrelated business income
        (Churches are not exempt although it is usually not a problem)......... **32**

Political activity
        (Churches are prohibited from participating in political campaigns).................. **44**

Compensation planning
        (Minimize taxable income by maximizing fringe benefits)
        Housing allowances **48**
        Vehicles provided to employees **51**
        Tax-sheltered annuity... **54**
        Dependent care assistance plan **55**
        Medical expense reimbursement plan.. **56**
        Loans to ministers... **57**
        Social security reimbursement... **58**
        Property transfers.. **59**
        Moving expenses **59**
        Allowances.. **60**
        Expense reimbursements **61**

Workers at the church
        (The classification of workers paid by the church is a critical issue)
        Employees **66**
        Independent contractors.. **66**
        Special tax provisions for ministers.. **68**
        Are ministers employees or independent contractors?.................... **69**
        Assignment of ministers **69**

Withholding FICA taxes **70**
Withholding federal income taxes **71**
Depositing withheld payroll taxes **73**
Filing quarterly payroll tax returns.. **74**
Filing Form W-2 .... **78**
Unemployment taxes **85**

Information return filings

(It is easy to overlook the filing of information returns)

Receipt of mortgage interest.. **89**
Real estate proceeds... **90**
Interest payments... **91**
Payments to nonresident aliens.. **93**
Payment for other services... **93**
Payment to volunteers.. **95**
Payment of moving expenses **96**

Financial records of the church

(Design a practical recordkeeping system that fits your church)

Budgeting.. **99**
Cash receipts... **100**
Cash disbursements **107**
Petty cash system **109**
Bank reconciliation... **114**
Accounting records... **115**
Financial reports **118**
Chart of accounts **119**
Audits of church records... **124**

Charitable contributions

(Help your donors obtain the maximum tax benefits from their gifts)

Types of charitable gifts **131**
Gifts that are not tax-deductible **134**
When is a gift tax-deductible?... **135**
Reporting gifts to the IRS... **137**
Letter to noncash donors **138**
Receipting charitable contributions... **142**
Gifts of $250 or more **142**

Part gift/part payment for goods and services 148

Church-operated schools 159

Contributions to support: specific workers 159

other than workers or the needy 160

the needy 160

Contributions designated for missionaries.. 162

Contributions by volunteers... 164

Insurance for the church

(An annual insurance review with a good agent or broker is a must)

Abuse and molestation.. 168

Automobile 168

Disability 170

General liability 170

Group life.. 171

Health.. 171

Professional liability 174

Property 174

Travel and accident... 175

Umbrella liability.. 175

Workers' Compensation 175

Key laws that apply to churches

(Though confusing or downright intimidating, you need a basic understanding of certain laws)

Fair Labor Standards Act.. 180

Immigration control 182

Mailing at third-class rates 182

National Child Care Act 185

State taxes and fees... 186

Sample Board Resolutions

Conflict of interest 17-18
Housing allowance 49
Tax-sheltered annuity agreement 54
Dependent care assistance plan 55
Medical expense reimbursement plan 57
Accountable expense reimbursement plan 62
Assignment of a minister 69
Benevolence fund 161

CAUTION: You may need to consult with a tax or legal professional before adapting these resolutions to the specific needs of your organization.

Sample Charitable Contribution Letters and Forms

Letter to donors of noncash property 138
Receipts for gifts when *no* goods or services were provided in exchange for
    the gift:
    • Receipt for a single gift of $250 or more 144
    • Periodic or annual receipt for all gifts whether over or under $250 145
Receipts for gifts when goods or services *were* provided in exchange for the
    gift:
    • Receipt issued for a single gift of $250 or more 150
    • Periodic or annual receipt for all gifts whether over or under $250 151
Letter to volunteers 164

INTRODUCTION

Yes, you can understand the tax rules for churches and other nonprofit organizations. It is easier than ever with this year's edition of the Guide.

Taxes and finances can be very unpleasant aspects of your organization. You do not have time or the interest to master thousands of pages of complex tax laws and regulations. But you want a basic understanding of tax and financial reporting requirements and strategies.

This book is the one for you—written in plain English—clearly explained advice you can act on, with icons in the margins to direct your attention to the most important provisions in the book.

 Tip   This marks strategy recommendations for saving tax dollars for your organization and your employees.

 Planning Idea   This alerts you to ideas for tax, compensation, or administrative planning steps.

 Key Issue   These are the most basic provisions in the tax law that impact churches and other nonprofit organizations.

 Remember   This is a friendly reminder of information to review that you will definitely want to remember.

 Action Steps   This highlights easy-to-follow steps to structure your tax and financial planning.

 Caution   This marks subjects that you should carefully study to achieve the best tax and financial treatment.

 Warning!   This alerts you to some of the most serious tax mistakes sometimes made by churches and other non profit organizations.

 Cross Reference   This is a reminder that more material on a topic appears in the companion Guide, *The Zondervan Minister's Tax and Financial Guide.*

1995 Tax Highlights

As we go to press, Congress has not passed a major tax bill in 1995. However, it has not been a dull year on the tax front. Understanding the impact of court decisions, IRS ruling, regulations, and congressional initiatives continues to be important to churches and other nonprofit organizations.

New Era implications

The Foundation for New Era Philanthropy had promised to solicit matching-fund grants from anonymous wealthy donors for Christian colleges and ministries, as well as for secular nonprofit organizations. All the nonprofits had to do was to meet new fundraising targets, place the money on deposit with New Era, and in six months, they would receive double the amount. Then, three years after its promising beginnings, the dream became a nightmare. There were no anonymous benefactors. The ministries that had been depositing funds with New Era were actually funding each other's matching grants. The scheme demanded rapid and continual expansion to keep delivering on the "double-your-money" promises. And in May 1995, it all came crashing down.

The damage caused by the collapse of the Foundation for New Era Philanthrophy may have a long-term impact on future regulation of public charities. There will undoubtedly be a call for increased federal and state regulation.

The IRS has ample jurisdiction over charities' affairs at the federal level. Organizations must file a complex report at the outset to obtain tax exemption and they most must file extensive annual reports with the IRS. There are a number of rules on private inurement and private benefit. Some would question whether the rules are being adequately enforced.

Most states have comprehensive charitable solicitation statutes. Additional rules and regulations exist in many instances. Whether this mass of law is being adequately enforced is another matter.

New Era should be treated as a case of fraud with little impact on changes in the regulation of charities. Charities themselves must be more accountable and their board of directors must see that it happens.

Church loses tax exemption over anti-Clinton ads

Four days before the 1992 election, The Church at Pierce Creek in Vestal, New York, published ads in *The Washington Times* and *USA Today* attacking Bill Clinton's positions on abortion and other social issues. After a two-year investigation, the IRS, in an unusual move, revoked the church's tax exemption, charging the ads were directed at a particular candidate and election.

Current law clearly prohibits tax exemption for churches that come out for or against particular candidates. If Pierce Creek had limited its attack to abortion without mentioning Clinton's name, the IRS would not have objected, its audience would have gotten the message and the ad would have been all right.

The church has now sued the IRS, charging that the IRS has violated the First and Fifth Amendment guarantees of free speech, religion, and due process as well as the 1993 Religious Freedom Restoration Act. An attorney for the church, Jay Sekulow, has charged the IRS with a double standard of enforcement, claiming the tax agency was silent when Clinton campaigned in churches in 1992, and when he endorsed Mario Cuomo's 1994 reelection bid from the pulpit of the Bethel A.M.E. church in New York.

"Democratic nominees for office have gone from church to church and no one wants to interfere with them," Sekulow said. "But when religious conservatives speak out, it seems like it's easy pickings."

"The churches say what they're doing is theology; the IRS says what they're doing is politics," explained Frances Hill, University of Miami Law School Professor.

Token limitations are adjusted

Charities can give slightly more to contributors before the donors must trim their deductions. Donations are fully deductible when benefits to donor are small, part of a fund raiser and the charity says those benefits are insubstantial. Examples of these benefits might include mugs, key chains, posters, shirts, tote bags and so on.

The value of the benefit to the donor cannot top the lesser of 2% of the gift or $66. Or the donor can get a token item (T-shirt, for example) bearing the name or logo of the charity and costing $6.60 or less for contributions that exceed $33.

Simplified payroll tax reporting a possibility

Under current law, most employers must file W-2s with the state and the Social Security Administration. The new plan being proposed is for organizations to file W-2s with one agency, not two. That agency would then transmit the data to both the other federal agency and the state agency. Transmission would be done electronically by the government, even for returns from small employers who file their W-2 forms on paper.

The proposed changes would take effect gradually over the next few years, provided the states go along. Many states will have to amend their laws to do so.

IRS issues proposed regulations on spousal/children travel

The proposed regulations provide additional guidance regarding whether churches and other employers should report expense payments as compensation to the employee (on Form W-2) or the independent contractor (on Form 1099-MISC).

The Omnibus Budget Reconciliation Act of 1993 disallowed business expense deductions for travel expenses paid or incurred, effective January 1, 1994, with respect to a spouse or dependent (or other individual) accompanying an employee on business travel, unless

✓ the spouse or dependent is also an employee of the organization, e.g., the person paying for the travel;

✓ the travel of the spouse or dependent is for a bona fide business purpose; and

✓ the expenses would otherwise be deductible as a business expense by the spouse or dependent.

However the proposed regulations provide a more liberal approach in instances where the employee's spouse/child is not also an employee of the organization paying the travel. Under the proposed regulations, travel expense payments may qualify as non-taxable "working condition fringe benefits" if

✓ the employer has not treated such amounts as compensation

✓ the travel of the spouse or dependent is for a bona fide business purpose; and

✓ the employee substantiates the time, place, amount, and business purpose of the travel under an accountable business expense reimbursement plan.

If there is a bona fide purpose and accountable plan payment, no taxable income will result. If there is not a bona fide purpose or no accountable plan payment, the expenses must be included as income on the employee's Form W-2 or on Form 1099-MISC for a volunteer or independent contractor.

What is a bona fide business purpose? While the proposed regulations do not define what constitutes a "bona fide" business purpose, IRS rulings and court decisions over many years indicate that the following criteria are critical factors:

✓ The spouse's/dependent's function must be "necessary," e.g., result in desired business benefits to the organization.

✓ The spouse's contributions to the organization must be those which cannot efficiently be performed (or performed at all) by the taxpayer's employee alone.

✓ The spouse's services must augment the employee's purpose for the trip.

✔ The benefit to the organization's business or activities must be "substantial."

Documentation is necessary to establish a bona fide business purpose. If the paying organization desires to establish a bona fide business purpose for the travel, the presence of certain factors will help ensure that the spouse's presence is significantly helping to carry out a related (to the tax-exempt purpose) function of the organization. Here are some possibilities:

✔ Document the purpose for spousal/children attendance by having written requirements for the spouse/children—such as functions which must be attended, roles which must be served, and so on—during the meetings, and actively put these requirements into practice;

✔ Include the spouse/children in ministry as well as social functions.

✔ Reflect the spouse's children's business role and mandatory presence in employment contracts and meetings minutes; and

✔ If possible, pay the spouse/children something for services performed (such payments would be taxable as compensation).

For detailed examples applying these proposed regulations, see the 1996 Edition of *The Zondervan Minister's Tax & Financial Guide.*

Lawsuit challenges gift annuities

Attorneys for a woman challenging the right of charities to issue gift annuities have petitioned a federal court to add 29 defendants to the case, including the Baptist Foundation of Texas and the Southern Baptist Convention. The case could have billion-dollar ramifications for almost every charitable organization in the United States from churches to the Boy Scouts.

Attorneys have asked the court to include every donor and/or their beneficiaries and heirs who have given charitable gift annuities and every charity that has issued an annuity or acts as a trustee for a charitable trust.

Gift annuities of $200,000 were acquired in 1988 by an elderly woman, Louise Peter, in agreements with several Lutheran organizations. Her payout rate was fixed at 13.4%, the recommended rate for 88-year-olds at the time. The agreements have been challenged by her grand-niece whose attorneys argue that the charitable gift annuities are a "commercial" arrangement that should come under state banking and insurance laws.

The suit alleges that the distribution of actuarial tables by the American Council on Gift Annuities violated antitrust law—that it was price-fixing for charities to use the same tables to calculate lifelong payments. Shocked by the suit, the council did not issue recommended rates in 1995—something it has been doing for the past 68 years.

A preliminary ruling in the Texas suit has found that the Lutheran charities issued the gift annuities illegally and also lacked legal authority to act as trustees of the contributed funds used to pay the annuities. However, the Texas Legislature has unanimously approved and Governor George W. Bush has signed statutes declaring that Texas law affirms the validity of charities issuing charitable gift annuities and charities acting as trustee for charitable trusts. Similar legislation has been introduced in Congress.

Final and temporary regulations issued on club dues

The Omnibus Budget Reconciliation Act of 1993 (OBRA) broadened previous law on the deductibility (or lack thereof) of club dues. Because the IRS had never defined what types of organizations were "clubs," the regulations became necessary.

Organizations like Kiwanis and Rotary had bombarded the IRS with cards and letters asking that they be excluded from any definition of "club." The IRS took the comments to heart in the issuance of the final rule.

Before OBRA, no portion of club dues were treated as taxable income to the employee if a club was used predominantly for business purposes. The final rule does not address the issue of inclusion of non-deductible club dues in an individual's income. It would appear that the club dues do not constitute taxable income to the individual so long as the individual used the club totally for business purposes. If the club were used for personal, as well as business purposes, a portion of employer-paid dues might have to be included in income. The new rule is applicable to expenditures made after January 1, 1994.

Dues for downtown luncheon clubs generally do not result in income to the employee under the new rules. Dues for country clubs generally will result in income to the employee, particularly when there is substantial use of the club by the employee's family and personal guests.

Draft of tax guide for churches

The public comment period ended on June 30, 1995, for the IRS Tax Guide for Churches and Other Religious Organizations that was issued in 1994. A number of tax practitioners have suggested the various changed be made before the guide is published in final form. Some of the key recommendations to the IRS include:

✓ **Unduly restrictive definition of a "minister."** The guide states that an individual who is a minister of music or education is generally not considered to be a minister for federal tax purposes. The guide does not state a reason for this conclusion. Many denominations employ licensed or ordained ministers of music and education. These ministers are generally considered to be ministers for Federal tax purposes because they are duly ordained, licensed or commissioned. They simply perform their ministry within a specialized area.

✓ **Minister's status for income tax versus social security tax.** Although an excellent explanation of the difference between a minister's status for income tax and social security purposes is included in IRS Publication 517, the draft of the guide fails to cover these issues.

✓ **Employee versus independent contractor status.** IRS Publication 517 states that a minister may be either an employee or an independent contractor depending on certain factors. However, the guide makes the absolute statement that "a church is . . . required to report a minister's compensation to the IRS on a Form W-2." The suggestion has been made to change this wording to "A church is . . . required to report a minister's compensation to the IRS on Form W-2, if the minister is an employee, or on Form 1099-MISC, if the minister is self-employed for income tax purposes."

✓ **Housing allowance.** The guide could provide more clarity on clergy housing and a more complete list of allowable housing expenses. There is no mention in the guide about parsonage or housing allowances that may be made available to retired ministers.

✓ **Attempts to influence legislation.** The guide states that the "provision of a forum for expression of candidates' views on a partisan basis . . . would clearly violate the prohibition against political activity." Because churches often sponsor candidate forums and invite candidates to address their congregations, it has been suggested that the language be changed to: "Unless all candidates are invited to participate on a nonpreferential and nonpartisan basis, the provision of a forum for expression of candidates' views is a violation of the political campaign activity prohibition."

✓ **Unrelated business income.** The discussion of rental income does not adequately explain the special rules regarding unrelated debt-finances income.

The new guide will be helpful to ministers, churches and religious organizations. The compilation also appears to be a wake-up call to those who are still not complying with the tax rules.

IRS issues clergy audit guidelines to tax examiners

Trustees of a minister's retirement plan may designate a portion of each pension distribution as a parsonage allowance excludable from income tax. A new guide issued by the IRS to its examiners for use in audits of ministers' tax returns states that because amounts received by a retired minister as a parsonage allowance relate to the performance of prior services as a minister, they are includible in net earnings from self-employment and are subject to self-employment tax.

Although this position does not appear to be in accordance with a reasonable interpretation of the Internal Revenue Code, IRS agents will be instructed to tell retired ministers to pay this tax. Consult with a tax professional before paying self-employment taxes on prior year tax returns or before you prospectively change your tax return filings.

Student employees are subject to social security taxes

The IRS has focused on the tax withholding liability of colleges and universities and the social security liability of their students. The tax code provides an exemption to students from paying social security taxes. Most colleges apply the exemption to anyone enrolled in at least one class. However, in the instance of at least one university, the IRS took the position that student employees must be enrolled in at least 12 course credits and work no more than 20 hours per week to qualify for the exemption.

The University of Wisconsin at Madison was assessed $81 million in back taxes for failure to withhold taxes from payments it made to student research assistants. The university termed the payments scholarships, but the IRS took the position that the students performed regular jobs for which they received salaries subject to withholding.

IRS issues proposed regulations on charitable gift substantiation

The IRS issued proposed regulations in 1995 providing guidance on the allowance of certain charitable contribution deductions, the substantiation requirements for charitable contributions of $250 or more, and the disclosure requirements for quid pro quo contributions in excess of $75.

✓ **Membership benefits.** Under current law, a member of a charitable organization may only claim a charitable contribution deduction for the difference between the membership fee and the fair market value of the membership benefits. The trouble is, it is tough to value these benefits, especially unlimited rights or privileges, such as free or discounted admission or parking, and gift shop discounts. Under the proposed regulations, more benefits may be disregarded—but only if they are given as part of an annual membership offered in return for a payment of $75 or less. Plus, the benefits must fall into one of the two categories:

- admission to events that are open only to members and for which the organization reasonably projects that the cost per person for each event would be less than or equal to the standard for low-cost articles, or

- rights or privileges that members can exercise frequently during the membership period.

If a benefit falls into either of the above categories, it does not have to be taken into account in figuring the donor's charitable deduction.

✓ **Good faith estimate of benefit value.** The proposed regulations define a "good faith estimate" of the value of goods or services provided by a charitable organization as an estimate of the fair market value of those goods or services. That value may differ from their cost to your organization, and you may use any reasonable method to estimate value if you apply it in good faith. Your donors generally may rely on your estimate—if it is in the required written acknowledgment of disclosure statement.

✓ **Gifts via planned giving vehicles.** A donor who sets up a charitable lead trust, a charitable remainder annuity trust, or a charitable remainder unitrust is not required to designate a specific organization as the charitable beneficiary at the time he or she transfers property to the trust. As a result, there is often no designated charity available to provide a written acknowledgment to the donor. Also, even if a specific charity is named, the donor can always change his or her mind.

The proposed regulations indicate that transfers of property to charitable lead trusts, charitable remainder annuity trusts, and charitable remainder unitrusts are exempt from the substantiation rules.

✓ **Unreimbursed expenses.** Many times, individuals incur out-of-pocket expenses in connection with charitable work. The proposed regulations say that if these amounts are over the key thresholds (i.e., $250 or $75 for quid pro quo gifts), the expenses may be substantiated by the donor's normal records. But do you have to send them receipts that indicate the amount of their expenses—when you usually have no idea as to the amount?

Under the proposed regulations, you can send them an abbreviated written acknowledgment. It must contain a description of the services provided by the donor, the date the services were provided, whether your organization provided any goods or services in return (and, if so, a description and good-faith estimate of the fair market value of any good or services provided). If the goods or services provided consist solely of intangible religious benefits, the receipt must so state.

Court orders religious groups to return donation

The Court of Appeals for the Seventh Circuit has ruled that a receiver may, consistent with the Uniform Fraudulent Transfer Act, order five religious charities to refund monies donated to them in violation of the Act by three corporations and their lone shareholder, Michael Douglas.

In upholding a district court's judgement ordering the refund, the Court held that the churches may be forced to divert funds from its religious and other charitable activities because a donation it received in good faith had a tainted source.

The court's order stemmed from a civil suit filed by the Securities and Exchange Commission against Douglas and his three corporations in 1989 charging multiple violations of federal securities laws. According to the SEC, Douglas created three corporations and caused them in turn to create limited partnerships in which the corporations will be the general partners and will sell limited partner interests to the investing public.

A refund order was made against five religious charities of more than $500,000 donated to them by Douglas and his corporations. The Court rejected the charities' arguments that the statute should be interpreted to exclude gifts to religious groups and other charitable organizations, especially when the ultimate beneficiaries of the fraudulent conveyance suits are themselves at fault.

The implication of the Court's ruling against the religious organizations is that they will always be liable under the fraudulent conveyance statute once it is proven that the donor obtained his money fraudulently.

IRS may audit charitable remainder trusts

The IRS plans to conduct random audits of charitable remainder trust (CRT) returns and some district offices may elect to audit all CRT's. The audits are intended to combat abuses of "accelerated" CRT's. Those trusts attempt to convert appreciated assets into cash in the donor's pocket while avoiding practically all the capital gains tax.

Planners are paid to plan and legal, creative tax planning is the order of the day in the tax world. But when gifts are made with no donative intent, the planning process is generally too aggressive. The IRS has drawn "a line in the sand" regarding "accelerated" CRTs.

For example, assume that capital assets with a value of $1 million and a "zero basis" ("zero basis" means the donor originally acquired the asset at no cost) are contributed to the trust on January 1. Assume further that the assets pay no income and that the term of the trust is 2 years. The unitrust amount is set at 80% of the fair market value of the trust assets valued annually. An 80% payout means that the trust will pay 80% of its value, determined annually, to the donor each year.

The unitrust amount required to be paid for the first year is $800,000 (80% of its $1 million value), but during the first year no actual distributions are made from the trust to the donor as the recipient of the unitrust amount. At the beginning of the second year, all the assets are sold for $1 million, and the $800,000 unitrust amount for the first year is distributed to the donor between January 1 and April 15 of the second year. The unitrust amount for the second year is $160,000 (80% times the $200,000 net fair market value of the trust assets). At the end of the second year, the trust terminates, and what is left, $40,000, (its "remainder) is paid to the charity.

Proponents of this transaction contend that the tax treatment of this example would be as follows:

✓ Because no assets are actually sold or distributed to the donor during the first year, the entire $800,000 unitrust amount is characterized as a distribution of trust corpus.

✓ The $160,000 unitrust amount for the second year is characterized as capital gain, on which the donor pays tax of $44,800 ($160,000 times the 28% tax rate for capital gains).

✓ The donor is allowed a charitable tax deduction that is equal to the present value of the remainder to charity. If the donor's tax deduction is assumed to be about $35,000 and he or she is in the 36% tax bracket, the deduction would save $12,600 in taxes (36% times $35,000).

✓ The donor is left with net cash of $927,800 ($800,000 from the first year and $127,800 net from the second year.) If the donor had sold the assets directly, the donor would have paid tax of $180,000 on the $1 million capital gain, and would have net cash of only $720,000.

In some situations, the IRS will not treat the transaction as a sale by a tax-exempt charitable remainder trust. Gain on the sale of the trust assets may constitute gross income to the donor, not to the trust. The IRS may also question the qualification of the trust as a charitable remainder trust.

Cities, counties, and states turn to charities for taxes

Many governmental entities are desperate for money. While arguments of altruism and good works by nonprofit organizations are important, they often do not wash.

✓ Pennsylvania's Erie County collects more than $1.5 million a year from over 100 charities in property taxes.

✓ Buffalo, New York, is trying to raise revenue by making all property owners, including nonprofit groups, pay a new fee for such services as snow plowing and street cleaning.

✓ In Iowa, the City of Des Moines and other communities want the state legislature to help them get property-tax revenue from nonprofit groups.

✓ The city of Wilmington, Delaware, is considering ways to collect fees from nonprofit groups for the cost of police and fire services.

✓ In Marion, Indiana, storm water utility fees have been assessed against all property owners, including churches and other nonprofit groups.

At the heart of the debate over state and local taxes are fundamental questions about how much nonprofit groups benefit society. Many states and cities think the federal standard for tax exemption has been too lenient. Pennsylvania has become a national leader in the effort to toughen the rules. Its standards are so rigorous that it is virtually impossible for large nonprofit institutions to escape paying property taxes.

Recent rulings on state tax issues

Rulings on state tax issues that impact churches and other nonprofit organizations are frequently made. Here are just a few recent rulings:

✓ **Church property not subject to "tax day" limits.** Oklahoma authorities cannot deny exemption to religious property acquired after January 1 or any tax year. Ordinarily the taxable status of property is based on its ownership and use as of the first day of January each year. If not exempt on that date, property remains taxable until the following year even if it is acquired by an organization entitled to tax exemption. However, since the legislature can neither confer nor deny exemption to religious property, the state's intermediate appeals court ruled that religious property becomes exempt for the remainder of the year on the date of acquisition.

✓ **Prayer chapel tax exempt.** A church gained exemption for property abutting its church building and used as a prayer chapel and for overflow parking. Fearing vandalism if the church building remained unlocked, the church installed a converted house trailer on the abutting lot. The trailer is open twenty-four hours a day to any member of the public seeking a place to pray. An Ohio Board of Tax Appeals ruled that both the prayer chapel and the overflow parking were necessary for the use and enjoyment of the main building.

✓ **Church Sunday school building taxable.** Overruling the local county board, the Wyoming State Board of Equalization denied exemption to church property used for Sunday school and youth programs. However, the board affirmed exemption for a parking lot next to the Sunday school building because it was also used for supplemental church parking.

The board concluded that the Sunday school building did not qualify for exemption either as property used exclusively for public worship or as a church school. The property failed the first test because the board found that while Christian youth fellowship and church education advance religious purposes, they are not themselves a form of worship. The property also did not qualify as a church school because it was used for both school and noneducational purposes and the noneducation uses were more than *de minimis*.

✓ **Church schools not exempt from public services tax.** The Florida Attorney General has ruled that a statute authorizing municipalities to exempt churches from the state's public services tax generally does not extend to church-operated schools and child care centers. The public services tax applies to sales of electricity, gas, water, and telecommunications. The church exemption is limited to public services used exclusively for church purposes and does not include church schools, clinics, recreation areas, playgrounds, convents, or rectories unless the activity constitutes a direct adjunct of the church and the congregation. Schools that are essentially the same as public schools are not such a direct adjunct.

✓ **Church exempt from sales tax in Alabama.** Reversing an initial ruling against the church, an Alabama court ruled that the University Avenue Church of Christ qualifies for sales tax exemption. The court ruled that the church should receive similar status under the sales tax exemption statute as under the state's income tax statute.

✓ **Parsonage not exempt in Illinois.** A parsonage failed to gain property tax exemption when the Immanuel Evangelical Lutheran Church of Springfield sold it to its minister under a contract for deed. The court ruled that the church must own the parsonage if it is to qualify for exemption. While the contract for deed left title in the name of the church, the contract transferred all ownership rights to the minister and his wife, making them the actual owners of the property.

✓ **Church liable for storm drainage user fee in Oregon.** A storm drainage user fee imposed on property owned by the Roman Catholic Archdiocese of Portland was valid because the charge was based on the amount of impervious surface of the property, not its value. The Oregon statute exempts property only from ad valorem taxation.

Pending legislation

As this book goes to press, Congress is considering various legislative proposals that would impact churches and other nonprofit organizations. Some of the proposed legislation that would potentially impact churches and other nonprofit organizations and their employees include:

✓ **Foreign earned income exclusion.** The maximum exclusion would increase from $70,000 to $100,000 for 1995, and the exclusion would be indexed annually for inflation thereafter.

✓ **Definition of highly compensated employee.** An employee would be considered highly compensated if he had compensation for the preceding year in excess of $50,000 (adjusted for the cost of living). The rule requiring that the highest paid officer of an employer be treated as a highly compensated employee without regard to compensation would be repealed, beginning in 1996.

✓ **Separation payments.** Qualified separation payments received by an employee upon termination would be excludable from gross income to the extent the amounts are transferred to an Individual Retirement Account (IRA) within 60 days of receipt of the payment, beginning in 1996.

✓ **FUTA exemption for certain religious schools.** The proposal would exempt from FUTA service performed in an elementary or secondary school that is operated primarily for religious purposes. The exemption would be available to such schools even if they are not operated, supervised, controlled, or principally supported by a church or churches.

Financial Accountability

We need to practice what we preach about accountability.

In This Chapter

- Organizations promoting accountability
- Accountability to an independent board
- Accountability to donors
- Accountability to government

Scandals such as the New Era Foundation and the Common Fund continue to expose the pitfalls of weak accountability. The public has high expectations of religious organizations. Day after day, thousands in the nonprofit community work tirelessly and selflessly to address physical and spiritual needs worldwide, only to find the public casting a wary eye on them due to the highly publicized misdeeds of a few. Donors recognize that enormous needs exist and they want to respond generously to those needs. But they also want to be sure that optimum use of their sacrificial gifts is employed by the charities they support. There is no acceptable alternative to accountability.

For large nonprofit organizations, accountability issues often relate to complex issues of private inurement or conflicts of interest. In churches and small-to-medium-nonprofits, the issues may be as basic as whether to accept a gift that appears to be a pass-through contribution for the personal benefit of a designated individual.

Financial accountability is based on the principle of stewardship. A steward-manager exercises responsible care over entrusted funds. Good stewardship rarely occurs outside a system of accountability.

Financial accountability is the natural outgrowth of proper organizational leadership. Providing clear, basic explanations of financial activity starts with the daily record of transactions and evolves to the adequate reporting to donors and boards.

U.S. laws provide special tax treatment of religious and charitable institutions. The nonprofit organization that refuses to disclose its finances is shortchanging the public from which it derives its support. It also causes suspicions about how it is using the financial resources at its disposal.

Organizations Promoting Accountability

Being a member of organizations that promote stewardship principles often enhances accountability. Several organizations provide leadership in the area of financial accountability. These organizations include the Evangelical Council for Financial Accountability (ECFA), the Ethics and Financial Integrity Commission (EFICOM), the National Charities Information Bureau (NCIB), and the Council of Better Business Bureaus, Inc. (CBBB).

The National Committee on Planned Giving and the Committee on Gift Annuities (NCPG/CGA) have adopted model standards for those involved in planned giving. The National Society of Fund Raising Executives (NSFRE) has also prepared fund-raising guidelines.

For missionary organizations, the Interdenominational Foreign Mission Association (IFMA) and the Evangelical Fellowship of Mission Agencies (EFMA) (formerly Evangelical Foreign Missions Association) are groups which provide accountability for members.

The strong tenets of these organizations are proper accounting, an independent and responsible volunteer board of directors, full disclosure of finances, and fair treatment for donors.

Accountability to an Independent Board

Board governance

Strong leadership often shuns accountability. Many a board has not lived up to its responsibility to hold itself accountable and to demand accountability of the organizational leadership.

Can your organization's leadership be challenged and voted down? Are the board members permissive and passive or involved and active? Are your values and policies clearly articulated? Are they operative in the organization daily? Are annual evaluations made of the pastor(s) or the nonprofit chief executive officer (CEO)?

A board should generally meet at least semi-annually. Some boards meet monthly. Meetings should be more than listening to the CEO's report and rubber-stamping a series of resolutions prepared by the CEO.

ECFA and NCIB members must have a board of not less than five individuals. A majority of the board must be other than employees or staff, or those related by blood or marriage, to meet ECFA standards. No more than one paid staff member may be on the board to comply with NCIB standards.

Even when employee membership on the board is slightly less than a majority, the independence of the board may be jeopardized. Employees often lack independence and objectivity in dealing with many board-level matters. The CEO, in-house secretary, and treasurer are often members of an organization's board of directors. Department heads of organizations are generally not members of the board.

Recording board actions

The actions of an organization's board and its committees should be recorded by written minutes prepared within a few days after the meeting concludes. The minute books of some charities are almost nonexistent. Minutes of the most recent board meeting often appear to be placed in proper written form on the eve of the succeeding board meeting. Such lack of organization can be indicative of weak board governance and may leave a poor paper trail to document the board's actions.

The actions of an organization's board typically include the approval and revision of policies that should be organized and printed as the body of board policies. These policies, extracted from the board minutes, should be revised after each board meeting if new policies are adopted or previously existing policies are revised.

Financial reporting

ECFA members must have an independent annual audit according to generally accepted auditing standards (GAAS). Financial statements must be prepared following generally accepted accounting principles (GAAP). NCIB also requires a GAAP audit.

A subcommittee of the board should review the annual audit report. This committee often has finance/budget responsibilities and should not be controlled by employees or staff members.

Compensation review

An annual review of the local church minister's or nonprofit organization executive's compensation package is vital. The review should focus on all elements of pay, taxable and nontaxable.

Pay and fringe benefit packages should be determined by an objective evaluation of responsibilities, goals reached, and available resources. A comparison with positions in other organizations may be helpful. National salary surveys may provide meaningful data such as National Association of Church Business Administrators Church Staff Compensation Survey, and Christian Management Association Salary Survey.

The approved compensation package should be documented in board and/or subcommittee minutes. This action should include guidelines for disbursement of compensation-related funds by the organization's treasurer.

With increased scrutiny on nonprofit salaries, it is important that compensation amounts be accurately stated. Gross pay may include the following elements (some taxable and some tax-free or tax-deferred):

✓ Cash salary

✓ Fair rental value of a house, including utilities, provided by the organization

✔ Cash housing or furnishings allowance

✔ Tax-deferred payments (TSA/IRA)

✔ Expense advances that exceed documented business expenses

✔ Value of the personal use of organization-owned aircraft or vehicle

✔ Value of noncash goods and services

✔ Cash bonuses

In an attempt to minimize high compensation, nonprofit executives too often resort to reporting only the cash salary to the press or their publics. If the noncash compensation is significant, disclosure of only the cash salary is very deceiving.

Budget process

The organization should prepare a detailed annual budget consistent with the major classifications in the financial statements and approved by the board. The budget should allow meaningful comparison with the previous year's financial statements; recast if necessary.

Responsibility for budgetary performance should be clearly assigned to management as appropriate (for example, department heads, field directors, and so on). The controller or treasurer of an organization is normally responsible for budgetary enforcement and reporting. For more information on the budgeting process, see pages 99-100.

Conflicts of interest and related party transactions

Selecting board members

Information concerning prospective and current board members may reveal potential conflicts that will disqualify the individual. If a conflict is sufficiently limited, the director may simply need to abstain from voting on certain issues. If the conflict of interest is material, the election or re-election of the individual may be inappropriate. A sample conflict of interest policy and annual reporting form appears on page 17 and 18.

Conducting activities

Fairness in decision-making is more likely to occur in an impartial environment. Conflicts of interest and related-party transactions are often confused. However, the

Sample Conflict or Duality of Interest Policy Statement

All trustees, officers, agents and employees of this corporation shall disclose all real or apparent conflict or dualities of interest which they discover or which have been brought to their attention in connection with this corporation's activities. "Disclosure" shall mean providing properly, to the appropriate person, a written description of the facts comprising the real or apparent conflict or duality of interest. An annual disclosure statement shall be circulated to trustees, officers, and certain identified agents and employees to assist them in considering such disclosures, but disclosure is appropriate and required whenever conflicts or dualities of interest may occur. The written notices of disclosures shall be filed with the Chief Executive Officer or such other person designated by the Chief Executive Officer to receive such notifications. All disclosures of real or apparent conflict or duality of interests shall be noted for the record in the minutes of the meeting of the Board of Directors.

An individual trustee, officer, agent, or employee who believes that he/she or an immediate member of his/her immediate family might have a real or apparent conflict of interest, in addition to filing a notice of disclosure, must abstain from (1) participating in discussions or deliberations with respect to the subject of the conflict (other than to present factual information or answer questions), (2) using their personal influence to affect deliberations, (3) making motions, (4) voting, (5) executing agreements, or (6) taking similar actions on behalf of the corporations where the conflict or duality of interest might pertain by law, agreement or otherwise. At the discretion of the Board of Directors or a committee thereof, a person with a real or apparent conflict or duality of interest may be excused from all or any portion of discussion or deliberations with respect to the subject of the conflict.

A member of the Board of Directors or a committee thereof, who, having disclosed a conflict or duality of interest, nevertheless shall be counted in determining the existence of a quorum at any meeting where the subject of the conflict is discussed. The minutes of the meeting shall reflect the disclosure made, the vote thereon, the abstention from participation and voting by the individual making disclosure.

There shall be no business transactions, whether the nature of employment, contract, purchase, or sale, between the corporation and a trustee during his/her term in office, except in the case of employment, for a period of one year thereafter. For purposes of this section, the payment of any benefit to which the trustee might otherwise be entitled, shall not be deemed a business transaction.

The Chief Executive Officer shall ensure that all trustees, officers, agents, employees and independent contractors of the corporation are made aware of the corporation's policy with respect to conflicts or duality of interest.

Sample Conflict or Duality of Interest Disclosure Annual Reporting Statement

Certification

I have read and understand Conflict or Duality of Interest Policy. I hereby declare and certify the following real or apparent conflict or dualities of interest:

Disclosure Statement

_____

_____

_____

_____

_____

_____

_____

_____

_____

_____

_____

_____

(If necessary, attach additional documentation)

Date _____   _____
                                                      Signature

                                         _____
                                                          Title

distinction between the two concepts is useful.

The potential for a conflict of interest arises in situations in which a person has a responsibility to promote one interest, but has a competing interest at the same time. If the competing interest is exercised over a fiduciary interest, the conflict is realized. Conflicts of interest should be avoided.

Related-party transactions are transactions that occur between two or more parties that have interlinking relationships. These transactions should be disclosed to the governing board. Transactions should be evaluated to ensure they are made on a sound economic basis. Some related-party transactions are clearly to the advantage of the organization and should be pursued. Other related-party transactions are conflicts of interest and should be avoided.

Under ECFA guidelines, transactions with related parties may be undertaken only in the following situations:

✓ The audited financial statements of the organization fully disclose material related-party transactions.

✓ Related parties are excluded from the discussion and approval of related-party transactions.

✓ Competitive bids or comparable valuations exist.

✓ The organization's board approves the transaction as being in the best interest of the organization.

Example 1: An organization purchases insurance coverage through an insurance firm owned by a board member. This would constitute a conflict of interest unless the cost of the insurance is disclosed, the purchase is subject to proper approvals, the price is below the competition, and the purchase is in the best interests of the organization. If the purchase passes these tests, it is still a related-party transaction.

Example 2: The CEO and several employees are members of the board. When the resolution on salary and fringe-benefit adjustments comes to the board, should those affected by the resolution discuss and vote on the matter? No. To avoid the appearance of a conflict of interest, the employees should absent themselves from the meeting.

Example 3: A nonprofit board considers a significant loan to a company in which a board member has a material ownership interest. Should this loan even be considered? Only if it is in the best interest of the nonprofit and allowable under state laws and the organization's by-laws.

Board compensation

Most nonprofit board members serve without compensation. This practice reinforces an important distinction of nonprofits: the assets of a nonprofit should not be used for the private enrichment of directors, members, or employees.

Board members often have travel-related expenses reimbursed. Mileage may be reimbursed up to the standard IRS business rate (30 cents per mile for 1995) without reporting any taxable income to the board member. Travel expenses reimbursed for the spouse of a board member represent taxable income to the board member unless the spouse provides services to the nonprofit in conjunction with the trip.

Accountability to Donors

Donors are showing greater concern about the solicitation and use of their contributions. The primary areas of concern are:

Donor communication

All aspects of a proposed charitable gift shall be explained fully, fairly, and accurately to the donor. These items should be included in the explanation:

✓ **The charity's proposed use of the gift.** Realistic expectations should be communicated regarding what the donor's gift will do within the programs of the donee organization.

✓ **Representations of fact.** Any description of the financial condition of the organization, or narrative about events must be current, complete, and accurate. References to past activities or events must be appropriately dated. There must be no material omissions or exaggerations of fact or use of misleading photographs or any other communication tending to create a false impression or misunderstanding.

✓ **Valuation issues and procedures.** If an appraisal is required, the donor should fully understand the procedures and who is responsible to pay for the appraisal.

✓ **Tax consequences and reporting requirements.** While tax considerations should not be the primary focus of a gift, the donor should clearly understand the current and future income, estate and gift tax consequences, and reporting requirements of the proposed gift. A charitable gift should never be represented as a tax shelter.

✓ **Alternative arrangements for making the gift.** The donor should understand the current and deferred gift options that are available.

✓ **Financial and family implications.** In addition to the tax consequences, the overall financial implications of the proposed gift and the potential impact on family members should be carefully explained.

✓ **Possible conflicts of interest.** Disclose to the donor all relationships which might constitute, or appear to constitute, conflicts of interest. The disclosure should include how and by whom each party is compensated and any cost of managing the gift.

Accounting for restricted gifts

Donors often place temporary or permanent restrictions on gifts that limit their use to certain purposes. These stipulations may specify a use for a contributed asset that is more specific than broad limits relating to the nature of the organization, the environment in which it operates, and the purposes specified in its articles of incorporation or bylaws or comparable documents for unincorporated entities.

Many organizations lack the proper accounting structure to account for restricted gift income and to track the funds through to the point of expenditure. This may lead to the following problems:

✓ **Donations received for one project but spent on another.** Separate revenue and expense accounts must be maintained for each project to ensure the integrity of the funds.

✓ **Overfunding or underfunding of projects.** This may require communicating additional information to donors about the use of the funds. In some cases, donor approval may be needed to re-direct the use of funds. If the purpose of a designated gift cannot be fulfilled and the donor is unwilling to remove or change the designation, it may be necessary to make a refund to the donor (see pages 165-166).

✓ **Inadequate reporting to donors on projects.** ECFA requires members, on request, to provide a report, including financial information, on the project for which it is soliciting gifts. Without a proper accounting system, a report on specific projects may be impossible to prepare accurately and timely.

Communication and donor intent

ECFA requires that all statements made by an organization in its fund-raising appeals about the use of the gift must be honored by the organization. The donor's intent may be shaped by both the organization's communication of the appeal and by any donor instructions with the gift.

If the donor responds to a specific appeal, the assumption may be made that the donor's intent is that the funds be used as outlined in the appeal. There is a need for clear communication in the appeal to insure that the donor understands precisely how the funds will be used.

Written or verbal communication from the donor also determines donor intent. Any note or correspondence accompanying the gift or conversations between the donor and donee representatives indicate donor intent.

Use of funds

Most contributors believe that their contributions are being applied to the current program needs identified by the organization, unless there is other specific representation. It is prudent management for organizations to accumulate adequate unrestricted operating funds. The needs of the constituency served should be the most important factor in determining the adequacy of reserve funds.

Example: An organization has $250,000 in savings at the time a direct mail appeal asks for donations to cover operating expenses. A donor questions the ethics of the appeal. Was the appeal improper?

The size of the organization would have a significant bearing on the appropriateness of the appeal. The appeal may be inappropriate if the annual budget of the organization is $50,000 (in other words, the savings account would be five times the annual budget). Yet, an organization with an annual budget of $2M may justify a savings account of $250,000 for contingencies.

NCIB standards call for net assets available for the following fiscal year to be not more than twice the current year's expenses or the next year's budget, whichever is higher.

Projects unrelated to an organization's primary purpose

Nonprofits sometimes receive funds for programs that are not part of its present or prospective ministry, but are proper according to its exempt purpose (i.e., one of the exempt purposes under the Internal Revenue Code). In these instances the organization must treat them either as restricted funds and channel them through an organization that can carry out the donor's intent, or return the funds to the donor.

Reporting for incentives and premiums

Fund-raising appeals may offer premiums or incentives in exchange for a contribution. If the value of the premiums or incentives is not insubstantial, but significant in relation to the amount of the donation, the donee organization must advise the donor of the fair market value of the premium or incentive and that the value is not deductible for tax purposes (see page 149-150). ECFA members must comply with the IRS rules on incentives and premiums. NPGA/CGA has a general standard relating to compliance with all federal and state laws.

Reporting to donors

ECFA, EFICOM, NCIB and the CBBB require an organization to provide a copy of its current financial statements upon written request. NCIB also requires that a statement of functional allocation of expenses be provided. This type of statement reflects expenses by type—salaries, fringe benefits, and travel—as well as by function.

Compensation of gift planners

Payment of finders' fees, commissions, or other fees by a donee organization to an outside gift planner as a condition for delivery of a gift is never appropriate under NCPG/CGA standards. If such arrangements exist, ECFA requires full disclosure in the organization's audited financial statements. The disclosure must reflect the income and related expenses. Commission or contingency-based compensation to an organization's own employees is never appropriate.

Tax-deductible gifts for a named recipient's personal benefit

According to the Internal Revenue Code and other laws and regulations governing tax-exempt organizations, tax-deductible gifts may not be used to pass money or benefits to any named individual for personal use. Individuals often want to use charitable organizations as a conduit for funds to change the character of personal, nondeductible gifts to deductible charitable contributions. Gifts for the support of specific staff individuals may be deductible as charitable contributions if the donee organization controls the funds and follows proper procedures. Chapter 7 covers this topic in more detail.

Conflict of interest on royalties

ECFA requires that an officer, director, or other principal of the organization must not receive royalties for any product used for fund-raising or promotional purposes by his or her organization. The payment of reasonable royalties for items offered for sale is permissible.

Acknowledgment of gifts-in-kind

Property or gifts-in-kind received by an organization should be acknowledged, describing the property or gift accurately *without* an estimate of the gift's market value. It is the responsibility of the donor to determine the fair market value of the property for tax purposes.

Acting in the interest of the donor

Every effort should be made to avoid accepting a gift from or entering into a contract with a prospective donor that would knowingly place a hardship on the donor, or place the donor's future well-being in jeopardy.

Financial advice

Fund-raisers should recognize that it is almost impossible to properly represent the full interests of the donor and the charitable organization simultaneously.

When dealing with persons regarding commitments on major estate assets, gift planners should seek to guide and advise donors so that they may adequately consider the broad interests of the family and the various organizations they are currently supporting before they make a final decision. Donors should be encouraged to discuss the proposed gift with competent and independent attorneys, accountants, or other professional advisors.

Accountability to Government

Almost every church and nonprofit has some reporting requirements to one or more governmental agencies. Many organizations do not fully comply with reporting guidelines.

Churches and nonprofits abhor the thought of increased governmental regulation. Yet failure to self-regulate areas such as executive compensation, unrelated business activities, fund-raising practices, and political lobbying continues to draw the attention of the IRS and Congress.

A few organizations knowingly operate in or at the edge of fraudulent areas. But most organizations have good intentions and any violations are primarily based on ignorance of laws and regulations.

Key Concepts

■ Good stewardship rarely occurs outside a system of accountability.

■ Adequate board governance is the first step to proper accountability.

■ Accountability in donor solicitation and the use of contributions is vital.

■ Fulfillment of required reporting to governmental agencies is a must.

Tax Exemption

Your tax-exempt status is extremely valuable — guard it carefully!

In This Chapter

- Tax exemption for churches
- Advantages and limitations of tax exemption
- Starting a nonprofit
- Unrelated business income
- Private benefit and private inurement
- Filing federal returns
- Filing state returns
- Political activity

Qualifying tax-exempt organizations may have many advantages. One of the most important benefits is the eligibility to attract deductible charitable contributions from individual and corporate donors. Exemption from tax liability, primarily income, sales, and property tax, is also important.

The term "nonprofit organization" covers a broad range of entities such as churches, colleges, universities, health-care providers, business leagues, veterans groups, political parties, country clubs, and united-giving campaigns. Sources of revenue, ownership structure, and activities distinguish nonprofit from for-profit organizations. The most common type of nonprofits is the charitable organization.

The nonprofit organization concept is basically a state law creation. But tax-exempt organizations are based primarily on federal law. The Internal Revenue Code does not use the word "nonprofit." The Code refers to nonprofits as exempt organizations. Certain state statutes use the term "not-for-profit." A not-for-profit organization under state law may or may not be tax-exempt under federal law.

In this book, the term "nonprofit" refers to nonprofit organizations that are exempt from federal income tax. This is key because not all nonprofit organizations are necessarily tax-exempt.

Tax Exemption for Churches

Tax law and IRS regulations do not define "religious." But the courts have defined "religious" broadly. In part, because of these constitutional concerns, some religious organizations are subject to more lenient reporting and auditing requirements under federal tax law.

The "religious" category includes churches, conventions of churches, associations of churches, church-run organizations (such as schools, hospitals, orphanages, nursing homes, publishing entities, broadcasting entities, and cemeteries), religious orders, apostolic groups, integrated auxiliaries of churches, missionary organizations, and Bible and tract societies. IRS regulations define religious worship as: "What constitutes conduct of religious worship or the ministration of sacerdotal functions depends on the interests and practices of a particular religious body constituting a church."

Although not stated in the regulations, the IRS applies the following 14 criteria to decide whether a religious organization can qualify as a "church":

✔ Distinct legal existence

✔ Recognized creed and form of worship

✔ Definite and distinct ecclesiastical government

✔ Formal code of doctrine and discipline

✔ Distinct religious history

✔ Membership not associated with any other church or denomination

✔ Organization of ordained ministers

✔ Ordained ministers selected after completing prescribed courses of studies

✔ Literature of its own

✔ Established places of worship

✔ Regular congregations

✔ Regular religious services

✔ Sunday schools for religious instruction of the young

✔ Schools for preparation of its ministers

Churches receive favored status in that they are not required to file either an application for exemption (Form 1023) or annual report (Form 990) with the IRS. A church is still subject to the possibility of filing an annual report on unrelated business income (Form 990-T) and Form 5578 for private schools as well as payroll tax, sales tax, and other forms.

Advantages and Limitations of Tax Exemption

Upon approval by the IRS, tax exemption is available to organizations that meet the requirements of the tax code. This exemption provides relief from federal income tax. This income tax exemption may or may not extend to local and state income taxes. Even if an organization receives tax-exempt status, certain federal taxes may still be imposed. Possible taxes are the unrelated business income tax, tax on certain "political" activities, and tax on excessive legislative activities.

Tax exemption advantages

Besides the basic exemption from federal income and excise tax, an organization that is recognized as a charitable organization under the Internal Revenue Code enjoys several advantages:

✓ Its donors can be offered the benefit of a deduction for contributions.

✓ It can benefit from lower postal rates on third-class bulk mailings.

✓ It is in a favored position to seek funding from foundations and other philanthropic entities, many of which will not support organizations other than those recognized under 501(c)(3).

✓ It is eligible for government grants available only to entities exempt under 501(c)(3).

✓ It often qualifies for exemption not only from state and local income tax but from property taxes (for property used directly for its exempt function) and certain sales and use taxes as well.

✓ It may qualify for exemption from the Federal Unemployment Tax Act in certain situations.

✓ Its employees may participate in 403(b) annuities.

✓ It is an exclusive beneficiary of free radio and television public service announcements (PSAs) provided by local media outlets.

✓ If it is a church or a qualified church-controlled organization, it may exclude compensation to employees from the FICA social security base. The organization must be opposed on religious grounds to the payment of FICA social security taxes. The social security liability shifts to the employees of the electing organizations in the form of SECA social security tax.

Tax exemption limitations

Offsetting the advantages of tax-exempt status are some strict requirements:

✓ An organization must be engaged "primarily" in qualified charitable or educational endeavors.

✓ There are limitations to the extent to which it can engage in substantial legislative activities or other political activities.

✓ An organization may not engage in unrelated business activities or commercial activities to an impermissible extent.

✓ There is a prohibition against private inurement or private benefit.

✓ Upon dissolution, the organization's assets must be distributed for one or more exempt purposes.

Starting a Nonprofit

The choice of a nonprofit organizational form is a basic decision. Most churches are unincorporated. However, an increasing number of churches are incorporating for the purpose of limiting legal liability. Most other nonprofit organizations are corporations. While incorporation may usually be desirable, it is generally not mandatory.

Organizations using the corporate form will need articles of incorporation and bylaws. An unincorporated organization will typically have the same instruments although the articles may be in the form of a constitution.

Several planning questions should be asked. If the organization is formed for charitable purposes, is public status desired or is a private foundation acceptable? Are any business activities contemplated and to what degree will the organization be incorporated? Is an attorney competent in nonprofit matters available to help with the preparation of the legal documents? What provisions will the bylaws contain? Who will serve on the board of directors? What name will be used for the organization?

The following materials may be needed or useful when starting a church or other nonprofit organization:

Package 1023   Application for Recognition of Exemption with Instructions

Publication 557   Tax-Exempt Status for Your Organization

Obtaining an employer identification number

All entities, whether exempt from tax or not, must obtain an Employer Identification Number (EIN) by filing IRS Form SS-4. An EIN is required for each church even though churches are not required to file with the IRS for tax-exempt status. This number is not a "tax-exempt number," but is simply the organization's unique identifier in the IRS's records, similar to an individual's social security number.

When the IRS approves an organization for exemption from federal income tax (not required for churches), it will receive a "determination letter." This letter does not assign the organization a "tax-exempt number."

If an organization is a "central organization" that holds a "group exemption letter," the IRS will assign that group a four-digit number, known as its Group Exemption Number (GEN). This number must be supplied with the central organization's annual report to the IRS (updating its list of included subordinate organizations). The number also is inserted on Form 990 (if required) of the central organization and the subordinate organizations included in the group exemption.

When an organization applies for exemption from state or local income, sales, or property taxes, the state or local jurisdiction may provide a certificate or letter of exemption, which, in some jurisdictions, includes a serial number. This number is often called a "tax-exempt number." This number should not be confused with an EIN.

Application for recognition of tax-exempt status

Although churches are not required to apply to the IRS for tax exempt status under Section 501(c)(3) of the Internal Revenue Code and are exempt from filing Form 990, it may be appropriate to apply for recognition in some situations:

 Independent local churches that are not a part of a national denominational body often file for tax-exempt status to provide evidence of their status. The local congregation may wish to file for group exemption if it is a parent church of other local congregations or separately organized ministries.

National denominations typically file for group exemption to cover all local congregations. A copy of the national body's IRS determination letter may be used by the local group to provide evidence of tax-exempt status.

| Form **SS-4** (Rev. December 1993) Department of the Treasury Internal Revenue Service | **Application for Employer Identification Number** (For use by employers, corporations, partnerships, trusts, estates, churches, government agencies, certain individuals, and others. See instructions.) | EIN OMB No. 1545-0003 Expires 12-31-96 |

Please type or print clearly.

1 Name of applicant (Legal name) (See instructions.)
Lynn Haven Church

2 Trade name of business, if different from name in line 1

3 Executor, trustee, "care of" name

4a Mailing address (street address) (room, apt., or suite no.)
P. O. Box 4382

5a Business address, if different from address in lines 4a and 4b
3801 North Florida Avenue

4b City, state, and ZIP code
Miami, FL 33168

5b City, state, and ZIP code
Miami, FL 33168

6 County and state where principal business is located
Dade County, Florida

7 Name of principal officer, general partner, grantor, owner, or trustor—SSN required (See instructions.) ►

8a Type of entity (Check only one box.) (See instructions.)
- ☐ Sole Proprietor (SSN) _____
- ☐ REMIC
- ☐ State/local government   ☐ National guard
- ☐ Other nonprofit organization (specify) _____
- ☐ Other (specify) ►
- ☐ Estate (SSN of decedent) _____
- ☐ Plan administrator-SSN _____
- ☐ Other corporation (specify) _____
- ☐ Federal government/military   ☒ Church or church controlled organization
- ☐ Personal service corp.
- ☐ Trust
- ☐ Partnership
- ☐ Farmers' cooperative

(enter GEN if applicable) _____

8b If a corporation, name the state or foreign country (if applicable) where incorporated ►   State   Foreign country

9 Reason for applying (Check only one box.)
- ☐ Started new business (specify) ► _____
- ☒ Hired employees
- ☐ Created a pension plan (specify type) ► _____
- ☐ Banking purpose (specify) ►
- ☐ Changed type of organization (specify) ► _____
- ☐ Purchased going business
- ☐ Created a trust (specify) ► _____
- ☐ Other (specify) ►

10 Date business started or acquired (Mo., day, year) (See instructions.)
2/1/96

11 Enter closing month of accounting year. (See instructions.)
June

12 First date wages or annuities were paid or will be paid (Mo., day, year). Note: If applicant is a withholding agent, enter date income will first be paid to nonresident alien. (Mo., day, year)   2/1/96

13 Enter highest number of employees expected in the next 12 months. Note: If the applicant does not expect to have any employees during the period, enter "0." ►

Nonagricultural	Agricultural	Household
3		

14 Principal activity (See instructions.) ►   Church

15 Is the principal business activity manufacturing? . . . . ☐ Yes ☒ No
If "Yes," principal product and raw material used ►

16 To whom are most of the products or services sold? Please check the appropriate box. ☐ Business (wholesale)
☐ Public (retail)   ☐ Other (specify) ►   ☒ N/A

17a Has the applicant ever applied for an identification number for this or any other business? . . . . ☐ Yes ☒ No
Note: If "Yes," please complete lines 17b and 17c.

17b If you checked the "Yes" box in line 17a, give applicant's legal name and trade name, if different than name shown on prior application.
Legal name ►   Trade name ►

17c Enter approximate date, city, and state where the application was filed and the previous employer identification number if known.
Approximate date when filed (Mo., day, year)   City and state where filed   Previous EIN

Under penalties of perjury, I declare that I have examined this application, and to the best of my knowledge and belief, it is true, correct, and complete.   Business telephone number (include area code)

Name and title (Please type or print clearly.) ►   Mike R. Thomas, Treasurer   305-688-7432

Signature ►   Mike R. Thomas   Date ►   1/31/96

Note: Do not write below this line.   For official use only.

| Please leave blank ► | Geo. | Ind. | Class | Size | Reason for applying |

For Paperwork Reduction Act Notice, see attached instructions.   Cat. No. 16055N   Form **SS-4** (Rev. 12-93)

Note: Nearly every church or other nonprofit organization needs an Employer Identification Number (EIN) obtained by filing this form.

✓ Some donors, or their professional advisors, may ask if a local church is listed in IRS Publication 78, the Cumulative List of Organizations to which tax deductible contributions may be made. Only churches that have applied and been approved for tax-exempt status are listed in Publication 78.

There is no requirement for churches to be listed in Publication 78. However, a listing in the publication generally eliminates any question about the deductibility of contributions to the church as charitable contributions.

✓ If a local congregation ordains ministers, it may be helpful to apply for tax-exempt status. Ministers that are ordained by a local church may be required to provide evidence that the church is tax-exempt. This could be particularly true if the minister files Form 4361 applying for exemption for self-employment tax.

Churches or other charitable organizations desiring recognition of tax-exempt status should submit Form 1023. If approved, the IRS will issue a determination letter describing the category of exemption granted.

The IRS must be notified that the organization is applying for recognition of exemption within 15 months from the end of the month in which it was organized. Applications made after this deadline will not be effective before the date on which the application for recognition of exemption is filed.

Large and small organizations often find that obtaining an exemption letter from the IRS is an intimidating process. Organizations faced with the process are typically new, with a general mission in mind. The mission is often not fully developed and therefore it may not be clearly articulated. It may be helpful to have your application reviewed by a CPA or attorney before it is filed.

Determination letter request

A user fee of $465 (with Form 8718) must accompany applications for recognition of tax-exempt status where the applicant has gross receipts that annually exceed $10,000. For an organization that has had annual gross receipts of $10,000 or less during the past four years, the fee is $150. Start-ups may qualify for the reduced fee if they anticipate those receipts. Group exemption letter fees are $500.

Granting tax exemption

Upon approval of the application for exemption, the IRS will provide a determination letter. This letter may be an advance determination or a definitive (or final) determination. The exempt status is usually effective as of the date of formation of the organization, if filing deadlines are met.

An advance determination letter provides tentative guidance regarding status but is a final determination relating to operations and structure of the organization. An advance determination is effective for five years. Before the end of the advance determination period, the organization must show that it qualifies for nonprivate foundation status. During the advance determination period, contributors may make tax-deductible donations to the organization.

A newly created organization seeking status as a publicly supported organization is entitled to receive, if it so elects, a definitive ruling if it has completed a tax year consisting of eight full months as of the time of filing the application.

A definitive (or final) determination letter represents a determination by the IRS position that the organizational and operational plans of the nonprofit entitle it to be classified as exempt.

Group exemption

An affiliated group of organizations under the common control of a central organization can obtain a group exemption letter. Churches that are part of a denomination are not required to file a separate application for exemption if they are covered by the group letter.

The central organization is required to report annually its exempt subordinate organizations to the IRS (the IRS does not provide a particular form for this reporting). The central organization is responsible to evaluate the tax status of its subordinate groups.

Unrelated Business Income

All income of tax-exempt organizations is presumed to be tax-exempt from federal income tax unless the income is generated by an activity that is

✓ not substantially related to the organization's exempt purpose or function,

✓ a trade or business, and

✓ regularly carried on.

Unrelated business income (UBI) is permitted for tax-exempt organizations. However, churches and other nonprofits may have to pay tax on income derived from activities unrelated to their exempt purpose. UBI must not comprise a substantial part of the organization's operation. There is no specific percentage limitation on how much UBI is "substantial." However, organizations with 50% to 80% of their activities classified as unrelated have faced revocation of their tax-exempt status.

Form 990-T must be completed to report the source(s) of UBI and related expenses and to compute any tax. UBI amounts are also reportable on Form 990 (if the filing of Form 990 is required).

Although churches are exempt from filing Form 990, they must file Form 990-T if they have $1,000 or more of gross UBI in a year. There is a specific deduction of $1,000 in computing unrelated business taxable income. This specific deduction applies to a diocese, province of a religious order, or a convention or association of churches with respect to each parish, individual church, district, or other local unit.

The reporting of UBI and payment of the tax is significantly abused by non-profits. Recent studies have shown that less than 10% of the organizations filing Form 990 also file Form 990-T.

Unrelated business income consequences

Some church and nonprofit executives are paranoid about UBI to the point that they feel it must be avoided altogether. Some people equate UBI with the automatic loss of exempt status. A more balanced view is to understand the purpose of the UBI and minimize the UBI tax through proper planning.

The most common adverse result of having UBI is that all or part of it may be taxed. A less frequent, but still possible, result is that the organization will lose its tax exemption. It is possible that the IRS will deny or revoke the tax-exempt status of an organization when it regularly derives over one-half of its annual revenue from unrelated activities.

Congress recognized that some nonprofits may need to engage in unrelated business activities to survive. For example, a nonprofit with unused office space might rent the space to another organization. Also, nonprofits are expected to invest surplus funds to supplement the primary sources of the organization's income.

A trade or business regularly carried on

A trade or business means any activity regularly carried on which produces income from the sale of goods and services and where there is a reasonable expectation of a profit. To decide whether a trade or business is regularly carried on, the IRS considers whether taxable organizations would carry on a business with the same frequency and continuity. Intermittent activities may escape the "regularly carried on" definition.

Example 1: If a church sells sandwiches at an area bazaar for only two weeks, the IRS would not treat this as the regular conduct of a trade or business.

Example 2: A one-time sale of property is not an activity that is regularly carried on and therefore does not generate unrelated business income.

Example 3: A church is located in the downtown section of a city. Each Saturday, the church parking lot is operated commercially to accommodate shoppers. Even though the business activity is carried on for only one day each week on a year-round basis, this constitutes the conduct of a trade or business. It is subject to the unrelated business income tax.

Substantially related

According to the IRS regulations, a trade or business must "contribute impor-

Form **990**

Return of Organization Exempt From Income Tax

Under section 501(c) of the Internal Revenue Code (except black lung benefit trust or private foundation) or section 4947(a)(1) nonexempt charitable trust

OMB No. 1545-0047

1995

This Form is Open to Public Inspection

Department of the Treasury
Internal Revenue Service

Note: The organization may have to use a copy of this return to satisfy state reporting requirements.

A For the 1994 calendar year, OR tax year period beginning _____, 1994, and ending _____, 19___

B Check if:
☐ Change of address
☐ Initial return
☐ Final return
☐ Amended return (required also for State reporting)

Please use IRS label or print or type. See Specific Instructions.

C Name of organization
Athens Children's Home

Number and street (or P.O. box if mail is not delivered to street address) Room/suite
1212 South Palo Verde

City, town, or post office, state, and ZIP code
Phoenix, AZ 85035

D Employer identification number
35 : 7438041

E State registration number

F Check ► ☐ if exemption application is pending

G Type of organization ► ☒ Exempt under section 501(c)(3) ◄ (insert number) OR ► ☐ section 4947(a)(1) nonexempt charitable trust

Note: *Section 501(c)(3) exempt organizations and 4947(a)(1) nonexempt charitable trusts MUST attach a completed Schedule A (Form 990).*

H(a) Is this a group return filed for affiliates? . . . . ☐ Yes ☒ No

I If either box in H is checked "Yes," enter four-digit group exemption number (GEN) ► _____

(b) If "Yes," enter the number of affiliates for which this return is filed: . ► _____

(c) Is this a separate return filed by an organization covered by a group ruling? ☐ Yes ☒ No

J Accounting method: ☐ Cash ☒ Accrual
☐ Other (specify) ►

K Check here ► ☐ if the organization's gross receipts are normally not more than $25,000. The organization need not file a return with the IRS; but if it received a Form 990 Package in the mail, it should file a return without financial data. Some states require a complete return.

Note: *Form 990-EZ may be used by organizations with gross receipts less than $100,000 and total assets less than $250,000 at end of year.*

Part I Statement of Revenue, Expenses, and Changes in Net Assets or Fund Balances

1	Contributions, gifts, grants, and similar amounts received:			
a	Direct public support	1a	314,812	
b	Indirect public support	1b	41,042	
c	Government contributions (grants)	1c		
d	**Total** (add lines 1a through 1c) (attach schedule—see instructions) (cash $ 355,854 noncash $ _____) . . .		1d	355,854
2	Program service revenue including government fees and contracts (from Part VII, line 93)		2	
3	Membership dues and assessments (see instructions)		3	
4	Interest on savings and temporary cash investments		4	10,483
5	Dividends and interest from securities		5	
6a	Gross rents	6a		
b	Less: rental expenses	6b		
c	Net rental income or (loss) (subtract line 6b from line 6a)		6c	
7	Other investment income (describe ►		7	
8a	Gross amount from sale of assets other than inventory	(A) Securities / 8a	(B) Other	
b	Less: cost or other basis and sales expenses .	8b		
c	Gain or (loss) (attach schedule)	8c		
d	Net gain or (loss) (combine line 8c, columns (A) and (B))		8d	
9	Special events and activities (attach schedule—see instructions):			
a	Gross revenue (not including $ 51,842 of contributions reported on line 1a) . .	9a	74,712	
b	Less: direct expenses other than fundraising expenses .	9b	29,003	
c	Net income or (loss) from special events (subtract line 9b from line 9a)		9c	45,709
10a	Gross sales of inventory, less returns and allowances . .	10a		
b	Less: cost of goods sold	10b		
c	Gross profit or (loss) from sales of inventory (attach schedule) (subtract line 10b from line 10a) .		10c	
11	Other revenue (from Part VII, line 103)		11	
12	**Total revenue** (add lines 1d, 2, 3, 4, 5, 6c, 7, 8d, 9c, 10c, and 11)		12	412,046
13	Program services (from line 44, column (B)—see instructions)		13	259,028
14	Management and general (from line 44, column (C)—see instructions)		14	84,933
15	Fundraising (from line 44, column (D)—see instructions)		15	59,012
16	Payments to affiliates (attach schedule—see instructions)		16	
17	**Total expenses** (add lines 16 and 44, column (A))		17	402,973
18	Excess or (deficit) for the year (subtract line 17 from line 12)		18	9,073
19	Net assets or fund balances at beginning of year (from line 74, column (A))		19	144,098
20	Other changes in net assets or fund balances (attach explanation)		20	
21	Net assets or fund balances at end of year (combine lines 18, 19, and 20)		21	153,171

For Paperwork Reduction Act Notice, see page 1 of the separate instructions.   Cat. No. 11282Y   Form **990** (1994)

Note: Form 990 has a total of five pages. Schedule A of Form 990 has five pages and is used to furnish additional information.

tantly to the accomplishment of the exempt purposes of an organization" if it is to be considered "substantially related." Even if all the profits from a business go to support the work of the nonprofit, the profits may still be taxed.

> **Example:** If a church operated a restaurant and devoted all the proceeds to mission work, the church could not escape taxation on the restaurant's income.

Types of income that may be "related" are

✓ the sale of products made by handicapped individuals as a part of their rehabilitation;

✓ the sale of homes constructed by students enrolled in a vocational training course; and

✓ a retail grocery store operated to provide emotional therapy for disturbed adolescents.

Tours conducted by nonprofits usually create UBI. Tours may be exempt from UBI only if they are strongly educationally oriented, with reports, daily lectures, and so on. Tours with substantial recreational or social purposes are not exempt.

The definition of "unrelated trade or business" *does not* include

✓ activities in which unpaid volunteers do most of the work for an organization;

✓ activities provided primarily for the convenience of the organization's members; or

✓ activities involving the sale of merchandise mostly donated to the organization.

Rental income

Nonprofits often rent facilities, equipment, and other assets for a fee. Rental income usually represents UBI with the following exceptions:

✓ Renting to another nonprofit may be termed "related" if the rental expressly serves the landlord's exempt purposes.

✓ Mailing lists produce UBI, with specific exceptions.

✓ Rental of real estate is excluded from UBI unless the excludable property is acquired or improved with indebtedness. Rental income from the property becomes UBI to the extent of the ratio of the "average acquisition indebtedness" during the year to the total purchase price. The nonprofit may deduct the

Form **990-T**	**Exempt Organization Business Income Tax Return** (and proxy tax under section 6033(e))	OMB No. 1545-0687
Department of the Treasury Internal Revenue Service	For calendar year 1994 or other tax year beginning .... , 1994, and ending .... , 19 .... ▶ **See separate instructions.**	**1995**

A ☐ Check box if address changed		Name of organization	**D** Employer identification number (Employees' trust, see instructions for Block D.)
B Exempt under section ☒ 501(**c**)(**3**) or ☐ 408(e)	Please Print or Type	Family Bible Crusades	35 : 4427081
		Number, street, and room or suite no. (If a P.O. box, see page 5 of instructions.)	**E** Unrelated business activity codes (see instructions for Block E)
		400 North Sunset Avenue	
C Book value of all assets at end of year		City or town, state, and ZIP code	6512 :
		Lemon Grove, CA 92045	

F Group exemption number (see instructions for Block F) ▶

G Check type of organization. ▶ ☒ 501(c) Corporation ☐ 501(c) Trust ☐ Section 401(a) trust ☐ Section 408(a) trust

H Describe the organization's primary unrelated business activity. (See instructions for Block H.)
Rental of building that is subject to a mortgage

I During the tax year, was the corporation a subsidiary in an affiliated group or a parent-subsidiary controlled group? . ▶ ☐ Yes ☒ No
If "Yes," enter the name and identifying number of the parent corporation. (See instructions for Block I.) ▶

Part I — Unrelated Trade or Business Income

			(A) Income	(B) Expenses	(C) Net
1a	Gross receipts or sales				
b	Less returns and allowances ___ c Balance ▶	1c			
2	Cost of goods sold (Schedule A, line 7)	2			
3	Gross profit (subtract line 2 from line 1c)	3			
4a	Capital gain net income (attach Schedule D)	4a			
b	Net gain (loss) (Form 4797, Part II, line 20) (attach Form 4797)	4b			
c	Capital loss deduction for trusts	4c			
5	Income (loss) from partnerships (attach statement)	5			
6	Rent income (Schedule C)	6			
7	Unrelated debt-financed income (Schedule E)	7	79,410	52,301	27,109
8	Interest, annuities, royalties, and rents from controlled organizations (Schedule F)	8			
9	Investment income of a section 501(c)(7), (9), or (17) organization (Schedule G)	9			
10	Exploited exempt activity income (Schedule I)	10			
11	Advertising income (Schedule J)	11			
12	Other income (see instructions—attach schedule)	12			
13	TOTAL (combine lines 3 through 12)	13	79,410	52,301	27,109

Part II — Deductions Not Taken Elsewhere (See instructions for limitations on deductions.)
(Except for contributions, deductions must be directly connected with the unrelated business income.)

14	Compensation of officers, directors, and trustees (Schedule K)	14	
15	Salaries and wages	15	
16	Repairs and maintenance	16	
17	Bad debts	17	
18	Interest (attach schedule)	18	
19	Taxes and licenses	19	
20	Charitable contributions (see instructions for limitation rules)	20	
21	Depreciation (attach Form 4562) . . . 21		
22	Less depreciation claimed on Schedule A and elsewhere on return . 22a	22b	
23	Depletion	23	
24	Contributions to deferred compensation plans	24	
25	Employee benefit programs	25	
26	Excess exempt expenses (Schedule I)	26	
27	Excess readership costs (Schedule J)	27	
28	Other deductions (attach schedule)	28	
29	TOTAL DEDUCTIONS (add lines 14 through 28)	29	
30	Unrelated business taxable income before net operating loss deduction (subtract line 29 from line 13)	30	27,109
31	Net operating loss deduction	31	
32	Unrelated business taxable income before specific deduction (subtract line 31 from line 30)	32	27,109
33	Specific deduction	33	1,000
34	Unrelated business taxable income (subtract line 33 from line 32). If line 33 is greater than line 32, enter the smaller of zero or line 32	34	26,109

For Paperwork Reduction Act Notice, see page 1 of separate instructions.   Cat. No. 11291J   Form **990-T** (1994)

Note: Form 990-T has a total of four pages. Only page one is shown here.
Caution: Professional assistance may be needed to complete this form.

same portion of the expenses directly connected with the production of the rental income. Depreciation is allowable using only the straight-line method.

Debt-financed income

To discourage exempt organizations from borrowing money to purchase passive income items, Congress imposed a tax on debt-financed income. An organization may have debt-financed income if

✔ it incurs debt to purchase or improve an income-producing asset; and

✔ some of that debt remains within the 12 months prior to when income is received from the asset.

An organization also may have debt-financed income if it accepts gifts or bequests of mortgaged property in some circumstances.

There are exceptions to the debt-financed income rules, including

✔ substantially all (85% or more) of any property is used for an organization's exempt purposes;

✔ use of property by a related exempt organization to further its exempt purposes;

✔ life income contracts, if the remainder interest is payable to an exempt charitable organization;

✔ neighborhood land rule, if an organization acquires real property in its "neighborhood" (the neighborhood restriction does not apply to churches) mainly to use it for exempt purposes within ten years (15 years for churches).

Activities that are not taxed

Income from the following sources is generally not considered as UBI:

✔ **Passive income.** Income earned from most passive investment activities is not UBI unless the underlying property is subject to debt. Types of passive income include

● dividends, interest, and annuities

● capital gains or losses from the sale, exchange, or other disposition of property

- rents from real property (some rent is UBI if the rental property was purchased or improved subject to a mortgage)

- royalties (oil and gas working interest income generally constitute UBI)

✓ **Volunteers.** Any business where volunteers perform most of the work without compensation does not qualify as UBI. To the IRS, "substantially" means at least 85% of total work performed.

Example: A used-clothing store operated by a nonprofit orphanage where volunteers do all the work in the store would likely be exempt.

✓ **Convenience.** A cafeteria, bookstore, or residence operated for the convenience of patients, visitors, employees, or students is not a business. Stores, parking lots, and other facilities may be dually used (part related and part unrelated).

✓ **Donated goods.** The sale of merchandise, mostly received as gifts or contributions, does not qualify as UBI. A justification for this exemption is that contributions of property are merely being converted into cash.

✓ **Low-cost items.** Items (costing no more than $6.60—1995 adjusted amount) distributed incidental to the solicitation of charitable contributions are not subject to UBI. The amounts received are not considered as an exchange for the low-cost articles and therefore they do not create UBI.

✓ **Mailing lists.** Mailing lists exchanged with or rented to another exempt organization are excluded from UBI, although the commercial sale of the lists will generally create UBI. The structuring of the agreement as a royalty arrangement may make the income exempt from UBI treatment.

Calculating the unrelated business income tax

Income tax rules applicable to businesses, such as depreciation method limitations and rates, apply to the UBI computation. Direct and indirect costs may be used to offset income. The first $1,000 of annual net unrelated income is exempt from taxation.

For 1995, the corporate tax rates are

Taxable Income			Tax Rate
$ 0	to	$50,000	15% plus
$ 50,001	to	$75,000	25% plus
$ 75,001	to	$100,000	34% plus
$100,001	to	$335,000	39% plus
$335,000	to	$10,000,000	34%

Unrelated business income summary

Be aware of the type of activities that may create UBI in your organization.

✓ Maintain careful records of income and related expenses (both direct and indirect, including depreciation) for any activities that might be considered unrelated to the exempt purpose of your organization. These records should include allocations of salaries and fringe benefits based on time records or, at a minimum, time estimates.

It may be wise to keep a separate set of records on potential unrelated activities. This separate set of records would need to be submitted to the IRS only upon audit.

✓ Be sure that board minutes, contracts, and other documents reflect the organization's view of relatedness of various activities to the exempt purpose of the entity.

✓ If the organization has over $1,000 of gross UBI in a given fiscal (tax) year, file Form 990-T.

Private Benefit and Private Inurement

Tax laws and regulations impose prohibitions on nonprofit organizations concerning private benefit and private inurement.

Private benefit

Nonprofit organizations must serve public, and not private, interests. The private benefit prohibition applies to anyone outside the intended charitable class. The law does allow some private benefit if it is incidental to the public benefits involved. It is acceptable if the benefit to the public cannot be achieved without necessarily benefiting private individuals.

> **Example:** The IRS revoked exemption of a charity where it served the commercial purposes and private interests of a professional fund-raiser where the fund-raiser distributed only 3% of the amount collected to the nonprofit organization.

Private inurement

Private inurement is a subset of private benefit. This is an absolute prohibition that generally applies to a distinct class of private interests. These "insiders" may be founders, trustees or directors, officers, managers, or significant donors. Transactions involving these individuals are not necessarily prohibited, but they must be subject to reasonableness, documentation, and applicable reporting to the IRS.

Inurement arises whenever a financial benefit represents a transfer of resources to an individual solely by virtue of the individual's relationship with the organization, without regard to accomplishing its exempt purposes. When an individual receives something for nothing or less than it is worth, private inurement may have occurred. Excessive, and therefore unreasonable, compensation can also result in prohibited inurement. The IRS may ask the following questions to determine if private inurement exists:

✔ Did the expenditure further an exempt purpose, and, if so, how?

✔ Was the payment at fair market value or did it represent reasonable compensation for goods and services?

✔ Does a low- or no-interest loan to an employee or director fall within a reasonable compensation package?

✔ On an overseas trip for the nonprofit, did the employee (and perhaps a spouse) stay an additional week for a personal vacation and charge the expenses to the organization?

Example 1: An organization lost its exemption where it engaged in numerous transactions with an insider, including the purchase of a 42-foot boat for the personal use of the insider. The insider also benefitted from several real estate transactions, including donations and sales of real property to the organization which were never reflected on its books.

Example 2: A church lost its tax-exemption after it operated commercial businesses and paid substantial private expenses of its founders, including expenses for jewelry and clothing in excess of $30,000 per year. The church also purchased five luxury cars for the founders' personal use. None of these benefits were reported as personal income to the founders.

Example 3: A tax-exempt organization transfers an auto to an employee for $100. The transfer was not approved by the board and does not constitute a portion of a reasonable pay package. The fair market value of the auto is $2,000. The net difference of $1,900 is not reported to the IRS as compensation. Private inurement has occurred.

Example 4: Same facts as Example 3, except the transfer was approved by the board and properly constituted a portion of the reasonable pay package, and the $1,900 was added to the employee's Form W-2 as compensation. There is no private inurement.

Filing Federal Returns

Nearly all nonprofit organizations must file an annual return with the IRS (churches are exempt from filing Form 990 or 990-EZ). The basic filing requirements are

FORM TO BE FILED	CONDITIONS
No form filed	Gross annual receipts normally under $25,000
Form 990-EZ	Gross annual receipts between $25,000 and $100,000 with total assets of less than $250,000
Form 990	Gross annual receipts over $100,000 or assets over $250,000 with gross annual receipts between $25,000 and $100,000
Form 990-T	Any organization exempt under Sec. 501(a) with $1,000 or more gross income from an unrelated trade or business
Form 1120	Any nonprofit corporation that is not tax-exempt
Form 5500	Pension, profit-sharing, medical benefit, cafeteria, and certain other plans must file annually one of several series 5500 Forms.

Public inspection of information returns

Nonprofit organizations must make copies of Forms 990 and 990-EZ for the three most recent years available to the public at any of their offices (with three or more employees) during regular business hours. Copies of the application for tax exemption (if applicable) also must be made available. There are penalties for failure to comply.

The following procedures may be followed to meet this requirement:

✓ Make copies of the information returns for the last three years, excluding only the list of contributions required to answer: (1) Part I, question 1d, (2) Schedule A, Part IV, question 26b. The details of the officers' annual salaries and expense reimbursements (in Part IV and in Schedule A, Part I)

are available to the public. Also make a copy of the tax-exempt application and related correspondence or supporting documents.

✓ When someone comes in and asks to see the documents, tell the guest that (1) the copies of the forms are ready and available for them to review, (2) a staff member will be happy to answer any questions about the documents, (3) the copies must be returned to the organization and may not be retained by the guest, and (4) that copies can be obtained by writing to the IRS on Form 4506-A.

✓ Keep a log showing the names and addresses of the individuals who reviewed the documents.

Reporting substantial organizational changes

An organization's tax-exempt status remains in effect if there are no material changes in the organization's character, purposes, or methods of operation. Significant changes should be reported by letter to the IRS soon after the changes occur.

Example: An organization received tax-exempt status for the operation of a religious radio ministry. Several years later, the organization decided to add a facility for homeless children. This change would likely be deemed to be material and should be reported to the IRS.

Change in accounting methods

A nonprofit organization may adopt any reasonable method of accounting to keep its financial records that clearly reflects income. These methods include the cash receipts and disbursements method; the accrual method; or any other method (including a combination of methods) that clearly reflects income.

An organization that wishes to change from one method of accounting to another must secure the consent of the IRS to make that change. Consent must be obtained both for a general change of method, and for any change of method with respect to one or more particular items. Thus, a nonprofit organization that generally uses the cash method, but uses the accrual method with respect to publications for which it maintains inventories may change its method of accounting by adopting the accrual method for all purposes. But the organization must secure the IRS consent to do so.

To obtain the consent of the IRS to change an accounting method, the organization should file IRS Form 3115, Application for Change in Accounting Method. The form must be filed within 180 days after the beginning of the tax year in which the change is made. There is a more expeditious consent for a change from the cash to accrual method filed under Revenue Procedure 85-37.

Change of fiscal years

Generally, an exempt organization may change its fiscal year simply by timely filing Form 990 with the appropriate Internal Revenue Service Center for the "short year." The return for the short year should indicate at the top of page 1 that a change of accounting period is being made. It should be filed not later than the 15th day of the fifth month following the close of the short year.

If neither Form 990 nor Form 990-T must be filed, the ministry is not required to notify the IRS of a change in the fiscal year, with one exception. The exception applies to exempt organizations that have changed their fiscal years within the previous ten calendar years. For this exception, Form 1128 must be filed with the IRS.

Other

✓ **Form 5578.** Form 5578 may be completed and furnished to the IRS to provide information regarding nondiscrimination policies of private schools instead of completing the information at item 31 of Form 990, Schedule A. If Form 990 is not required to be filed, Form 5578 should be submitted, if applicable. Form 5578 must be filed for schools operated by a church, including pre-schools.

✓ **Form 8717 and 8718.** Nonprofits wishing IRS private letter rulings on exempt organization information or on employee plans must include new forms 8717 or 8718, respectively, with the appropriate fees.

✓ **Form 8282.** If a nonprofit donee sells or otherwise disposes of gift property for which an appraisal summary is required on Form 8283 within two years after receipt of the property, it generally must file an information return (Form 8282) with the IRS. See Chapter 7 for more information on these reporting rules.

✓ **Employee and nonemployee payments.** As an employer, a nonprofit organization must file federal and state forms concerning payment of compensation and the withholding of payroll taxes. Payments to nonemployees may require the filing of information returns. See Chapters 4 and 5 for more coverage on these requirements.

Filing State Returns

Separate filings are often necessary to obtain exemption from state income tax. The requirements vary from state to state. In some states it is also possible to obtain exemption from sales, use, and property taxes.

A nonprofit organization may be required to report to one or more states in relation to its exemption from or compliance with state income, sales, use, or property taxation.

Many states accept a copy of Form 990 as adequate annual reporting for tax-exempt status purposes. Annual reporting to the state in which the organization is incorporated is normally required even if there is no requirement to file Form 990 with the IRS. Check with the offices of the secretary of state and attorney general to determine required filings.

Do not send a list of major contributors to the state unless it is specifically required. While this list is not open to public inspection with respect to the federal filing, it may not be confidential for state purposes.

Political Activity

Churches and other organizations exempt from federal income tax under section 501(c)(3) of the Internal Revenue Code are prohibited from participating or intervening, directly or indirectly, in any political campaign on behalf of or in opposition to any candidate for public office.

To avoid violating the political campaign provisions of the law:

✔ Do not use a rating program to evaluate candidates.

✔ Do not endorse a candidate directly or indirectly through a sermon, speech, newsletter, or sample ballot.

✔ Do not publish a candidate's statement.

✔ Do not publish the names of candidates who agree to adhere to certain practices.

✔ Do not publish candidate responses to a questionnaire that evidences a bias on certain issues.

✔ Do not publish responses to an unbiased questionnaire focused on a narrow range of issues.

✔ Do not raise funds for a candidate.

✔ Do not provide volunteers, mailing lists, publicity, or free use of facilities unless all parties and candidates in the community receive the same services.

✔ Do not pay campaign expenses for a candidate.

✔ Do not distribute statements about candidates or display campaign literature on organization's premises.

If the IRS finds that an organization has engaged in these activities, it could result in a loss of exempt status. Also, the IRS may assess an excise tax on the amount of the funds spent on the activity.

Are there any political campaign activities that may legally be engaged in by a church or nonprofit? Forums or debates may be conducted to educate voters at which all candidates are treated equally, or a mailing list may be rented to candidates on the same basis as it is made available to others. Organizations may engage in voter registration or get-out-the-vote activities. However, it is wise to avoid defining a target group by political or ideological criteria (e.g., encouraging individuals to vote who are "registered Republicans").

Key Concepts

- Tax exemption is a privilege—not to be taken lightly.

- Churches are generally tax-exempt from federal income taxes without applying for this status.

- Most nonchurch organizations must apply for federal tax-exempt status.

- Churches and other nonprofits may be subject to the unrelated business income tax.

- Tax-exempt funds must be diverted for personal use. This is called private inurement or benefit.

- Exemption from federal income tax does not automatically provide exemption from state taxes such as property, sales, and use tax.

| Form **5578** (Rev. February 1993) Department of the Treasury Internal Revenue Service | **Annual Certification of Racial Nondiscrimination for a Private School Exempt From Federal Income Tax** (For use by organizations that do not file Form 990 or Form 990-EZ) | OMB No. 1545-0213 Expires 1-31-96 For IRS use ONLY ▶ |

For the period beginning __July 1__, 19 95 and ending __June 30__, 19 96

1a Name of organization that operates, supervises, and/or controls school(s)		1b Employer identification number
Liberty Grove Church		
Address (number and street or P.O. box no. if mail is not delivered to street address)	Room/suite	35 : 1047863
1533 North Andrews Avenue		
City or town, state, and ZIP code		
Ft. Lauderdale, FL 33308		

2a Name of central organization holding group exemption letter covering the school(s). (If same as 1a above, write "Same" and complete 2c.) If the organization in 1a above holds an individual exemption letter, write "Not Applicable."		2b Employer identification number
Not applicable		
Address (number and street or P.O. box no. if mail is not delivered to street address)	Room/suite	2c Group exemption number (see instructions under Definitions)
City or town, state, and ZIP code		

3a Name of school (if more than one school, write "See Attached," and attach list of the names, addresses, ZIP codes, and employer identification numbers of the schools. If same as 1a above, write "Same."		3b Employer identification number, if any
Liberty Grove Christian School		
Address (number and street or P.O. box no. if mail is not delivered to street address)		Room/suite
2100 Cook Lane		
City or town, state, and ZIP code		
Ft. Lauderdale, FL 33308		

Under penalties of perjury, I hereby certify that I am authorized to take official action on behalf of the above school(s) and that to the best of my knowledge and belief the school(s) has (have) satisfied the applicable requirements of section 4.01 through 4.05 of Revenue Procedure 75-50 for the period covered by this certification.

Roy L. Crawford (Signature)　　　_Superintendent_ (Title or authority of signer)　　　_7/31/96_ (Date)

Instructions

This form is open to public inspection.

Paperwork Reduction Act Notice.—We ask for the information on this form to carry out the Internal Revenue laws of the United States. You are required to give us the information. We need it to ensure that you are complying with these laws.

The time needed to complete and file this form will vary depending on individual circumstances. The estimated average time is 4 hours and 45 minutes. If you have comments concerning the accuracy of this time estimate or suggestions for making this form more simple, we would be happy to hear from you. You can write to both the **Internal Revenue Service,** Washington, DC 20224, Attention: IRS Reports Clearance Officer, T:FP; and the **Office of Management and Budget,** Paperwork Reduction Project (1545-0213), Washington, DC 20503. **DO NOT** send the form to either of these offices. Instead, see **Where To File** below.

Purpose of Form

Form 5578 may be used by organizations that operate tax-exempt private schools to provide the Internal Revenue Service with the annual certification of racial nondiscrimination required by Rev. Proc. 75-50, 1975-2 C.B. 587.

Who Must File

Every organization that claims exemption from Federal income tax under section 501(c)(3) of the Internal Revenue Code and that operates, supervises, or controls a private school or schools must file a certification of racial nondiscrimination. If an organization is required to file **Form 990,** Return of Organization Exempt From Income Tax, or **Form 990-EZ,** Short Form Return of Organization Exempt From Income

Tax, either as a separate return or as part of a group return, the certification must be made on **Schedule A (Form 990),** Organization Exempt Under Section 501(c)(3), rather than on this form.

An authorized official of a central organization may file one form to certify for the school activities of subordinate organizations that would otherwise be required to file on an individual basis, but only if the central organization has enough control over the schools listed on the form to ensure that the schools maintain a racially nondiscriminatory policy as to students.

Definitions

A **racially nondiscriminatory policy as to students** means that the school admits the students of any race to all the rights, privileges, programs, and activities generally accorded or made available to students at that school and that the school does not discriminate on the basis of race in the administration of its educational policies, admissions policies, scholarship and loan programs, and other school-administered programs.

The IRS considers discrimination on the basis of race to include discrimination on the basis of color or national or ethnic origin.

A **school** is an educational organization that normally maintains a regular faculty and curriculum and normally has a regularly enrolled body of pupils or students in attendance at the place where its educational activities are regularly carried on. The term includes primary, secondary, preparatory, or high schools and colleges and universities, whether operated as a separate legal entity or as an activity of a church or other organization described in Code section 501(c)(3). The term also includes preschools and any other organization that is a school as defined in Code section 170(b)(1)(A)(ii).

A **central organization** is an organization that has one or more subordinates under its general supervision or control. A subordinate is a chapter, local, post, or other unit of a central organization. A central organization may also be a subordinate, as in the case of a state organization that has subordinate units and is itself affiliated with a national organization.

The **group exemption number (GEN)** is a 4-digit number issued to a central organization by the IRS. It identifies a central organization that has received a ruling from the IRS recognizing on a group basis the exemption from Federal income tax of the central organization and its covered subordinates.

When To File

Under Rev. Proc. 75-50, a certification of racial nondiscrimination must be filed annually by the 15th day of the 5th month following the end of the organization's calendar year or fiscal period.

Where To File

If the principal office of the organization is located in	Use the following Internal Revenue Service Center address
Alabama, Arkansas, Florida, Georgia, Louisiana, Mississippi, North Carolina, South Carolina, or Tennessee	Atlanta, GA 39901
Arizona, Colorado, Kansas, New Mexico, Oklahoma, Texas, Utah, or Wyoming	Austin, TX 73301
Indiana, Kentucky, Michigan, Ohio, or West Virginia	Cincinnati, OH 45999
Alaska, California, Hawaii, Idaho, Nevada, Oregon, or Washington	Fresno, CA 93888

Cat. No. 42658A　　　　Form **5578** (Rev. 2-93)

Note: Private schools must complete this form annually. This form need not be filed if Form 990 is required and item 31 of Schedule A is completed.

CHAPTER THREE

Compensation Planning

In This Chapter

- Reasonable compensation
- Organization-provided housing
- Maximizing fringe benefits
- Nondiscrimination rules
- Paying employee expenses

Compensation plans should provide tax-effective benefits. A dollar of benefit costs to the organization may be multiplied when received by the employee through proper planning.

Reasonable Compensation

Employees of churches and nonprofit organizations may receive reasonable compensation for their efforts. Excessive compensation can result in private inurement and may jeopardize the tax-exempt status of the organization. Reasonable compensation is based on what would ordinarily be paid for like services by a like organization under like circumstances.

Compensation packages over the $150,000-$200,000 level for even larger nonprofit organizations could be challenged by the IRS. Lower compensation packages could be termed excessive for smaller churches or ministries.

A review of the changes in the Consumers Price Index from one year to the next may be helpful when projecting salary increases:

1981	8.9%	1986	1.1%	1991	3.1%
1982	3.8%	1987	4.4%	1992	2.9%
1983	3.8%	1988	4.4%	1993	2.7%
1984	3.9%	1989	4.6%	1994	2.7%
1985	3.8%	1990	6.1%	1995	3.0% (est.)

47

Organization-Provided Housing

Nonminister employees

Housing provided to nonminister employees by a church or nonprofit organization for its convenience, as a condition of employment, and on its business premises is

✓ exempt from income tax and FICA tax withholding by the church; and

✓ excluded from wages reporting by the church and employee.

If these criteria are not met, the fair rental value should be reported as compensation on Form W-2 and is subject to withholding and FICA taxation.

Minister's housing allowance

Qualified ministers receive preferred treatment for their housing. If a minister has a home provided as part of compensation, the minister pays no income tax on the rental value of the home. If a home is not provided but the minister receives a rental or housing allowance, the minister pays no tax on the allowance if it is used for housing expenses subject to certain limitations.

Every minister should have a portion of salary designated as a housing allowance. For a minister living in organization-owned housing, the housing allowance may have only modest value to cover incidental expenses such as maintenance, furnishings, and utilities. But a properly designated housing allowance may be worth thousands of dollars in tax savings for ministers living in their own homes or rented quarters. For the minister without a housing allowance, every dollar of compensation is taxable for federal income tax purposes.

Ministers may exclude the housing allowance under the following rules:

✓ The allowance must be officially designated before payment by the organization. The designation should be evidenced in writing, preferably by board resolution, in an employment contract, or, at a minimum, in the church budget and payroll records.

  If the only reference to the housing allowance is in the organization's budget, the budget should be formally approved by the official board.

✓ Only actual expenses can be excluded from income. The expenses must be paid from ministerial income earned in the current year.

Sample Housing Allowance Resolutions

PARSONAGE OWNED BY OR RENTED BY A CHURCH

Whereas, The Internal Revenue Code permits a minister of the gospel to exclude from gross income "the rental value of a home furnished as part of compensation" or a church-designated allowance paid as a part of compensation to the extent that actual expenses are paid from the allowance to maintain a parsonage owned or rented by the church;

Whereas, Nelson Street Church compensates the senior minister for services in the exercise of ministry; and

Whereas, Nelson Street Church provides the senior minister with the rent-free use of a parsonage owned by (rented by) the church as a portion of the compensation for services rendered to the church in the exercise of ministry;

Resolved, That the compensation of the senior minister is $2,500 per month of which $200 per month is a designated housing allowance; and

Resolved, That the designation of $200 per month as a housing allowance shall apply until otherwise provided.

HOME OWNED OR RENTED BY MINISTER

Whereas, The Internal Revenue Code permits a minister of the gospel to exclude from gross income a church-designated allowance paid as part of compensation to the extent used for actual expenses in owning or renting a home; and

Whereas, Nelson Street Church compensates the senior minister for services in the exercise of ministry;

Resolved, That the compensation of the senior minister is $3,500 per month of which $1,250 per month is a designated housing allowance; and

Resolved, That the designation of $1,250 per month as a housing allowance shall apply until otherwise provided.

EVANGELISTS

Whereas, The Internal Revenue Code permits a minister of the gospel to exclude from gross income a church-designated allowance paid as part of compensation to the extent used in owning or renting a permanent home; and

Whereas, Nelson Street Church compensates Rev. John Doe for services in the exercise of ministry as an evangelist;

Resolved, That the honorarium paid to Rev. Doe shall be $1,500 consisting of $312 travel expenses (with documentation provided to the church), $500 housing allowance, and a $688 honorarium.

Standing housing resolution

It is a good practice to establish a standing housing allowance resolution in the organization's minutes. A standing resolution specified that a portion of the salary of a qualified minister shall be designated as a housing allowance and that it shall continue in force until changed. This standing resolution provides a back-up housing allowance in instances of ministerial staff changes.

Amending the housing designation

If a minister's actual housing expenses are or will be higher than initially estimated and designated, the organization may prospectively amend the designation during the year. The increase in the housing allowance only applies to housing dollars expended after the allowance is amended.

Multiple ministers of one organization receiving housing allowances

There is no limit on how many ministers may be given housing allowances by one organization. If there are multiple pastors on staff, the organization may designate a housing allowance for each of them.

Some organizations, not providing an organization-owned parsonage, erroneously set the housing allowance at the same dollar amount for each minister. Properly designated, the dollar amount should vary depending on the estimated housing expenses of the respective ministers.

Housing allowance as a percentage of salary

Some organizations set the housing allowance by applying a percentage to the total cash salary. Housing allowance percentages are often in a range of 40% to 60% of the total cash salary. Setting the housing designation based on an estimate of housing expenses for each minister is highly preferable over the percentage method. By using the percentage approach, the organization may unintentionally permit an excessive housing exclusion from income or preclude a legitimate exclusion.

Housing allowance limited to one home

Only one housing allowance may be provided to a minister. For example, a minister may have a summer home on a lake in addition to a home that is regularly used during most of the year. The housing allowance cannot be extended to the second home.

Cost of the housing allowance to the organization

Some organizations mistakenly believe that the provision of a housing allowance to a minister will increase the organization's budget. This is not true. If a portion of the minister's compensation is designated as a housing allowance, it costs the organization nothing.

Maximizing Fringe Benefits

Personal use of employer-provided vehicles

Vehicles provided by organizations to employees for business use are often used for personal purposes. The IRS treats most types of personal use of an employer-provided vehicle as a noncash fringe benefit, and generally requires the fair market value of such use to be included in the employee's gross income (to the extent that the value is not reimbursed to the employer).

If the employee reimburses the employer in a chargeback system for the full dollar value of the personal use, it will cost the employee more than if the employer includes the personal use value in the income of the employee.

Example: The personal use value of an automobile provided to a lay employee is determined to be $100; a chargeback system would require the employee to pay $100 to the employer. If, on the other hand, the employer includes the $100 in the employee's income, the employee will be subject to payroll taxes on $100 of income. Assuming a federal income tax rate of 31% and an FICA rate of 7.65% (based on annual gross pay of $61,200 or less for 1995) for a total of $38.65, compared with the $100 cash out-of-pocket chargeback.

Valuation of personal vehicle use

There are three special valuation rules, besides a set of general valuation principles, which may be used under specific circumstances for valuing the personal use of an employer-provided vehicle. This value must be included in the employee's compensation if it is not reimbursed by the employee.

Under the general valuation rule, the value is based on what the cost would be to a person leasing from a third party the same or comparable vehicle on the same or comparable terms in the same geographic area.

The special valuation rules, which are used by most employers, are:

 Cents-per-mile valuation rule. Generally, this rule may be used if the employer reasonably expects that the vehicle will be regularly used in the employer's trade or business, and if the vehicle is driven at least 10,000

miles a year and the vehicle is primarily used by employees. This valuation rule is available only if the fair market value of the vehicle, as of the date the vehicle was first made available for personal use by employees, does not exceed a specified value set by the IRS. For 1995, this value is $15,500.

The value of the personal use of the vehicle is computed by multiplying the number of miles driven for personal purposes by the current IRS standard mileage rate (30 cents per mile for 1995). For this valuation rule, personal use is "any use of the vehicle other than use in the employee's trade or business of being an employee of the employer."

✓ **Commuting valuation rule.** This rule may be used to determine the value of personal use only where the following conditions are met:

- The vehicle is owned or leased by the employer and is provided to one or more employees for use in connection with the employer's trade or business and is used as such.

- The employer requires the employee to commute to and/or from work in the vehicle for bona fide noncompensatory business reasons. One example of a bona fide noncompensatory business reason is the availability of the vehicle to an employee who is on-call and must have access to the vehicle when at home.

- The employer has a written policy that prohibits employees from using the vehicle for personal purposes other than for commuting or de minimis personal use (such as a stop for a personal errand on the way home from work).

- The employee required to use the vehicle for commuting is not a "control" employee of the employer. A control employee is generally defined as any employee who is an officer of the employer whose compensation equals or exceeds $50,000 or is a director of the employer whose compensation equals or exceeds $100,000.

  The personal use of an employer-provided vehicle that meets the above conditions is valued at $1.50 per one-way commute.

✓ **Annual lease valuation rule.** Under this rule, the fair market value of a vehicle is determined and that value is used to determine the annual lease value amount by referring to an annual lease value table published by the IRS (see page 53). The annual lease value corresponding to this fair market value, multiplied by the personal use percentage, is the amount to be added to the employee's gross income. Amounts reimbursed by the employee are offset.

The fair market value of a vehicle owned by an employer is generally the employer's cost of purchasing the vehicle (including taxes and fees). The fair market value of a vehicle leased by an employer generally is either the manufacturer's suggested retail price less 8%, or the retail value as reported in a nationally recognized publication that regularly reports automobile retail values.

If the three special valuation rules described above do not apply, the value of the personal use must be determined by using a set of general valuation principles. Under these principles, the value must be generally equal to the amount that the employee would have to pay in a normal business transaction to obtain the same or comparable vehicle in the geographic area in which that vehicle is available for use.

ANNUAL LEASE VALUE TABLE

Annual Fair Market Value of Car			Lease Value	Fair Market Value of Car			Annual Lease Value
$0	-	$999	$600	$19,000	-	$19,999	$5,350
1,000	-	1,999	850	20,000	-	20,999	5,600
2,000	-	2,999	1,100	21,000	-	21,999	5,850
3,000	-	3,999	1,350	22,000	-	22,999	6,100
4,000	-	4,999	1,600	23,000	-	23,999	6,350
5,000	-	5,999	1,850	24,000	-	24,999	6,600
6,000	-	6,999	2,100	25,000	-	25,999	6,850
7,000	-	7,999	2,350	26,000	-	27,999	7,250
8,000	-	8,999	2,600	28,000	-	29,999	7,750
9,000	-	9,999	2,850	30,000	-	31,999	8,250
10,000	-	10,999	3,100	32,000	-	33,999	8,750
11,000	-	11,999	3,350	34,000	-	35,999	9,250
12,000	-	12,999	3,600	36,000	-	37,999	9,750
13,000	-	13,999	3,850	38,000	-	39,999	10,250
14,000	-	14,999	4,100	40,000	-	41,999	10,750
15,000	-	15,999	4,350	42,000	-	43,999	11,250
16,000	-	16,999	4,600	44,000	-	45,999	11,750
17,000	-	17,999	4,850	46,000	-	47,999	12,250
18,000	-	18,999	5,100	48,000	-	49,999	12,750

Federal income tax withholding on auto benefits

Withholding of federal income tax is required on auto benefits for lay employees unless the employee is notified that the employer elects not to withhold by January 31 of the calendar year to which the election applies or, if later, within 30 days after the employee is given the automobile. The notification must be provided in writing and the employer must still withhold social security taxes if required to normally do so. If withholding is provided, the employer can treat the compensation as regular wages subject to the regular withholding rates or as supplemental wages subject to a flat 20% rate.

Tax-sheltered annuity

Employees of churches and other nonprofit organizations may have a Section 403(b) salary reduction arrangement based on a written plan. These plans are also called tax-sheltered annuities (TSAs).

Both nonelective and elective employer contributions for a minister-employee to a TSA are excludable for income and social security tax (SECA) purposes. Voluntary salary reduction TSA contributions for lay employees are subject to social security/Medicare taxes. The housing allowance amount must be excluded from a minister's gross pay before multiplying 20% times compensation to determine the maximum annual TSA contribution. See the 1996 Edition of *The Zondervan Minister's Tax & Financial Guide* for additional information on TSA contribution limitations.

Tax-Sheltered Annuity Agreement

Agreement for Salary Reduction by and between the undersigned Employer and Employee:

In order to provide benefits for retirement, the Employee desires to have contributions made on his behalf to purchase a non-forfeited annuity contract from _____ Life Insurance Company.

The Employer and Employee hereby agree that, with respect to the Employee's compensation for services rendered to the Employer commencing on the annual period ending _____, 199__ such compensation shall be reduced by $_____ or _____% per _____(period).

Each Employee shall ensure that the reduction in compensation shall in no event exceed the Employee's "exclusion allowance" as defined in Section 403(b)(2), or the limitation set forth in Section 415 and 402(g) of the Internal Revenue Code.

The Employee may, from time to time, by written instruction to the Employer, change from one division to another under the annuity contract.

This agreement must be amended by an instrument in writing signed by the Employer and the Employee and may be terminated by either the Employer or the Employee upon not less than 30 days' notice to the other. No amendment shall be made in the calendar year in which the Agreement is signed and not more than one amendment shall be made in any other calendar year. No designation or redesignation of investments or withdrawal shall be construed as an amendment or termination of this Agreement.

This Agreement is not a contract of employment between the parties hereto, and no provision hereof shall restrict the right of the Employer to discharge the Employee or the right of the Employee to terminate his employment.

Note: The above plan includes wording related to the stringent nondiscrimination rules. However, if your organization is a church or elementary or secondary school that is controlled, operated, or principally supported by a church or convention of association of churches, the nondiscrimination rules do not apply.

Employer-provided dependent care assistance plan

A church or nonprofit organization can provide employees with child care or disabled dependent care services to allow employees to work. The amount excludable from tax is limited to the smaller of the employee's earned income, the spouse's earned income, or $5,000 ($2,500 if married filing separately).

The dependent care assistance must be provided under a separate written plan that does not favor highly compensated employees and that meets other qualifications (see sample plan below).

Dependent care assistance payments are excluded from income if the payments cover expenses that would be deductible by the employee as child and dependent care expenses on Form 2441 if the expenses were not reimbursed. If the employee is married, both spouses must be employed. There are special rules if one spouse is a student or incapable of self-care.

Sample Dependent Care Assistance Plan

Whereas, Willowbrook Church desires to establish a dependent care assistance plan under Section 129 of the Internal Revenue Code,

Resolved, That a dependent care assistance plan shall be established as follows:
1. The plan will not discriminate in favor of highly compensated employees.
2. Notification of the availability of the plan will be provided to all eligible employees.
3. Each year, on or before January 31, the plan will furnish to each employee, a written statement showing the amounts paid or expenses incurred by the employer in providing dependent care assistance to such employee during the previous calendar year.
4. Dependent care assistance will be reported in Box 10 of Form W-2.
5. If dependent care assistance is provided to highly compensated employees, only those employees must include benefits provided under the plan in gross income.
6. Payments from the plan must be for expenses that would be deductible by the employee as child and dependent care expenses incurred to enable the employee to work.
7. The plan will only cover dependents of common-law employees of the church.
8. The exclusion for dependent care assistance payments is limited to $5,000 a year ($2,500 in the case of a married individual filing separately).
9. If child care services are provided on the premises of the church, the value of the services made available to the employee is excludable from income.

Resolved, That this dependent care assistance plan shall become effective on _____, 199__.

Medical expense reimbursement plan

Organizations often provide benefit plans covering an employee's major medical expenses. Some plans even cover some dental and optometry expenses.

With even the best employee benefit plans, there are usually after-tax expenses that the employee must pay out-of-pocket. These expenses may relate to the plan deductible, co-insurance, or simply noncovered items.

A medical expense reimbursement plan (MERP) is an excellent way to pay expenses not covered under another employee benefit plan—tax-free! With a MERP, the employee merely submits the otherwise out-of-pocket medical bills to the organization and receives a reimbursement. Since the nondiscrimination rules apply to these plans, it is often wise to make the benefit available to all full-time employees. MERP payments to individuals that are self-employed for income tax purposes represent taxable income.

Here's how a medical reimbursement plan could work for your organization:

✓ **Determine the relation of the MERP to the compensation package and set any limits.** Determine if the medical reimbursement benefit will be handled as:

- strictly a salary reduction (for example, an employee chooses to have $50 withheld each month under the medical reimbursement plan and may submit documentation for medical expenses up to $600 per year for reimbursement), or

- funded by the employer in addition to present gross pay and fringe benefits (for example, the organization elects to pay up to $500 per year without any salary reduction), or

- salary reduction plus employer funding (for example, the employer agrees to pay $500 plus the employee has a salary reduction of $600 per year. In this example, expenses of up to $1,100 could be reimbursed).

✓ **Formally adopt the plan.** The plan should be approved by the organization's board annually based on the structure and amounts determined. This action would generally occur in December for the following year.

✓ **Reimburse expenses under the plan.** Employees submit documentation after the primary carrier has considered the claims. If a particular expense is noncovered under the primary plan, it could be submitted under the medical reimbursement plan without being denied by the carrier.

A MERP established with employee-provided funds is a "use it or lose it" concept. If the employee does not submit sufficient expenses in the course of a year to use up the amount set aside under the plan, the amount remaining in the plan cannot

Sample Medical Expense Reimbursement Plan

Whereas, Valley View Church desires to provide medical care benefits relating to expenses not covered under the medical policy of the Church;

Resolved, That Valley View Church establishes a Medical Reimbursement Plan effective _____, 199__ for the benefit of all full-time employees (working at least 30 hours or more per week) and their dependents (employee's spouse and minor children) under Sections 105 and 106 of the Internal Revenue Code;

Resolved, That medical reimbursement accounts shall be maintained for each full-time employee from which covered expenses (as defined in Section 213 of the Internal Revenue Code) for the employee or their dependents shall be reimbursed. Reimbursements to an employee shall not exceed $_____ during one calendar year, plus any additional amount contributed by the employee under a written salary reduction agreement to the Plan for that year;

Resolved, That there shall be only one salary reduction election by each employee each year. This election may be changed during the year only in the following situations: (1) change in family status, e.g., marriage or divorce; birth, adoption, or death of a family member; (2) change of spousal employment status and/or health plan coverage; or (3) change in coverage under the employer's own health insurance policy;

Resolved, That the submission of medical expenses must be in a form and in sufficient detail to meet the requirements of the Church. Expenses may be submitted until March 31 for the previous calendar year. At that time, any balance remaining in an employee's account as of the end of the calendar year, shall be forfeited by the employee; and

Resolved, That the plan shall be administered in a nondiscriminatory manner and shall remain in effect until modified or terminated by a later resolution.

be paid over to the employee without causing all benefits paid under the plan to become taxable. Therefore, it is important that the employee estimate expenses conservatively.

File Form 5500 (or 5500-C or 5500-R) for employee-funded MERPs. There is no filing requirement for employer-funded MERPs.

A medical reimbursement plan does require administrative effort to establish it, annually review it, and process claim payments. However, the benefit can easily save several hundreds of dollars per year for each employee.

Compensation-related loans

Some churches and nonprofit organizations make loans to employees. The loans are often restricted to the purchase of land or a residence or the construction of a residence.

Before a loan is made, the organization should determine if the transaction is legal under state law. Such loans are prohibited in many states. Congress is considering prohibiting them for all nonprofits.

If an organization receives interest of $600 or more in a year relating to a loan secured by real estate, a Form 1098 (see page 89) must be provided to the payor. For the interest to be deductible as an itemized deduction, an employee loan must be secured and properly recorded.

If an organization makes loans to employees at below-market rates, the organization may be required to report additional compensation to the employee. If the loan is below $10,000, there is no additional compensation to the borrower. For loans over $10,000, additional compensation is calculated equal to the foregone interest that would have been charged if the loan had been made at a market rate of interest. The market rate of interest is the "applicable federal rate" for loans of similar duration. The IRS publishes these rates monthly. The additional compensation must be reported on Form W-2, box 1.

There are certain exceptions to the general rules on below-market loans. These exceptions relate to loans secured by a mortgage and employee relocation bridge loans that are not secured by the new residence.

Social security tax reimbursement

Churches and nonprofit organizations often reimburse ministers for a portion or all their self-employment tax (SECA) liability. Reimbursement also may be made to lay employees for all or a portion of the FICA tax that has been withheld from their pay. Any social security reimbursement must be reported as taxable income for both income and social security tax purposes. The FICA reimbursement to a lay employee is subject to FICA withholding.

Because of the deductibility of the self-employment tax in both the income tax and self-employment tax computations, a full reimbursement is effectively less than the gross 15.3% rate:

Marginal Tax Rate	Effective SECA Rate
0%	14.13%
15	13.07
28	12.15
31	11.94

For missionaries who are not eligible for the income tax deduction of one-half of the self-employment tax due to the foreign earned-income exclusion, the full reimbursement rate is effectively 14.13%.

It is usually best to reimburse an employee for self-employment tax on a monthly or quarterly basis. An annual reimbursement may leave room for misunderstanding between the organization and the employee. This is especially true if the employee is no longer employed at the time the reimbursement is due.

Property transfers

✓ **Unrestricted.** If an employer transfers property (for example, a car, residence, equipment, or other property) to an employee at no charge, this constitutes taxable income to the employee. The amount of income is generally the fair market value of the property transferred.

✓ **Restricted.** To recognize and reward good work, some churches or nonprofits transfer property to an employee subject to certain restrictions. The ultimate transfer will occur only if the employee lives up to the terms of the agreement. Once the terms are met, the property is transferred free and clear. Property that is subject to substantial risk of forfeiture and is nontransferable is substantially not vested. No tax liability will occur until title to the property is vested with the employee.

The exclusion is not an exemption from tax but is a deferral of tax. When restricted property becomes substantially vested, the employee must report the transfer as taxable income. The amount reported must be equal to the excess of the fair market value of the property at the time it becomes substantially vested, over the amount the employee pays for the property.

Example: A church transfers a house to the pastor subject to the completion of 20 years of service for the church. The pastor does not report any taxable income from the transfer until the 20th year.

✓ **Property purchased from employer.** If the employer allows an employee to buy property at a price below its fair market value, the employer must include in income as extra wages the difference between the property's fair market value and the amount paid and liabilities assumed by the employee.

Moving expenses

Moving expenses reimbursed by an employer, based on substantiation, are excludable from an employee's gross income. Prior to 1994, reimbursed moving expenses were includible in gross income. To qualify for this exclusion, the expenses must be deductible as moving expenses if they are not reimbursed.

The definition of deductible moving expenses is quite restrictive. For example, meals consumed while traveling and while living in temporary quarters near the new workplace are not deductible. The new place of work must be at least 50 miles farther from the taxpayer's former residence than the former residence was from the old place of work.

Reimbursements to nonminister employees that do not exceed deductible moving expenses are not subject to withholding. However, excess payments are subject to FICA and federal income tax withholding. Excess reimbursements to minister-employees are only subject to income tax withholding if a voluntary withholding agreement is in force.

Excess payments to minister or nonminister employees must be included as taxable compensation, for income tax purposes, on Form W-2 and Form 4782 must be provided to the employee.

Reimbursements to a self-employed individual (for income tax purposes) are reportable on Form 1099-MISC and are not deductible for purposes of the social security calculation on Schedule SE.

Example: A nonprofit paid a moving company $2,200 in 1995 for an employee's move. The employer also reimbursed the employee $350 for deductible moving expenses. The employer should report $2,550 on Form W-2, only in Box 13, using Code P.

Allowances and other nonaccountable expense reimbursements

Many organizations pay periodic allowances to employees for car expenses, library, entertainment, and so on. Other organizations reimburse employees for professional expenses with no requirement to account adequately for the expenses. (This is a nonaccountable plan). Allowances or reimbursements under a nonaccountable plan must be included in the taxable income of the employee and are subject to income tax and FICA withholding for nonminister employees.

Gifts

All cash gifts to employees must be included in taxable compensation. Noncash gifts of nominal value to employees are tax-free. Gifts to certain non-employees up to $25 may be tax-free.

Nondiscrimination Rules

To qualify for exclusion from income, many fringe benefits must be nondiscriminatory. This is particularly true for many types of benefits for certain key employees. Failure to comply with the nondiscrimination rules does not disqualify a fringe benefit plan entirely. The benefit simply is fully taxable for the highly compensated or key employees.

The nondiscrimination rules apply to the following types of fringe benefit plans:

✓ qualified tuition and fee discounts,

✓ eating facilities on or near the employer's premises,

✓ educational assistance benefits,

✔ dependent care plans,

✔ tax-sheltered annuities (TSAs) and other deferred compensation plans,

✔ group-term life insurance benefits, and

✔ medical reimbursement and cafeteria plans.

Fringe benefit plans that limit benefits only to officers or highly compensated employees are clearly discriminatory. An officer is an employee who is appointed, confirmed, or elected by the board of the employer. A highly compensated employee for 1995 is

✔ paid more than $99,000,

✔ paid more than $66,000 and is in the top 20% of paid employees for the year,

✔ an officer and is paid more than $59,400, or

✔ highest-paid officer if there is no one paid over $59,400.

Paying Employee Expenses

An accountable plan is a reimbursement or expense allowance arrangement that requires (1) a business purpose for the expenses, (2) employees to substantiate the expenses and (3) the return of any excess reimbursements.

The substantiation of expenses and return of excess reimbursements must be handled within a reasonable time. The following methods meet the "reasonable time" definition:

✔ The fixed date method applies if

- an advance is made within 30 days of when an expense is paid or incurred;

- an expense is substantiated to the employer within 60 days after the expense is paid or incurred; and

- any excess amount is returned to the employer within 120 days after the expense is paid or incurred.

Sample Accountable Expense Reimbursement Plan

Whereas, Income tax regulations provide that an arrangement between an employee and employer must meet the requirements of business connection, substantiation, and return of excess payments in order to be considered a reimbursement;

Whereas, Plans that meet the three requirements listed above are considered to be accountable plans, and the reimbursed expenses are generally excludable from an employee's gross compensation;

Whereas, Plans that do not meet all the requirements listed above are considered nonaccountable plans, and payments made under such plans are includible in gross employee compensation; and

Whereas, Poplar Grove Church desires to establish an accountable expense reimbursement policy in compliance with the income tax regulations;

<u>Resolved</u>, That Poplar Grove Church establish an expense reimbursement policy effective _____, 199__ whereby ministers serving the church may receive advances for or reimbursement of expenses if

    A. There is a stated business purpose of the expense related to the ministry of the church and the expenses would qualify for deductions for federal income tax purposes if the expenses were not reimbursed,

    B. The employee provides adequate substantiation to the church for all expenses, and

    C. The employee returns all excess reimbursements within a reasonable time.

and,

<u>Resolved</u>, That the following methods will meet the "reasonable time" definition:

    A. An advance is made within 30 days of when an expense is paid or incurred;

    B. An expense is substantiated to the church within 60 days after the expense is paid or incurred; or

    C. An excess amount is returned to the church within 120 days after the expense is paid or incurred.

and,

<u>Resolved</u>, That substantiation of business expenses will include business purpose, business relationship (including names of persons present), cost (itemized accounting), time, and place. Auto mileage reimbursed must be substantiated by a daily mileage log separating business and personal miles. The church will retain the original copies related to the expenses substantiated.

✓ The periodic statement method applies if

- the employer provides employees with a periodic statement that sets forth the amount paid under the arrangement in excess of substantiated expenses;

- statements are provided at least quarterly; and

- the employer requests that the employee provide substantiation for any additional expenses that have not yet been substantiated and/or return any amounts remaining unsubstantiated within 120 days of the statement.

If employees substantiate expenses and return any unused excess payments to the church or nonprofit organization, payments to the employee for business expenses have no impact on tax reporting. They are not included on Form W-2 for the employee or Form 1099-MISC for the self-employed.

Nonaccountable expense-reimbursement plans

If business expenses are not substantiated by the employee to the church or nonprofit organization, or if the amount of the reimbursement to the employee exceeds the actual expenses and the excess is not returned within a reasonable period of time, reporting is required.

Nonaccountable reimbursements and excess reimbursements over IRS limits must be reported as wages on Form W-2. They are generally subject to federal income tax and FICA withholding for employees other than ministers.

Accountable plans and the self-employed

Nonaccountable reimbursements and excess reimbursements over IRS limits paid to self-employed workers must be reported as compensation on Form 1099-MISC. No reporting to the IRS is required for accountable expense reimbursements to self-employed workers.

Reimbursement of an organization's operating expenses

The reimbursement of operating expenses of an organization should be distinguished from reimbursements of employee business expenses. Accountable expense reimbursement plans generally relate to payments for employee business expenses.

Many organizations set a limit on over-all accountable expense plan reimbursements. If organization operating expenses are mixed with employee business expenses, the employee may be penalized.

Example: A minister uses personal funds to pay for the printing of the weekly church bulletin. This printing is a church operating expense not an employee business expense. If the church has imposed an over-all expense reimbursement limit on the minister, the inclusion of the bulletin printing in the employee reimbursement plan would improperly count these dollars against the plan limit.

Per diem allowance

The federal per diem rate, which is the sum of the federal lodging rate and meals and incidental expenses rate, was $152 for 1995 for the 47 high-cost areas and $95 per day for all other areas. The federal meals and incidental expense rate is $36 for the high-cost areas and $28 for any other locality. The federal lodging rate is $116 for the high-cost areas and $67 for other localities. Allowances that do not exceed these rates need not be reported to the IRS. The high-cost areas are identified in IRS Publication 463.

Key Concepts

◼ Your organization will benefit from compensation planning as you try to stretch ministry dollars to cover personnel costs.

◼ Maximizing tax-free fringe benefits by adequate planning is vital for your employees.

◼ Proper use of the housing allowance for ministers who work for your organization is crucial.

◼ Do not ignore the nondiscrimination rules that apply to certain fringe benefits.

◼ The use of an accountable expense reimbursement plan for all employees of your organization is vital.

CHAPTER FOUR
Employer Reporting

In This Chapter
- The classification of workers
- Reporting compensation
- Payroll tax withholding
- Depositing withheld payroll taxes
- Filing the quarterly payroll tax forms
- Filing the annual payroll tax forms
- Refunds and abatements

The withholding and reporting requirements with which employers must comply are complicated. The special tax treatment of qualified ministers simply adds another level of complexity.

Churches and nonprofit organizations are generally required to withhold federal (and state and local, as applicable) income taxes and social security taxes, and pay employer social security tax on all wages paid to all full-time or part-time employees (except qualified ministers) who earn at least $100 during the year.

The Classification of Workers

Whether an individual is classified as an employee or independent contractor has far-reaching consequences. This decision determines an organization's responsibility under the Federal Insurance Contributions Act (FICA), income tax withholding responsibilities, potential coverage under the Fair Labor Standards Act (see pages 180-181), and coverage under an employer's benefit plans. Misclassification can lead to significant penalties.

Questions frequently arise about the classification of certain nonprofit workers. Seasonal workers and those working less than full-time such as secretaries, custodi-

KEY ISSUE

65

ans, and organists require special attention for classification purposes. If a custodian or secretary receives pay at an hourly rate, it will be difficult to justify independent contractor status. This conclusion would be true even if the workers are part-time.

Since 1935, the IRS has relied on 20 common law factors (see bottom of this page) to determine whether workers are employees or independent contractors. Pressure continues to build on Congress and the IRS to provide clearer guidance on who can be an independent contractor and when.

Employee

If a worker is an employee, the employer must meet the overhead costs of withholding income and Federal Insurance Contributions Act (FICA) taxes; match the employee's share of FICA taxes; and, unless exempted, pay unemployment taxes on employee's wages. In addition, the employer may incur obligations for employee benefit plans such as vacation, sick pay, health insurance, and pension plan contributions.

Among other requirements, employees comply with instructions, have a continuous relationship, perform work personally, work full- or part-time, are subject to dismissal, can quit without incurring liability, are often reimbursed for expenses, and must submit reports.

Independent contractor

If the worker is classified as an independent contractor, quarterly estimated taxes are paid by the worker on income as well as social security taxes under the Self-Employment Contributions Act (SECA). There is no unemployment tax liability or income or social security tax withholding requirement for independent contractors.

Independent contractors normally set the order and sequence of work, set their hours of work, work for another at the same time, are paid by the job, offer their services to the public, have an opportunity for profit or loss, furnish their tools, and may do work on another's premises, and there is often substantial investment by the worker.

Common law rules

The IRS generally applies the common law rules to decide if an individual is an employee or self-employed (independent contractor) for income tax purposes. Generally the individual is an employee if the employer has the legal right to control both what and how it is done, even if the individual has considerable discretion and freedom of action.

Workers are generally considered employees if they

■ ✔ Must follow the church's work instructions;

Independent Contractor Status Myths

- *Myth*: A written contract will characterize a person as an independent contractor.

  Fact: It is the substance of the relationship that governs.

- *Myth*: Casual labor or seasonal workers are independent contractors or their classification is a matter of choice.

  Fact: There is never a choice. The classification is determined by the facts and circumstances.

- *Myth*: If a person qualifies as an independent contractor for federal payroll tax purposes, he or she is automatically exempt for Workers' Compensation and state unemployment tax purposes.

  Fact: State Workers' Compensation and unemployment tax laws are often broader and an individual may actually be covered under these laws even though qualifying as an independent contractor for federal payroll tax purposes.

✔ Receive on-the-job training;

✔ Provide services that must be rendered personally;

✔ Provide services that are integral to the church;

✔ Hire, supervise, and pay assistants for the church;

✔ Have an ongoing work relationship with the church;

✔ Must follow set hours of work;

✔ Work full-time for the church;

✔ Work on the church's premises;

✔ Must do their work in an church-determined sequence;

✔ Receive business expense reimbursements;

✓ Receive routing payments of regular amounts;

✓ Need the church to furnish tools and materials;

✓ Do not have a major investment in job facilities;

✓ Cannot suffer a loss from their services;

✓ Work for one church at a time;

✓ Do not offer their services to the general public;

✓ Can be fired by the church;

✓ May quit work at any time without penalty.

Key issue: The amount of control and direction the church has over a worker's services is the most important overall issue. So some of the above factors may be given greater weight than others.

Special Tax Provisions for Ministers

- Exclusion for income tax purposes of the housing allowance and the fair rental value of a church-owned parsonage provided rent-free to clergy.

- Exemption of clergy from self-employment tax under very limited circumstances.

- Treatment of clergy (who do not elect social security exemption) as self-employed for social security tax purposes for income from ministerial services.

- Exemption of clergy compensation from mandatory income tax withholding.

- Eligibility for a voluntary income tax withholding arrangement between the minister-employee and the church.

- Potential "double deduction" of mortgage interest and real estate taxes as itemized deductions and as housing expenses for housing allowance purposes.

The classification of ministers

It is important that the organization decide if the services of ministers employed by the organization qualify for special tax treatment as ministerial services.

Most ordained, commissioned, or licensed ministers serving local churches will qualify for the above six special tax provisions with respect to services performed in the exercise of ministry. The IRS applies certain tests to these ministers including whether the minister administers the sacraments, conducts worship services, is considered a spiritual leader by the church, and if the minister performs services in the "control, conduct, or maintenance of a religious organization." It may not be necessary for a minister to meet all of these tests to qualify for the special tax treatment. For a complete discussion of this topic, see the 1996 Edition of the *Zondervan Minister's Tax & Financial Guide.*

Ordained, commissioned, or licensed ministers not serving local churches may qualify as ministers for federal tax purposes without meeting additional tests if their duties include the following:

 Administration of church denominations and their integral agencies, including teaching or administration in parochial schools, colleges, or universities that are under the authority of a church or denomination.

✓ Performing services for an institution that is not an integral agency of a church pursuant to an assignment or designation by ecclesiastical superiors, but only if the services relate to church purposes.

Sample Board Resolution for Ministerial Assignment

Whereas, _____ Name of assigning church _____ recognizes the calling of _____ Name of minister assigned _____ as a minister and is (ordained, licensed, or commissioned) and

Whereas, We believe that the assignment of ___ Name of minister assigned ___ will further the efforts and mission of our church and we desire to provide support and encouragement;

Resolved, That _____ Name of minister assigned _____ is hereby assigned to _____ Name of ministry to which assigned _____ effective _____, 199__ to serve as _____ Position Title _____ and

Resolved, That this assignment is made for a period of one year upon which time it will be reviewed and may be renewed, and

Resolved, That this assignment is contingent upon the quarterly submission of activity and financial reports by ___ Name of minister assigned ___ to our church.

If a church does not assign or designate the minister's services, they will be qualified services only if they involve performing sacerdotal functions or conducting religious worship.

Reporting Compensation

Minister-employees

Form W-2s are annually provided to minister-employees. There is no requirement to withhold income taxes, but they may be withheld under a voluntary agreement. Social security taxes are not withheld.

Nonminister-employees

If an employee does not qualify for tax treatment as a "minister," the organization is liable to withhold and pay FICA and income taxes. Certain FICA tax exceptions are discussed later.

Nonemployees

A self-employed minister and other self-employed recipients of compensation should receive Form 1099-MISC instead of Form W-2 (if the person has received compensation of at least $600 for the year).

Payroll Tax Withholding

FICA social security

Most churches and nonprofit organizations must withhold FICA taxes from their employees' wages and pay it to the IRS along with the employer's share of the tax. Minister-employees are an exception to this rule. In 1995 both the employer and the employee pay a 6.2% tax rate on the social security wage base of up to $61,200. Similarly, both the employer and the employee pay a 1.45% medicare tax rate on all pay above $61,200. The rates remain the same for 1996. The 1996 social security wage base is estimated to be $63,000.

There are a few exceptions to the imposition of FICA. Generally wages paid to an employee of less than $100 in a calendar year are not subject to FICA. Services excluded from FICA include

✓ services performed by a minister of a church in the exercise of ministry or by a member of a religious order in the exercise of duties required by such order;

✔ services performed in the employ of a church or church-controlled organization that is opposed for religious reasons to the payment of social security taxes (see later discussion of filing Form 8274);

✔ services performed by a student in the employ of a school, college, or university.

Churches and church-controlled organizations opposed to social security taxes

In 1984 the law was changed to allow qualifying churches and church-controlled organizations to claim exemption from payment of FICA taxes. An organization must certify opposition "for religious reasons to the payment of employer social security taxes." Very few organizations qualify to file Form 8274.

Organizations in existence on September 30, 1984, were required to file Form 8274 by October 30, 1984. Any organization created after September 30, 1984, must file before the first date on which a quarterly employment tax return is due from the organization.

Organizations desiring to revoke their exemption made earlier by filing Form 8274 should file Form 941 with full payment of social security taxes for that quarter.

Federal income tax

Most nonprofit organizations are exempt from the payment of federal income tax on the organization's income (see page 32 for the tax on unrelated business income). But they must withhold and pay federal, state, and local income taxes on the wages paid to each employee. Minister-employees are an exception to this rule.

An employee-minister may have a voluntary withholding agreement with a church or nonprofit employer relating to the minister's income taxes. An agreement to withhold income taxes from wages must be in writing. There is no required form for the agreement. A minister may request voluntary withholding by submitting Form W-4 (Employee Withholding Allowance Certificate) with the employer indicating the additional amount to be withheld in excess of the tax table or the written request may be in another form.

The self-employed minister for income tax purposes reports and pays income taxes through the estimated tax (Form 1040-ES) procedure. There is no provision for federal income tax withholding from payments made to independent contractors, even on a voluntary basis.

Federal income taxes for all employees (except ministers) are calculated based on the chart and tables shown in IRS Publication 15. State and local income taxes are usually required to be withheld according to state withholding tables.

✔ **Form W-4.** All employees, part- or full-time, must complete a W-4 form. (Ministers are an exception to this requirement unless they elect voluntary

Form **W-4**	**Employee's Withholding Allowance Certificate**	OMB No. 1545-0010
Department of the Treasury Internal Revenue Service	▶ For Privacy Act and Paperwork Reduction Act Notice, see reverse.	19**96**

1 Type or print your first name and middle initial	Last name	2 Your social security number
Walter R. Knight		511 20 7943

Home address (number and street or rural route)	3 ☐ Single ☒ Married ☐ Married, but withhold at higher Single rate.
601 Oakridge Boulevard	Note: *If married, but legally separated, or spouse is a nonresident alien, check the Single box.*
City or town, state, and ZIP code	4 If your last name differs from that on your social security card, check
Vinton, VA 24179	here and call 1-800-772-1213 for more information ▶ ☐

5 Total number of allowances you are claiming (from line G above or from the worksheets on page 2 if they apply) . **5** 4
6 Additional amount, if any, you want withheld from each paycheck . . . . **6** $
7 I claim exemption from withholding for 1994 and I certify that I meet BOTH of the following conditions for exemption:
  ● Last year I had a right to a refund of ALL Federal income tax withheld because I had NO tax liability; AND
  ● This year I expect a refund of ALL Federal income tax withheld because I expect to have NO tax liability.
  If you meet both conditions, enter "EXEMPT" here . . . . ▶ **7**

Under penalties of perjury, I certify that I am entitled to the number of withholding allowances claimed on this certificate or entitled to claim exempt status.

Employee's signature ▶ *Walter R. Knight* Date ▶ January 31 19 96

8 Employer's name and address (Employer: Complete 8 and 10 only if sending to the IRS)	9 Office code (optional)	10 Employer identification number

Cat. No. 10220Q

Note: This form must be completed by all lay employees, full- or part-time. If a minister completes this form, it can be the basis to determine income tax withholding under a voluntary agreement.

Form **W-5**	**Earned Income Credit Advance Payment Certificate**	OMB No. 1545-1342
Department of the Treasury Internal Revenue Service	▶ This certificate expires on December 31, 1994.	19**96**

Type or print your full name	Your social security number
Daniel L. Wheeler	304 78 6481

Note: *If you get advance payments of the earned income credit for 1994, you must file a 1994 Form 1040A or Form 1040. To get advance payments, your filing status must be any status except married filing a separate return and you must have a qualifying child.*

		Yes	No
1	I expect to be able to claim the earned income credit for 1994, I do not have another Form W-5 in effect with any other current employer, and I choose to get advance EIC payments	X	
2	Do you have a qualifying child?	X	
3	Are you married?	X	
4	If you are married, does your spouse have a Form W-5 in effect for 1994 with any employer?		X

Under penalties of perjury, I declare that the information I have furnished above is, to the best of my knowledge, true, correct, and complete.

Signature ▶ *Daniel L. Wheeler* Date ▶ 1/1/96

Cat. No. 10227P

Note: This form should be completed if an employee elects to receive advance payments of the earned income credit.

withholding.) The withholding allowance information completed on this form gives the basis to determine the amount of income tax to be withheld. A Form W-4 remains valid until a new one is submitted to the employer.

✓ **Form W-5.** An eligible employee uses Form W-5 to elect to receive advance payments of the earned income credit. Employees with a qualifying child and expecting 1995 earned income and adjusted gross income each to be less than $26,673 may be eligible for the earned income credit.

   If eligible for the earned income credit, they may choose to receive an advance instead of waiting until they file their annual Form 1040.

Self-employment tax

Self-employment taxes (SECA) may not be withheld from the salary of an employee. But under the voluntary withholding agreement for ministers' federal income taxes, additional federal income tax may be withheld sufficient to cover the minister's self-employment tax liability. When these withheld amounts are paid to the IRS, they must be identified as "federal income tax withheld" (and not social security taxes withheld).

Personal liability for payroll taxes

Church and nonprofit officers and employees may be personally liable if payroll taxes are not withheld and paid to the IRS. If the organization has willfully failed to withhold and pay the taxes, the IRS has the authority to assess a 100% penalty (of withheld income and social security taxes).

This penalty may be assessed against the individual responsible for withholding and paying the taxes, even if the person is an unpaid volunteer such as a church treasurer.

Depositing Withheld Payroll Taxes

The basic rules for depositing payroll taxes are

✓ If your total accumulated and unpaid employment tax is less than $500 in a calendar quarter, taxes can be paid directly to the IRS when the organization files Form 941. These forms are due one month after the end of each calendar quarter.

✓ If payroll taxes are over $500 for a quarter, deposits must be made monthly or before the 15th day of each month for the payroll paid during the preceding month. Large organizations with total employment taxes of over $50,000 per year, will be subject to more frequent deposits.

To determine if an organization is a monthly depositor under the new rules, you must determine if the accumulated liabilities in the "look-back period" reached a threshold of $50,000. Those with an accumulated liability of less than $50,000 in the look-back period are generally monthly depositors (except those qualifying for quarterly deposits with liabilities of $500 or less).

A new organization (or one filing payroll tax returns for the first time) will be required to file monthly until a "look-back" period is established. A look-back period begins on July 1 and ends on June 30 of the preceding calendar year.

The cost of missing deposit deadlines can be very high. Besides interest, the organization can be hit with penalties at progressively stiffer rates. These range from 2% if you deposit the money within five days of the due date, to 15% if it is not deposited within 10 days of the first delinquency notice or on the day that the IRS demands immediate payment, whichever is earlier.

Deposit coupons

✓ **Form 8109.** Use Form 8109 deposit coupons to make deposits of the taxes covered by the following forms: Form 940, Form 941, Schedule A, and Form 990-T.

The preprinted name and address of the organization and the Employer's Identification Number (EIN) appear on the coupons. Deliver or mail the completed coupon with the appropriate payment to a qualified depository for federal taxes.

✓ **Form 8109-B.** Use Form 8109-B deposit coupons to make tax deposits only in the following two situations:

- You have reordered preprinted deposit coupons (Form 8109) but have not yet received them.

- You are a new entity and have already been assigned an EIN, but have not yet received your initial supply of preprinted deposit coupons (Form 8109).

Form 8109-B may be obtained only from the IRS.

Filing the Quarterly Payroll Tax Forms

Employers must report covered wages paid to their employees by filing Form 941 with the IRS.

Form 941

Church and other nonprofit employers who withhold income tax and both social security and medicare taxes, must file Form 941 quarterly. There is no requirement to file Form 941 if your organization has not been required to withhold payroll taxes even if you have one or more employee-ministers (but without any voluntary withholding).

Most common errors made on Form 941

The IRS has outlined the most common errors discovered during the processing of Form 941, Employer's Quarterly Federal Tax Return, and the best way to avoid making these mistakes. A checklist for avoiding errors follows:

✓ Make sure that taxable social security wages and the social security tax on line 6a, the social security tax on line 6b, and the taxable medicare wages and the medicare tax on line 7 are reported separately. Most employers will need to complete both lines 6a and 7.

✓ The preprinted form sent by the IRS should be used. If the return is prepared by a third-party preparer, make certain that the preparer uses exactly the name that appears on the preprinted form that was sent.

✓ Check the math for lines 5, 10, 13, and 14. Line 14 should always be the sum of lines 5, 10, and 13.

✓ Make sure the social security tax on line 6a is calculated correctly (12.4% x social security wages).

✓ Make sure the medicare tax on line 7 is calculated correctly (2.9% x medicare wages).

✓ Be sure to use the most recent Form 941 that the IRS sends. The IRS enters the date the quarter ended after the employer identification number. If the form is used for a later quarter, the IRS will have to contact the employer.

✓ Make sure there is never an entry on both lines 18 and 19. There cannot be a balance due and a refund.

✓ Always sign the return and print name and title in the space provided.

Form 941c

Form 941c may be used to correct income, social security, and medicare tax

Form **941**
(Rev. January 1995)
Department of the Treasury
Internal Revenue Service

4141

Employer's Quarterly Federal Tax Return

▶ See separate instructions for information on completing this return.

Please type or print.

OMB No. 1545-0029

Enter state code for state in which deposits made . ▶ **A:L** (see page 3 of instructions).

Name (as distinguished from trade name)

Barnett Ridge Church
Trade name, if any

Date quarter ended

3/31/96
Employer identification number

35-7849201

Address (number and street)

P. O. Box 517

City, state, and ZIP code

Selma, AL 36701

T	
FF	
FD	
FP	
I	
T	

If address is different from prior return, check here ▶

IRS Use

1 1 1 1 1 1 1 1 1 1   2   3 3 3 3 3   4 4 4   10 10 10 10 10 10 10 10 10 10
5 5 5   6   7   8 8 8 8 8   9 9 9   10 10 10 10 10 10 10 10 10 10

If you do not have to file returns in the future, check here ▶ ☐   and enter date final wages paid ▶

If you are a seasonal employer, see **Seasonal employers** on page 1 of the instructions and check here ▶ ☐

1	Number of employees (except household) employed in the pay period that includes March 12th ▶		4
2	Total wages and tips, plus other compensation	2	24,811
3	Total income tax withheld from wages, tips, and sick pay	3	4,642
4	Adjustment of withheld income tax for preceding quarters of calendar year	4	
5	Adjusted total of income tax withheld (line 3 as adjusted by line 4—see instructions)	5	4,642
6a	Taxable social security wages . . . . $ 16,340 × 12.4% (.124) =	6a	2,026
b	Taxable social security tips . . . . $ × 12.4% (.124) =	6b	
7	Taxable Medicare wages and tips . . . . . $ 16,340 × 2.9% (.029) =	7	474
8	Total social security and Medicare taxes (add lines 6a, 6b, and 7). Check here if wages are not subject to social security and/or Medicare tax . . . . ▶ ☐	8	2,500
9	Adjustment of social security and Medicare taxes (see instructions for required explanation) Sick Pay $ _____ ± Fractions of Cents $ _____ ± Other $ _____ =	9	
10	Adjusted total of social security and Medicare taxes (line 8 as adjusted by line 9—see instructions)	10	2,500
11	**Total taxes** (add lines 5 and 10)	11	7,142
12	Advance earned income credit (EIC) payments made to employees, if any	12	
13	Net taxes (subtract line 12 from line 11). **This should equal line 17, column (d) below** (or line D of Schedule B (Form 941))	13	7,142
14	Total deposits for quarter, including overpayment applied from a prior quarter	14	7,142
15	**Balance due** (subtract line 14 from line 13). Pay to Internal Revenue Service	15	-0-
16	**Overpayment,** if line 14 is more than line 13, enter excess here ▶ $ _____ and check if to be: ☐ Applied to next return **OR** ☐ Refunded.		

- **All filers:** If line 13 is less than $500, you need not complete line 17 or Schedule B.
- **Semiweekly depositors:** Complete Schedule B and check here . . . . ▶ ☐
- **Monthly depositors:** Complete line 17, columns (a) through (d), and check here . . . . ▶ ☐

17	Monthly Summary of Federal Tax Liability.		
(a) First month liability	(b) Second month liability	(c) Third month liability	(d) Total liability for quarter

Sign Here

Under penalties of perjury, I declare that I have examined this return, including accompanying schedules and statements, and to the best of my knowledge and belief, it is true, correct, and complete.

Signature ▶ *Alan W. Dunn*   Print Your Name and Title ▶ *Alan W. Dunn, Treas.*   Date ▶ *4/30/96*

For Paperwork Reduction Act Notice, see page 1 of separate instructions.   Cat. No. 17001Z   Form **941** (Rev. 1-95)

Note: File this form to report social security (FICA) and medicare taxes and federal income tax withheld.

Form **941c** (Rev. January 1994) Department of the Treasury Internal Revenue Service	**Supporting Statement To Correct Information** **Do Not File Separately** ▶ Attach to the employment tax return on which adjustments are made.	OMB No. 1545-0256 Expires 11-30-96 Page No.

Name: **Little Valley Church**   Employer identification number: **35-6309294**

Telephone number:

A This form supports adjustments to: Check one box.
- ☒ Form 941
- ☐ Form 941-M
- ☐ Form 941-SS
- ☐ Form 943
- ☐ Form 945

B This form is filed with the return for the period ending (month, year) ▶ **3/31/96**

C Enter the date you discovered the error(s) reported on this form. (If you are making more than one correction and they were not discovered at the same time, please explain in Part V.) . . . ▶ **3/1/96**

Part I Signature and Certification (You **MUST** complete this part for the IRS to process your adjustments for overpayments.)

I certify that Forms W-2c, Statement of Corrected Income and Tax Amounts, have been filed (as necessary) with the Social Security Administration, and that (check appropriate boxes):

☐ All overcollected income taxes for the current calendar year and all social security and Medicare taxes for the current and prior calendar years have been repaid to employees. For claims of overcollected employee social security and Medicare taxes in earlier years, a written statement has been obtained from each employee stating that the employee has not claimed and will not claim refund or credit of the amount of the overcollection.

☐ All affected employees have given their written consent to the allowance of this credit or refund. For claims of overcollected employee social security and Medicare taxes in earlier years, a written statement has been obtained from each employee stating that the employee has not claimed and will not claim refund or credit of the amount of the overcollection.

☐ The social security tax and Medicare tax adjustments represent the employer's share only. An attempt was made to locate the employee(s) affected, but the affected employee(s) could not be located or will not comply with the certification requirements.

☐ None of this refund or credit was withheld from employee wages.

Sign Here Signature ▶ *Curtis R. Lee* Title ▶ Treasurer Date ▶ 4/30/96

Part II Income Tax/Backup Withholding Adjustment

	(a) Period Corrected (Quarterly returns, enter date quarter ended. Annual returns, enter year.)	(b) Withheld Income Tax Previously Reported for Period	(c) Correct Withheld Income Tax for Period	(d) Withheld Income Tax Adjustment
1	12/31/95	400	600	200
2				
3				
4				
5	Net withheld income tax/backup withholding adjustment. If more than one page, enter total of all columns (d) on first page only. Enter here and on the **appropriate** line of the return with which this form is filed . . . ▶		**5**	200

Part III Social Security Tax Adjustment (Use the tax rate in effect during the period(s) corrected. You must also complete Part IV for return periods beginning after 12/31/90.)

	(a) Period Corrected (Quarterly returns, enter date quarter ended. Annual returns, enter year.)	(b) Wages Previously Reported for Period	(c) Correct Taxable Wages for Period	(d) Tips Previously Reported for Period	(e) Correct Taxable Tips for Period	(f) Social Security Tax Adjustment
1	12/31/95	2,000	4,500			155
2						
3						
4						
5	Totals.—If more than one page, enter totals on first page only. ▶					
6	Net social security tax adjustment. If more than one page, enter total of **ALL** columns (f) on first page only. Enter here and on the appropriate line of the return with which this form is filed . . ▶				**6**	155
7	Net wage adjustment. If more than one page, enter the total of **ALL** lines 7 on first page only. If 5(c) is smaller than 5(b), enter difference in parentheses . . . . ▶				**7**	2,500
8	Net tip adjustment. If more than one page, enter the total of **ALL** lines 8 on first page only. If 5(e) is smaller than 5(d), enter difference in parentheses . . . . ▶				**8**	

For Paperwork Reduction Act Notice, see page 3.   Cat. No. 11242O   Form **941c** (Rev. 1-94)

Note: Use this form to correct income, social security (FICA), and medicare tax information reported on Form 941. It may be necessary to issue Form W-2c to employees relating to prior year data.

information reported on Forms 941, 941-M, 941SS, or 943. Attach it to the tax return on which you are claiming the adjustment (Form 941, and so on) or to Form 843, Claim for Refund and Request for Abatement. Also issue the employee(s) a Form W-2c for the prior year, if applicable.

Filing the Annual Payroll Tax Forms

Form W-2

By January 31 each employee must be given a Form W-2. To help you in the completion of the 1995 version of the Form W-2, an explanation of certain boxes is provided. For additional help, call any local IRS office or 800-TAX-FORM.

Void. Put an X in this box when an error has been made.

Box 1—Wages, tips, other compensation. Items to include in box 1 before any payroll deductions are

- ✔ total wages paid during the year (including love offerings paid by the church to a minister or other church employee);

- ✔ the value of noncash payments, including taxable fringe benefits;

- ✔ business expense payments under a nonaccountable plan;

- ✔ payments of per diem or mileage allowance paid for business expense purposes that exceed the IRS specified rates;

- ✔ payments for nonexcludable moving expenses;

- ✔ all other compensation, including taxable fringe benefits. "Other compensation" represents amounts an organization pays to an employee from which federal income tax is not withheld. If you prefer, you may show other compensation on a separate Form W-2; and

- ✔ the cash housing allowance or the fair market rental value of housing and utilities must be reported as taxable income for lay employees unless furnished on the employer's premises and the employee is required to accept the lodging as a condition of employment.

Exclude the following:

- ✔ the fair rental value of a church-provided parsonage or a properly designated housing allowance for ministers;

Checklist for Completing Box 1 of Form W-2

Data Included for

Minister Only	Both	Nonminister Only	
	yes		Salary
no		yes	Housing/furnishings allowance (designated in advance)
no		yes	Parsonage rental value
no		yes	Utilities paid by church or nonprofit
	yes		Social security/Medicare "allowance" or reimbursement
	no		Transportation/travel and other business and professional expense reimbursements *only if* paid under a board adopted accountable reimbursement plan
	yes		"Reimbursements" if not paid under an accountable reimbursement plan
	yes		Church love offerings or cash gifts in excess of $25
	no		Contributions to a tax-sheltered annuity plan
	no		Health/dental insurance premiums paid directly or reimbursed by the employer
	no		Group term life insurance premiums (for up to $50,000 coverage) paid directly by the employer
	no		Excludable moving expense paid for or reimbursed to an employee
	yes		Nonexcludable moving expenses paid for or reimbursed to an employee
	yes		Value of personal and nonbusiness use of organization's vehicle

✓ auto or business expense reimbursements paid through an accountable expense plan; and

✓ contributions to a 403(b) tax-sheltered annuity plan.

Box 2—Federal income tax withheld. Enter the total federal income tax withheld according to the chart and tables in IRS Publication 15.

A qualified minister may enter into a voluntary withholding arrangement with the employing organization. Based on a completed Form W-4 or other written withholding request, federal income tax withholding may be calculated from the chart and tables in Publication 15 excluding any housing allowance amount.

The minister may request that an additional amount of income tax be withheld to cover any self-employment tax that may be due. The additional amount withheld is reported as income tax withheld on the quarterly Form 941 and in box 2 of Form W-2.

An organization that provides additional compensation to the employee-minister to cover part or all of the self-employment tax liability may:

a Control number		OMB No. 1545-0008			
b Employer's identification number 35-2946039			1 Wages, tips, other compensation 15786.00	2 Federal income tax withheld 2039.00	
c Employer's name, address, and ZIP code ABC Charity 2670 N. Hull Road Traverse City, MI 49615			3 Social security wages 15786.00	4 Social security tax withheld 979.00	
			5 Medicare wages and tips 15786.00	6 Medicare tax withheld 229.00	
			7 Social security tips	8 Allocated tips	
d Employee's social security number 517-28-6451			9 Advance EIC payment	10 Dependent care benefits	
e Employee's name, address, and ZIP code Michael A. Black 15550 Cleveland Avenue Traverse City, MI 49615			11 Nonqualified plans	12 Benefits included in box 1	
			13 See Instrs. for Form W-2 E 1200.00 P 984.73	14 Other	
			15 Statutory employee ☐ Deceased ☐ Pension plan ☐ Legal rep. ☐ Hshld. emp. ☐ Subtotal ☐ Deferred compensation ☐		
16 State Employer's state I.D. No. MI 6309294	17 State wages, tips, etc. 15786.00	18 State income tax 205.00	19 Locality name	20 Local wages, tips, etc.	21 Local income tax

Department of the Treasury—Internal Revenue Service

Form **W-2** Wage and Tax Statement **1995**

Copy D For Employer

For Paperwork Reduction Act Notice,
see separate instructions.

✓ pay the additional compensation directly to the IRS by entering that amount on the organization's Form 941 and in boxes 1 and 2 of Form W-2 or

✓ pay the additional compensation to the minister with the minister being responsible for remitting the amounts to the IRS with a Form 1040-ES. If this procedure is followed, the organization reports this amount only as additional compensation on Form 941 and only in box 1 of Form W-2.

Box 3—Social security wages. Show the total wages paid (before payroll deductions) subject to employee social security tax (FICA). This amount must not exceed $61,200 in 1995 (the maximum social security tax wage base). Generally all cash and noncash payments reported in box 1 must be shown in box 3. Include nonaccountable employee business expenses reported in box 1. Voluntary salary reduction tax-sheltered annuity contributions for nonminister employees are included in Box 3.

Box 3 should be blank for qualified ministers.

Box 4—Social security tax withheld. Show the total FICA social security tax (not including your share) withheld or paid by you for the employee. The amount shown must equal 6.2% of the amount in box 3 and must not exceed $3,794.40 for 1995. Do not include the matching employer FICA tax.

Some organizations pay the employee's share of FICA tax for some or all nonminister employees instead of deducting it from the employee's wages. These amounts paid by the organization must be included in boxes 1, 3, and 5 as wages and proportionately in boxes 4 and 6 as social security and medicare tax withheld. In these instances, the effective cost to the employer is 8.28% instead of 7.45% for wages up to $61,200 and 1.47% rather than 1.45% for wages above $61,200.

Box 4 should be blank for qualified ministers. Any amount of withholding to meet the minister's SECA tax liability must be reported in Box 2, not in Box 4 or Box 6.

Box 5—Medicare wages. The wages subject to medicare tax are the same as those subject to social security tax (box 3). However, there is no wage limit for the medicare tax.

> **Example:** You paid a nonminister employee $65,000 in wages. The amount shown in box 3 (social security wages) should be $61,200, but the amount shown in box 5 (Medicare wages) should be $65,000. If the amount of wages paid was less than $61,200, the amounts entered in boxes 3 and 5 will be the same.

Box 5 should be blank for qualified ministers.

Box 6—Medicare tax withheld. Enter the total employee medicare tax (not your share) withheld or paid by you for your employee. The amount shown must equal 1.45% of the amount in box 5. Box 6 should be blank for qualified ministers.

Box 9—Advance EIC payment. Show the total paid to the employee as advance earned income credit payments.

Box 10—Dependent care benefits. Show the total amount of dependent care benefits under Section 129 paid or incurred by you for your employee including any amount over the $5,000 exclusion. Also include in box 1, box 3, and box 5 any amount over the $5,000 exclusion.

Box 11—Nonqualified plans. Enter the total amount of distributions to the employee from a nonqualified deferred compensation plan. Include an amount in Box 11 only if it is also includable in Box 1 or Boxes 3 and 5.

Box 12—Benefits included in box 1. Show the total value of the taxable fringe benefits included in box 1 as other compensation.

If the organization owns or leases a vehicle for an employee's use, the value of the personal and nonbusiness use of that vehicle is taxable income. The value of the use of the vehicle is established by using one of the methods described on pages 51-53. The amount of the personal and nonbusiness use must be included in Boxes 1 and 12 (and in Boxes 3 and 5 if a lay employee). The employee is required to maintain a mileage log or similar records to substantiate business and personal use of the vehicle and submit this to the employer. If not substantiated, the employer must report 100 percent of the use of the vehicle as taxable income.

If the employee fully reimburses the employer for the value of the personal use of the vehicle, then no value would be reported in either Box 1 or in Box 12.

Box 13—Additional entries. Complete and code this box for only the following items:

C—Group-term life insurance. If you provided your employee more than $50,000 of group-term life insurance, show the cost of the coverage over $50,000. Also include the amount in box 1, (also in Boxes 3 and 5 if a lay employee).

D—Section 401(k) cash or deferred arrangement

E—Section 403(b) voluntary salary reduction agreement to purchase an annuity contract. This amount would not be included in Box 1 for either ministerial or lay employees. This amount would be included in Boxes 3 and 5 for a lay employee.

F—Section 408(k)(6) salary reduction simplified employee pension (SEP)

G—Section 457 deferred compensation plan

H—Section 501(c)(18)(D) tax-exempt organization plan

L—Generally payments made under an accountable plan are excluded from the employee's gross income and are not required to be reported on Form W-2. But if you pay a per diem or mileage allowance, and the amount paid exceeds the amount substantiated under IRS rules, you must report as wages on Form W-2 the amount in excess of the amount substantiated. Report the amount treated as substantiated (the nontaxable portion) in box 13. In box 1, show the portion of the reimbursement that is more than the amount treated as substantiated. For lay employees the excess amount is subject to income tax withholding, social security tax, medicare tax, and possibly federal unemployment tax.

P—Excludable moving expenses paid for or reimbursed to an employee must be reported on Form W-2, only in Box 13, using Code P to identify them as nontaxable reimbursements. Report nonexcludable moving expense reimbursements and payments in Boxes 1, 3, and 5.

Do not include any per diem or mileage allowance or other reimbursements for employee business expenses in boxes 1 or 13 if the total reimbursement is less than or equal to the amount substantiated.

Example 1: An employee receives mileage reimbursement at the rate of 30 cents per mile in 1995 and substantiates the business miles driven to the church. The mileage reimbursement is not reported on Form W-2.

Example 2: An employee receives a mileage allowance of $2,000 per year and does not substantiate the business miles driven. The $2,000 allowance is includible in box 1 as compensation. The business mileage is deductible as a miscellaneous deduction on the employee's Schedule A, subject to limitations.

Payments made to nonminister employees under a nonaccountable plan are reportable as wages on Form W-2 and are subject to income tax withholding, social security tax, medicare tax, and possibly federal unemployment tax.

Payments made to minister-employees under a nonaccountable plan are reportable as wages on Form W-2 and may be subject to income tax withholding under a voluntary agreement, but are not subject to mandatory withholding or social security (FICA) or medicare tax.

Box 14—Other. You may use this box for any other information you want to give your employee. Label each item and include information such as health insurance premiums deducted, or educational assistance payments.

Do not include the minister's housing allowance in this box. Provide the minister with a separate statement reflecting the housing allowance amount.

Box 15—Check the appropriate boxes. The boxes that apply to employees of churches and nonprofit organizations are:

Pension plan. Check this box if the employee was an active participant (for any part of the calendar year) in a retirement plan (including a 401(k) plan and a simplified employee pension plan) maintained by the organization. An employee is an active participant for purposes of this box if the employee participated in a Section 401(a) qualified plan, Section 403(a) qualified annuity plan (nonvoluntary contributions), Section 403(b) annuity contract or custodial account, Section 408(k) simplified employee pension, or Section 501(c)(18) trust.

Subtotal. Check this box only when submitting 42 or more Forms W-2.

Deferred compensation. Check this box if you made contributions for the employee to a Section 401(k) cash or deferred arrangement, Section 403(b) annuity contract or custodial account (voluntary salary reduction), Section 408(k)(6) salary reduction (SEP), Section 457 deferred compensation plan, or Section 501(c)(18)(D) trust.

Form W-3

A Form W-3 is submitted to the IRS as a transmittal form with Form W-2s. Form W-3 and all attached W-2s must be submitted to the Social Security Administration Center by February 28. No money is sent with Form W-3.

Form W-2c

Use Form W-2c to correct errors on a previously filed Form W-2.

Form W-3c

Use Form W-3c to transmit corrected W-2c forms to the Social Security Administration.

DO NOT STAPLE

a Control number	33333	For Official Use Only ▶ OMB No. 1545-0008		

b Kind of Payer ▶	941 ☒	Military ☐	943 ☐	1 Wages, tips, other compensation 243987.00	2 Federal income tax withheld 29142.00
	CT-1 ☐	Hshld. ☐	Medicare govt. emp. ☐	3 Social security wages 236431.00	4 Social security tax withheld 14659.00

c Total number of statements 19	d Establishment number	5 Medicare wages and tips 243987.00	6 Medicare tax withheld 3538.00

e Employer's identification number 35-2946039	7 Social security tips	8 Allocated tips

f Employer's name ABC Charity	9 Advance EIC payments	10 Dependent care benefits
	11 Nonqualified plans	12 Deferred compensation
2670 N. Hull Road Traverse City, MI 49615	13 Adjusted total social security wages and tips	
	14 Adjusted total Medicare wages and tips	
g Employer's address and ZIP code		
h Other EIN used this year	15 Income tax withheld by third-party payer	

i Employer's state I.D. No.						

Under penalties of perjury, I declare that I have examined this return and accompanying documents, and, to the best of my knowledge and belief, they are true, correct, and complete.

Signature ▶ *Donald L. Lewis*　　Title ▶ Treasurer　　Date ▶ 1/31/96

Telephone number (　)

Form **W-3** Transmittal of Wage and Tax Statements **1995**　　Department of the Treasury Internal Revenue Service

---

a Year/Form corrected 19 95 / W- 2	Void ☐	OMB No. 1545-0008		

b Employee's name, address, and ZIP code　☐ Corrected	c Employer's name, address, and ZIP code　☐ Corrected
Norman R. Tice 418 Trenton Street Springfield, OH 45504	Little Valley Church 4865 Douglas Road Springfield, OH 45504

d Employee's correct SSN 304-64-7792	e Employer's SSA number 69-	f Employer's Federal EIN 35-6309294	g Employer's state I.D. number

h Previously reported ▶ Stat. emp. ☐　De-ceased ☐　Pension plan ☐　Legal rep. ☐　Def'd. comp. ☐　IRA/SEP ☐	Corrected ▶ Stat. emp. ☐　De-ceased ☐　Pension plan ☐　Legal rep. ☐　Def'd. comp. ☐　IRA/SEP ☐	j Employer's use

Complete k and/or l only if incorrect on the last form you filed. Show incorrect item here. ▶	k Employee's incorrect SSN	l Employee's name (as incorrectly shown on previous form)

Form W-2 box	(a) As previously reported	(b) Correct information	(c) Increase (decrease)
1 Wages, tips, other comp.	10000.00	12500.00	2500.00
2 Federal income tax withheld	1800.00	2000.00	200.00
3 Social security wages	10000.00	12500.00	2500.00
4 Social security tax withheld	620.00	775.00	155.00
5 Medicare wages and tips	10000.00	12500.00	2500.00
6 Medicare tax withheld	145.00	181.25	36.25
7 Social security tips			
8 Allocated tips			
17 State wages, tips, etc.			
18 State income tax			
20 Local wages, tips, etc.			
21 Local income tax			

CHANGES

Form **W-2c** (Rev. 10-94)　**Statement of Corrected Income and Tax Amounts**　Copy D　For Employer Department of the Treasury Internal Revenue Service

Unemployment taxes

The federal and state unemployment systems provide temporary unemployment compensation to workers who have lost their jobs. Employers provide the revenue for this program by paying federal unemployment taxes, under the Federal Unemployment Tax Act (FUTA), and state unemployment taxes. These are strictly employer taxes and no deductions are taken from employees' wages.

The current federal unemployment tax law exempts from coverage

✔ services performed in the employ of a church, a convention, or association of churches or an organization that is operated primarily for religious purposes and that is operated, supervised, controlled, or principally supported by a church or convention or association of churches;

✔ services performed by a duly ordained, commissioned, or licensed minister of a church in the exercise of ministry or by a member of a religious order in the exercise of duties required by such order.

States may expand their coverage of unemployment taxes beyond the federal minimum. In many states, exemption is also provided for

✔ services performed in the employ of a separately incorporated church school if the school is operated primarily for religious purposes and is operated, supervised, controlled, or principally supported by a church or convention or association of churches;

✔ services performed in the employ of an unincorporated church-controlled elementary or secondary school.

Recent court cases reflect attempts by states to subject religious organizations, including churches, to state unemployment taxes.

FUTA reporting requirements

Nonprofit organizations that are liable for FUTA taxes are required to file Form 940, or 940-EZ Employer's Annual Federal Unemployment Tax Return. This form covers one calendar year and is due on or before January 31. Tax deposits may be required before filing the annual return. You must use Form 8109, Federal Tax Deposit Coupon, when making each federal unemployment tax deposit.

The taxable wage base under the Federal Unemployment Tax Act is $7,000 for 1995. The gross FUTA tax rate is 6.2% for 1995. The credit against FUTA tax for payments to state unemployment funds remains at a maximum 5.4%. The net rate is 0.8%. There are no states with credit reductions for 1995, so employers in all states pay FUTA taxes at the net rate of 0.8% for 1995. The 0.2% FUTA surtax has been extended through 1996.

Refunds and Abatements

In certain instances, Form 843, Claim for Refund and Request for Abatement, is used to file a claim for refund of overpaid taxes, interest, penalties, and additions to tax.

Example 1: On your employment tax return you reported and paid more federal income tax than you withheld from an employee. Use Form 843 to claim a refund.

Example 2: The IRS assessed penalties or interest relating to your employment tax return. You paid the penalties or interest. You later realized that the penalties or interest had been incorrectly calculated or assessed. Use Form 843 to file a claim for refund.

Key Concepts

- The proper classification of all your workers as employees or self-employed is a crucial matter for both your organization and the workers.

- Understanding the special tax treatments for ministers is very important.

- The failure to timely file and pay payroll taxes will leave your organization open to scrutiny by the IRS.

- Reporting all taxable compensation to the IRS requires considerable understanding of the tax laws and regulations.

CHAPTER FIVE

Information Reporting

In This Chapter

- General filing requirements
- Reporting on the receipt of funds
- Reporting on the payment of funds
- Summary of payment reporting requirements

Information reporting may be required for many noncontribution funds received by your organization. Payments to nonemployees will often require filings with the IRS also.

General Filing Requirements

Information forms (1098 and 1099) must be provided to the payers/recipients on or before January 31 following the calendar year that the funds were paid or received. Copies of the forms (or magnetic media) must be filed with the IRS by February 28, following the year that the funds were paid or received.

An extension of time to file may be requested by filing Form 8809, Request for Extension of Time to File Information Returns, with the IRS by the due date of the returns.

Magnetic media reporting may be required for filing information returns with the IRS. If you are required to file 250 or more information returns, you must file on magnetic media. The 250-or-more requirement applies separately to each type of form. A Form 4419, Application for Filing Information Returns on Magnetic Media, must be filed to apply to use magnetic media.

Payers filing returns on paper forms must use a separate transmittal Form 1096, Annual Summary and Transmittal of U.S. Information Returns, for each different type of information form. For example, if you file Forms 1098, 1099-MISC, and 1099-S, complete one Form 1096 to transmit Forms 1098, another Form 1096 to transmit Forms 1099-MISC, and a third Form 1096 to transmit Forms 1099-S.

DO NOT STAPLE   6969

Form **1096**	**Annual Summary and Transmittal of U.S. Information Returns**	OMB No. 1545-0108
Department of the Treasury Internal Revenue Service		**1995**

FILER'S name

ABC Charity

Street address (including room or suite number)

2670 N. Hull Road

City, state, and ZIP code

Traverse City, MI 49615

Name of person to contact if the IRS needs more information

Telephone number
(   )

For Official Use Only

If you are not using a preprinted label, enter in box 1 or 2 below the identification number you used as the filer on the information returns being transmitted. Do not fill in both boxes 1 and 2.

1 Employer identification number	2 Social security number	3 Total number of forms	4 Federal income tax withheld	5 Total amount reported with this Form 1096
35-7431092		3	$	$ 5842.00

Enter an "X" in only one box below to indicate the type of form being filed.   If this is your FINAL return, enter an "X" here . . ▶ ☐

W-2G 32	1096 81	1099-A 80	1099-B 79	1099-C 85	1099-DIV 91	1099-G 86	1099-INT 92	1099-MISC 95	1099-OID 96	1099-PATR 97	1099-R 98	1099-S 75	5498 28
☐	☐	☐	☐	☐	☐	☐	☐	☒	☐	☐	☐	☐	☐

Please return this entire page to the Internal Revenue Service. Photocopies are NOT acceptable.

Under penalties of perjury, I declare that I have examined this return and accompanying documents, and, to the best of my knowledge and belief, they are true, correct, and complete.

Signature ▶ *Donald P. Williams*   Title ▶ Executive Director   Date ▶ 1/25/96

Obtaining correct identification numbers

Organizations required to file information returns with the IRS must obtain the correct taxpayer identification number (TIN) to report income paid, real estate transactions, and mortgage interest paid to or by the organization.

Form **W-9** (Rev. March 1994) Department of the Treasury Internal Revenue Service	**Request for Taxpayer Identification Number and Certification**	Give form to the requester. Do NOT send to the IRS.

Name (If joint names, list first and circle the name of the person or entity whose number you enter in Part I below. See instructions on page 2 if your name has changed.)

Richard K. Bennett

Business name (Sole proprietors see instructions on page 2.)

Please check appropriate box: ☒ Individual/Sole proprietor   ☐ Corporation   ☐ Partnership   ☐ Other ▶ ....   Requester's name and address (optional)

Address (number, street, and apt. or suite no.)

826 Garner Street

City, state, and ZIP code

Thomasville, NC 27360   List account number(s) here (optional)

Part I   Taxpayer Identification Number (TIN)

Enter your TIN in the appropriate box. For individuals, this is your social security number (SSN). For sole proprietors, see the instructions on page 2. For other entities, it is your employer identification number (EIN). If you do not have a number, see How To Get a TIN below.

Note: If the account is in more than one name, see the chart on page 2 for guidelines on whose number to enter.

Social security number
4 0 3 9 8 1 2 9 7

OR

Employer identification number

Part II   For Payees Exempt From Backup Withholding (See Part II instructions on page 2)

▶

Part III   Certification

Under penalties of perjury, I certify that:

1. The number shown on this form is my correct taxpayer identification number (or I am waiting for a number to be issued to me), and

2. I am not subject to backup withholding because: (a) I am exempt from backup withholding, or (b) I have not been notified by the Internal Revenue Service that I am subject to backup withholding as a result of a failure to report all interest or dividends, or (c) the IRS has notified me that I am no longer subject to backup withholding.

Certification Instructions.—You must cross out item 2 above if you have been notified by the IRS that you are currently subject to backup withholding because of underreporting interest or dividends on your tax return. For real estate transactions, item 2 does not apply. For mortgage interest paid, the acquisition or abandonment of secured property, cancellation of debt, contributions to an individual retirement arrangement (IRA), and generally payments other than interest and dividends, you are not required to sign the Certification, but you must provide your correct TIN. (Also see Part III instructions on page 2.)

Sign Here   Signature ▶ *Richard K. Bennett*   Date ▶ 3/12/96

Form W-9, Request for Taxpayer Identification Number and Certification, is used to furnish the correct TIN to the organization and in certain other situations to:

✓ certify that the TIN furnished is correct;

✓ certify that the recipient of the income is not subject to backup withholding; or

✓ certify exemption from backup withholding.

If the recipient does not furnish a completed Form W-9, the church or nonprofit organization is required to withhold 31% of the payment, deposit the withholding with Form 8109 or 8109-B, and report amounts withheld on Form 1099-INT, 1099-MISC, or 1099-R, as applicable.

Reporting on the Receipt of Funds

Receipt of interest on mortgages

Use Form 1098, Mortgage Interest Statement, to report mortgage interest of $600 or more received by your organization during the year from an individual, including a sole proprietor. You need not file Form 1098 for interest received from a corporation, partnership, trust, estate, or association. A transmittal Form 1096 must accompany one or more Form 1098s.

☐ CORRECTED (if checked)

RECIPIENT'S/LENDER'S name, street address, city, state, and ZIP code	* The amount shown may not be fully deductible by you on your Federal income tax return. Limitations based on the cost and value of the secured property may apply. In addition, you may only deduct an amount of mortgage interest to the extent it was incurred by you, actually paid by you, and not reimbursed by another person.	OMB No. 1545-0901 1995 Form 1098	Mortgage Interest Statement

Debra Heights Church
1517 Cedar St.
Rochester, MN 55902

RECIPIENT'S Federal identification no.	PAYER'S social security number	1 Mortgage interest received from payer(s)/borrower(s)*	Copy B For Payer
35-8814073	441-09-7843	$ 1819.00	

PAYER'S/BORROWER'S name

Julie M. Chapman

2 Points paid on purchase of principal residence (See Box 2 on back.)
$

Street address (including apt. no.)

125 Orchard Drive

3 Refund of overpaid interest (See Box 3 on back.)
$

City, state, and ZIP code

Cedar Falls, IA 50613

4

Account number (optional)

The information in boxes 1, 2, and 3 is important tax information and is being furnished to the Internal Revenue Service. If you are required to file a return, a negligence penalty or other sanction may be imposed on you if the IRS determines that an underpayment of tax results because you overstated a deduction for this mortgage interest or for these points or because you did not report this refund of interest on your return.

Form **1098**   (Keep for your records.)   Department of the Treasury - Internal Revenue Service

Proceeds from real estate transactions

Use Form 1099-S, Statement for Recipients of Proceeds From Real Estate Transactions, to report the sale or exchange of one-to-four-family and certain other real estate.

Reporting is required only if the transaction consists in whole or in part of the sale or exchange of commercial property, land, apartments, leaseholds, easements, one-to-four-family real estate for money, indebtedness, property, or services and certain time-shares. One-to-four-family real estate means any structure designed principally for the occupancy of one to four families, such as a house, townhouse, duplex, or four-unit apartment building. Excluded are mobile homes that include wheels and axles.

When a church sells property, the church does not have a Form 1099-S filing requirement. And when a church buys property, there will generally not be a filing requirement. However, if no mortgage lender or broker is involved in the transaction, the church does have the responsibility to file Form 1099-S and provide a copy to the seller.

☐ VOID ☐ CORRECTED			
FILER'S name, street address, city, state, and ZIP code Lakeside Church 70 Thompson Road Watertown, NY 13601	1 Date of closing 10/15/95	OMB No. 1545-0997 **1995** Form **1099-S**	Proceeds From Real Estate Transactions
	2 Gross proceeds $ 30450.00		
FILER'S Federal identification number 35-9431872	TRANSFEROR'S identification number 309-88-4659	3 Address or legal description (including city, state, and ZIP code) 702 Franklin Street Syracuse, New York	Copy C For Filer
TRANSFEROR'S name Craig J. Peters			For Paperwork Reduction Act Notice and instructions for completing this form, see **Instructions for Forms 1099, 1098, 5498, and W-2G.**
Street address (including apt. no.) P. O. Box 503			
City, state, and ZIP code Avon, NY 14414		4 Check here if the transferor received or will receive property or services as part of the consideration. ▶ ☐	
Account number (optional)		5 Buyer's part of real estate tax $	

Form **1099-S**   Department of the Treasury - Internal Revenue Service

Receipt of large amounts of cash

Form 8300, Report of Cash Payments Over $10,000 Received in a Trade or Business, is generally required if you receive more than $10,000 in cash in one transaction or two or more related transactions. This reporting requirement does not apply to churches or other nonprofit organizations.

Reporting on the Payment of Funds

Payments of interest

File Form 1099-INT, Statement for Recipients of Interest Income, for each person to whom you paid interest reportable in boxes 1 and 3 of at least $10 in any calendar year. This form is also required if you withheld any federal income tax under the backup withholding rules (31% rate), regardless of the amount of the payment. In certain instances, the $10 limit increases to $600.

The $10 limit applies if the interest is on "evidences of indebtedness" (bonds and promissory notes) issued by a corporation in "registered form." A note or bond

---

☐ VOID ☐ CORRECTED		
PAYER'S name, street address, city, state, and ZIP code Lancaster Community Church 1425 Spencer Avenue Logansport, IN 46947	Payer's RTN (optional)	OMB No. 1545-0112 **1995** **Interest Income** Form **1099-INT**

PAYER'S Federal identification number 35-7921873	RECIPIENT'S identification number 438-42-9973	1 Interest income not included in box 3 $ 923.00		Copy C For Payer
RECIPIENT'S name James R. Moore		2 Early withdrawal penalty $	3 Interest on U.S. Savings Bonds and Treas. obligations $	For Paperwork Reduction Act Notice and
Street address (including apt. no.) 604 Linden Avenue		4 Federal income tax withheld $		instructions for completing this
City, state, and ZIP code Wabash, IN 46992		5 Foreign tax paid	6 Foreign country or U.S. possession	form, see **Instructions for** **Forms 1099,**
Account number (optional)	2nd TIN Not. ☐	$		**1098, 5498,** **and W-2G.**

Form **1099-INT**   Department of the Treasury - Internal Revenue Service

---

is in "registered form" if its transfer must be effected by the surrender of the old instrument and either the reissuance by the corporation of the old instrument to the new holder or the issuance by the corporation of a new instrument to the new holder.

There is no requirement to file Form 1099-INT for payments made to a corporation or another tax-exempt organization.

> **Example 1:** Sleepy Hollow Church financed a new church by issuing registered bonds. 1099-INT forms must be provided to each bond investor receiving $10 or more in interest during any calendar year.
>
> If Sleepy Hollow engaged a bond broker to handle the issuance of the bonds, the broker would issue 1099-INT forms. If Sleepy Hollow issued the bonds without using a bond broker, the church would issue 1099-INT forms.

Example 2: Sleepy Hollow Church borrows funds from church members. The notes are transferrable. There is no requirement to return the bonds to the church for reissuance. The $600 limit applies for the issuance of 1099-INT forms for the payment of interest on these notes.

Payments to annuitants

File Form 1099-R for each person to whom you have made a designated distribution that is a total distribution from a retirement plan or a payment to an annuitant of $1 of more. If part of the distribution is taxable and part is nontaxable, Form 1099-R should reflect the entire distribution.

□ VOID □ CORRECTED			
PAYER'S name, street address, city, state, and ZIP code ABC Charity 8049 Riverside Blvd. Sacramento, CA 95831	1 Gross distribution $ 1425.00 2a Taxable amount $ 565.00	OMB No. 1545-0119 1995 Form **1099-R**	Distributions From Pensions, Annuities, Retirement or Profit-Sharing Plans, IRAs, Insurance Contracts, etc.
	2b Taxable amount not determined □	Total distribution □	Copy D For Payer
PAYER'S Federal identification number RECIPIENT'S identification number 35-4792142 703-41-3669	3 Capital gain (included in box 2a) $	4 Federal income tax withheld $	
RECIPIENT'S name Mary D. Hughes	5 Employee contributions or insurance premiums $	6 Net unrealized appreciation in employer's securities $	For Paperwork Reduction Act Notice and instructions for completing this form, see **Instructions for Forms 1099, 1098, 5498, and W-2G.**
Street address (including apt. no.) P. O. Box 9042	7 Distribution code IRA/ SEP □	8 Other $ %	
City, state, and ZIP code El Toro, CA 92630	9a Your percentage of total distribution %	9b Total employee contributions $	
Account number (optional)	10 State tax withheld $ $	11 State/Payer's state no.	12 State distribution $ $
	13 Local tax withheld $ $	14 Name of locality	15 Local distribution $ $
Form **1099-R**		Department of the Treasury - Internal Revenue Service	

Example: ABC Ministry makes payments of $1,000 during the year to one of their annuitants, Mary Smith. (Several years earlier, Mary entered into the charitable gift annuity agreement by giving a check to ABC.)

A portion of each annuity payment is a tax-free return of principal and the remainder is annuity income for Mary. ABC should report the entire $1,000 as annuity income on Form 1099-R.

Form W-4P, Withholding Certificate for Pension or Annuity Payments, should be completed by recipients of income from annuity, pension, and certain other deferred compensation plans to inform payers whether income tax is to be withheld and on what basis. Withholding is not required from pension and annuity payments unless the payments are more than $10,000 per year.

Form **W-4P** Department of the Treasury Internal Revenue Service	**Withholding Certificate for Pension or Annuity Payments**	OMB No. 1545-0415 **1996**

Type or print your full name Arnold B. Luther	Your social security number 505 ⋮ 19 ⋮ 4129
Home address (number and street or rural route) P. O. Box 185	Claim or identification number (if any) of your pension or annuity contract
City or town, state, and ZIP code Asheboro, NC 27203	

Complete the following applicable lines:

1 I elect not to have income tax withheld from my pension or annuity. (Do not complete lines 2 or 3.) . . . . . ▶ ☒

2 I want my withholding from each periodic pension or annuity payment to be figured using the number of allowances and marital status shown. (You may also designate a dollar amount on line 3.) . . . . ▶

   Marital status: ☐ Single ☐ Married ☐ Married, but withhold at higher Single rate   (Enter number of allowances.)

3 I want the following additional amount withheld from each pension or annuity payment. **Note:** *For periodic payments, you cannot enter an amount here without entering the number (including zero) of allowances on line 2* . . . ▶ $

Your signature ▶   Date ▶   1/5/96

Cat. No. 10225T

Payments to nonresident aliens

Payments for personal services made to non-citizens (nonresident aliens) who are temporarily in this country are often subject to federal income tax withholding at a 30% rate. A nonresident alien is a person who is neither a U.S. citizen nor a resident of the U.S. Some payments may be exempt from income tax withholding if the person is from a country with which the U.S. maintains a tax treaty. Salary payments to nonresident aliens employed in the U.S. are subject to income tax withholding based on the regular withholding tables.

Single, nonrecurring fixed or determinable payments to nonresident aliens are generally subject to withholding. Honoraria paid to visiting speakers usually fit this definition. It is not clear if love offerings are subject to withholding.

All payments to nonresident aliens, other than expense reimbursements and amounts reported on Form W-2, must be reported on Form 1042 and 1042-S. These forms are filed with the IRS Service Center in Philadelphia by March 15 for the previous calendar year, and a copy of Form 1042-S must be sent to the nonresident alien.

Payments of royalties and for other services

File Form 1099-MISC for each recipient (other than corporations) to whom you have paid

 ✓ at least $10 in royalties, or

 ✓ at least $600 in rents (for example, office rent or equipment rent), payments for services (nonemployee compensation), or medical health care payments.

Example: A charity has established a written, nondiscriminatory employee medical expense reimbursement plan under which the charity pays the medical expenses of the employee, spouse, and dependents.

If $600 or more is paid in the calendar year to a doctor or other provider of health care services, a Form 1099-MISC must be filed. Amounts paid to the employee under a medical reimbursement plan are not reportable on Forms W-2 or 1099-MISC.

☐ VOID ☐ CORRECTED			
PAYER'S name, street address, city, state, and ZIP code	1 Rents $	OMB No. 1545-0115	Miscellaneous Income
ABC Charity 110 Harding Avenue Cincinnati, OH 45963	2 Royalties $	**1995**	
	3 Other income $	Form 1099-MISC	
PAYER'S Federal identification number 35-1148942	RECIPIENT'S identification number 389-41-8067	4 Federal income tax withheld $	5 Fishing boat proceeds $	Copy C For Payer
RECIPIENT'S name Mark A. Mitchell	6 Medical and health care payments $	7 Nonemployee compensation $ 2400.00	For Paperwork Reduction Act Notice and instructions for completing this form, see **Instructions for Forms 1099, 1098, 5498, and W-2G.**
Street address (including apt. no.) 5412 Warren Avenue	8 Substitute payments in lieu of dividends or interest $	9 Payer made direct sales of $5,000 or more of consumer products to a buyer (recipient) for resale ▶ ☐	
City, state, and ZIP code Norwood, OH 45212	10 Crop insurance proceeds $	11 State income tax withheld $	
Account number (optional)	2nd TIN Not. ☐	12 State/Payer's state number	
Form **1099-MISC**			Department of the Treasury - Internal Revenue Service

Do not include the payment of a housing allowance to a minister on Form 1099-MISC (or Form W-2). The housing allowance is not reportable to the IRS.

Advances, reimbursements, or expenses for traveling and other business expenses of an employee are not reportable on Form 1099-MISC. These payments may be reportable on Form W-2 if they do not comply with the accountable expense plan rules.

Advances, reimbursements, or expenses for traveling and other business expenses of a self-employed person are not reportable on Form 1099-MISC if made under an accountable expense reimbursement plan. Under this type of plan, expenses are reimbursed only if they are substantiated as to amount, date, and business nature, and any excess reimbursements must be returned to the organization.

Advances, reimbursements, or expenses for traveling and other business expenses of a self-employed person that are not substantiated to the paying organization are reportable on Form 1099-MISC.

Example 1: ABC Ministry organizes a seminar and engages a speaker. The speaker is paid a $750 honorarium, and ABC reimbursed the travel expenses upon presentation of proper substantiation by the speaker. Form 1099-MISC should be issued to the speaker for $750.

Example 2: Same facts as Example 1, except of the $750 payment, $250 is designated for travel expenses and the speaker accounted to ABC for the travel. Since the honorarium of $500, after excluding the substantiated payments, is less than the $600 limit, there is no requirement to issue a Form 1099-MISC to the speaker.

    The answer to this example would be different if ABC paid an honorarium to the same speaker during the same calendar year of $100 or more, bringing the total for the year to the $600 level.

Example 3: Same facts as Example 1, except of the $750 payment, $250 is designated for travel expenses. But the speaker did not account to ABC for the travel expenses. A Form 1099-MISC should be issued to the speaker for $750.

Example 4: ABC Ministry contracts for janitorial services with an unincorporated janitorial service and pays $2,000 during the year for this service. ABC should issue a Form 1099-MISC for these payments.

Payments to volunteers

Payments to volunteers that represent a reimbursement under an accountable business expense reimbursement plan for expenses directly connected with the volunteer services are not reportable by the charity.

Payments for auto mileage up to the maximum IRS rate for business miles (30 cents for 1995) are generally considered to be tax-free for volunteers. When an organization provides liability insurance for its volunteers, the value of the coverage can be excluded from the volunteer's income as a working condition fringe benefit.

Payments to or on behalf of volunteers that are not business expenses are reported on Form W-2 or Form 1099-MISC, depending on whether or not a common law employee relationship exists. When the relationship between an organization takes the form of an employer-employee relationship, payments other than expense reimbursement are reported on Form W-2. Payments to volunteers for medical, education, or personal living expenses must be reported as nonemployee compensation. Payments to volunteers for lodging, meals, and incidental expenses may be made under the per diem rules if the duration of the travel is under one year.

Moving expenses

Qualified employee moving expense payments or reimbursements are reportable on Form W-2, only in Box 13, using Code P. The payments do not constitute compensation if the expenses would be otherwise deductible by the employee as moving expenses. The employer should provide an employee with Form 4782 only if the expenses were not substantiated by the employee or if the payments did not qualify as moving expenses.

Form **4782**
(Rev. September 1994)

Department of the Treasury
Internal Revenue Service

Employee Moving Expense Information

Payments made during the calendar year 19 9 5....

▶ **See instructions on back.**

OMB No. 1545-0182

Do not file.
Keep for your records.

Name of employee

Melvin L. Brown

Social security number

541 : 16 8194

Moving Expense Payments		(a) Amount paid to employee	(b) Amount paid to a third party for employee's benefit and value of services furnished in kind	(c) Total (Add columns (a) and (b).)
Part I **Expenses Incurred After 1993**				
1 Transportation and storage of household goods and personal effects	1	3,250	1,000	4,250
2 Travel and lodging payments for expenses of moving from old to new home. **Do not** include meals	2	200		200
3 List all other payments (specify). Note: *These amounts must be included in the employee's income* ▶	3			
4 Total payments for moving expenses incurred after 1993. Add the amounts in column (c) of lines 1 through 3. . . . . ▶	4			4,450
Part II **Expenses Incurred Before 1994**				
Section A—Transportation of Household Goods				
1 Transportation and storage of household goods and personal effects	1			
Section B—Expenses of Moving From Old To New Home				
2 Travel and lodging payments **not** including meals	2			
3 Meal payments for travel . . . . ▶	3			
Section C—Pre-move Househunting Expenses and Temporary Quarters for any 30 Days in a Row After Obtaining Employment (90 Days for a Foreign Move)				
4 Pre-move travel and lodging payments **not** including meals	4			
5 Temporary quarters payments **not** including meals	5			
6 Total meal payments for both pre-move househunting and temporary quarters . . .	6			
Section D—Qualified Real Estate Expenses				
7 Qualified expenses of selling, buying, or renting a home	7			
Section E—Miscellaneous Payments				
8 List all other payments (specify) ▶	8			
9 Total payments for moving expenses incurred before 1994. Add the amounts in column (c) of lines 1 through 8. Note: *This amount **must** be included in the employee's income* . . . . ▶	9			

For Paperwork Reduction Act Notice, see back of form.   Cat. No. 13079T   Form **4782** (Rev. 9-94)

Summary of Payment Reporting Requirements

Below is an alphabetical list of some payments and the forms to file to report them. It is not a complete list of payments, and the absence of a payment from the list does not suggest that the payment is not reportable.

Types of Payment	Report on Form
Advance earned income credit	W-2
Annuities, periodic payments	1099-R
Auto reimbursements (nonaccountable plan):	
Employee	W-2
Nonemployee	1099-MISC
Awards:	
Employee	W-2
Nonemployee	1099-MISC
Bonuses:	
Employee	W-2
Nonemployee	1099-MISC
Cafeteria/flexible benefit plan	5500, 5500-C or 5500-R
Car expense (nonaccountable plan):	
Employee	W-2
Nonemployee	1099-MISC
Christmas bonuses:	
Employee	W-2
Nonemployee	1099-MISC
Commissions:	
Employee	W-2
Nonemployee	1099-MISC
Compensation:	
Employee	W-2
Nonemployee	1099-MISC
Dependent care payments	W-2
Director's fees	1099-MISC
Education expense reimbursement (nonaccountable plan):	
Employee	W-2
Nonemployee	1099-MISC
Employee business expense reimbursement (nonaccountable plan)	W-2
Fees:	
Employee	W-2

```
       Nonemployee ................................... 1099-MISC
Interest .......................................... 1099-INT
Interest, mortgage ................................... 1098
Medical expense reimbursement plan ................... 5500, 5500-C or 5500-R
       (employee-funded)
Mileage (nonaccountable plan):
       Employee ....................................... W-2
       Nonemployee . . . . . . . . . . . . . . . . . . 1 0 9 9 - M I S C
Mortgage interest ................................... 1098
Moving expense:
       * Employee ..................................... W-2/4782
       Nonemployee ............................... 1099-MISC
Prizes:
       Employee ....................................... W-2
       Nonemployee ............................... 1099-MISC
** PS 58 costs ..................................... W-2 or 1099-R
Real estate proceeds ................................ 1099-S
Rents .......................................... 1099-MISC
Royalties ...................................... 1099-MISC
Severance pay ....................................... W-2
Sick pay .......................................... W-2
Supplemental unemployment ............................ W-2
Vacation allowance:
       Employee ....................................... W-2
       Nonemployee ............................... 1099-MISC
Wages ............................................ W-2
```

* For 1994 and later, qualified reimbursements or payments must be reported on Form W-2, only in Box 13, using Code P. Form 4782 must be prepared for excess or unubstantiated reimbursements.

** Relates to group-term life insurance

Key Concepts

■ The receipt of certain funds, such as mortgage interest, by your organization may trigger information reporting to the IRS.

■ Payments for rent, various services, and other items will often require the preparation of annual information returns.

■ Securing correct taxpayer identification numbers should routinely occur in connection with the ruling of information returns.

CHAPTER SIX

Your Financial Records

In This Chapter
- Budgeting
- The money comes in
- The money goes out
- Accounting records
- Financial reports
- Audit guidelines

It takes a practical set of accounting records and financial information to communicate how the finances are at your organization.

Controlling and managing the organization's money is also very important. It is essential that the procedures for the handling of finances be reduced to writing. The governing board should establish and maintain the basic financial procedures for the organization. Too often, a new treasurer is handed a file box of accounting records with no written guidelines to follow. It is little wonder that the accounting system functions effectively one year and is in shambles the next.

Sound procedures should be developed, installed, and maintained year after year. These procedures will be different for every organization depending on the size of the organization, capability, and availability of personnel.

Budgeting

It is possible for a small church or nonprofit organization to run without a budget. But a budget is an effective tool for allocating financial resources and planning and controlling your spending even for smaller organizations. For larger organizations, a budget is essential.

A budget matches anticipated inflows of resources with outflows of resources.

Preparing a budget requires considerable effort. It includes looking back at revenue and expense trends. Projected plans and programs must be converted into estimated dollar amounts. Too many organizations budget expenses with some degree of precision and then set the income budget at whatever it takes to cover the total expenses. This is often a disastrous approach.

Ideally, separate budgets should be prepared for all funds of an organization. Even capital and debt-retirement funds should be budgeted. The separate budgets are then to be combined into a unified budget.

Line-item budgets within each fund reflect the projected cost of salaries, fringe benefits, utilities, maintenance, debt retirement, and other expenses. The line-item approach is generally used by a treasurer in reporting to department heads or other responsible individuals.

Program budgets are often presented to the board of a nonprofit organization or a church's membership. In this approach, the cost of a program is reflected rather than the cost of specific line-items such as salaries or fringe benefits.

A good budgeting approach is to divide the budget into quarterly or monthly segments. If a monthly budget is used, the budget for each month is not necessarily one-twelfth of the annual amount. For example, if gifts are typically lower in summer months, the monthly budgets for the summer reflect the projected lower income. When actual activity is compared to monthly or quarterly budgets, it may be possible to make program adjustments as the year progresses.

The Money Comes In

All funds received should be recorded in detail. The bulk of the income for a church is received in Sunday offerings. Counting sheets are used to record the offerings in detail. Non-offering income for churches and other organizations should be receipted in detail.

Recording cash receipts

A cash receipts journal should be prepared manually or by computer. Entries in the journal come from the weekly offering counting sheets and other receipts.

For a manually-prepared cash receipts journal, the total of each deposit is generally the only information recorded in the "total received" column of the cash receipts journal. The monthly totals of the cash receipts journal should be posted to the general ledger.

Counting money

Be sure that at least two people are present when offerings and other cash receipts are counted and recorded. Two or more individuals counting offerings protects the organization from misappropriation and protects the counters from suspicion. After the money is counted in a controlled process, the funds could be assigned to one member of the counting committee for deposit.

Revenue Flow Chart

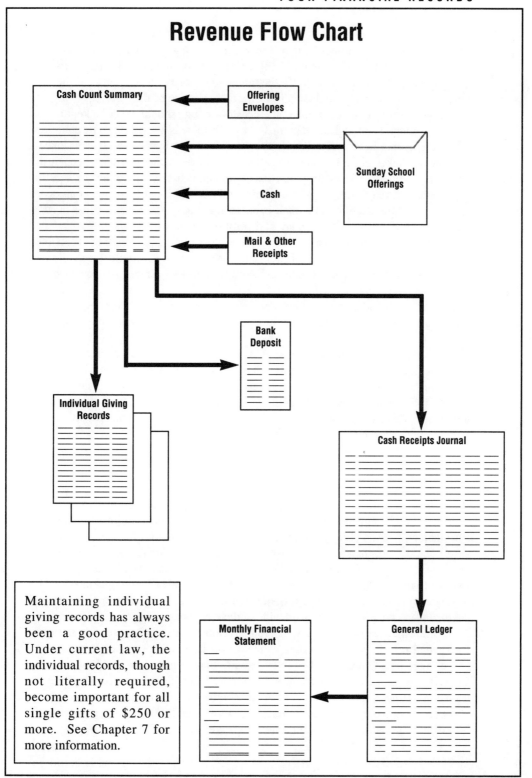

Maintaining individual giving records has always been a good practice. Under current law, the individual records, though not literally required, become important for all single gifts of $250 or more. See Chapter 7 for more information.

The treasurer should not be involved in the counting process. The exclusion of the treasurer is not a reflection on his or her honesty or integrity. It merely enables the counters to independently verify the amount of money received, record the designation of certain gifts, and then deposit the money in the bank.

Large sums of counted or uncounted cash offerings should never be kept on the church or nonprofit organization premises, even if there is a safe. At some churches, offering counting is completed while the service is in progress. In other instances, the counting takes place immediately after the service. Other churches deposit the uncounted funds in a bank drop-box during or immediately following the service. The funds are then retrieved from the bank and counted by at least two counters at the bank or at the church on the next bank business day. Churches located in rural areas may need to wait until Monday to deposit the Sunday offerings.

Provide a convenient place to count money. A calculator, counting sheets (see examples on page 103), coin holders and other supplies should be available. Offerings are usually separated into four groups: checks, currency, loose coins, and offering envelopes.

Counters should sign a written statement of confidentiality before participating in the counting process. If the commitment of confidentiality is broken, the individual(s) should be removed from the team of counters.

Offering reports should be completed each time offerings are counted with the counters signing the reports. One page should summarize the offerings with an indication of the various types of funds received. All checks should be listed on this report. Individual contributions should be listed on a sheet separate from the offering report. This listing is based on the list of checks from the offering report and the offering envelopes that are identified by donors.

Use of offering envelopes

The use of offering envelopes and writing checks when contributing to the church should be encouraged. Checks, payable to the church, are more difficult to steal than cash. And checks still provide proof of contributions for IRS purposes for single gifts of less than $250. The use of offering envelopes is essential when cash is given. Unless offering envelopes are used, loose cash could more easily be removed without detection during the cash collection and counting process. The money counters should verify that the contents of the offering envelopes are identical to any amounts written on the outside of the envelopes.

Some churches provide 52 numbered envelopes each year plus extra envelopes for special offerings. This system is ideal as a basis of posting contributions to church records. Other churches only provide blank envelopes in the pew racks. Either way, the recording of all gifts by donor with a periodic report of giving to each donor is necessary to provide adequate control over the money given.

Offering envelopes should be retained in the church office. Their retention is important if individual contributions need to be verified.

Contributions By Donor

March 6 , 1996 (x) A.M. ( ) P.M. ( )

Name of Contributor	Regular Tithes & Offerings	Sunday School	Building Fund	Missions	Other Description	Other Amount
M/M Mark Wilson	50.00		10.00	20.00		
Frank Young	35.00					
Ellen Jackson	60.00		15.00			
Lori Avery	40.00					
M/M Mike Floyd	100.00	10.00			Benevolence	40.00
M/M Harold Long	45.00		5.00	10.00		
Mary Martin	75.00			20.00		
M/M Steve Ross	80.00					
M/M Joe Harris	65.00		5.00		School Project	30.00
Kelly York	50.00					
Peggy Walker	30.00					
M/M Bob Franklin	75.00	5.00		15.00		
Don Gilles	40.00		10.00			
Lou Shields	200.00			20.00		
M/M Ron White	80.00					
Art Howe	100.00		20.00		Choir Robes	50.00
M/M Stan Plunkett	60.00	10.00				
Nancy Robbins	75.00				Youth Trip	40.00
M/M Bill Lyon	50.00			5.00		
M/M David Clark	80.00		20.00			
James Bowers	40.00				Parking Lot	20.00
Cindy Burr	60.00			10.00		
TOTALS	1,490.00	25.00	85.00	100.00		180.00

Cash Count Summary

March 6 , 1996

	Sunday School	Sunday A.M.	Sunday P.M.	Received During Week	TOTAL
Coins	83.12	21.82	10.42		115.36
Currency	320.00	431.00	108.00		859.00
Checks	25.00	1,855.00	360.00	185.00	2,425.00
TOTALS	428.12	2,307.82	478.42	185.00	3,399.36

Breakdown By Type Of Gift

	Sunday School	Sunday A.M.	Sunday P.M.	Received During Week	TOTAL
Regular Tithes and Offerings		1,942.81	368.42	140.00	2,451.24
Sunday School	428.12				428.12
Building Fund		85.00	50.00	15.00	150.00
Missions		100.00	30.00	20.00	150.00
Other Designated Funds:					
Benevolence Fund		40.00			40.00
School Project		30.00	10.00		40.00
Choir Robes		50.00			50.00
Youth Trip		40.00	20.00	10.00	70.00
Parking Lot		20.00			20.00
TOTALS	428.12	2,307.82	478.42	185.00	3,399.36

Counted by: Mike Anderson
Helen David
Bob Wells

Deposited on:
March 7 , 1996

CASH RECEIPTS JOURNAL

Date	Description	Total Received	Regular Tithes & Offerings	Sunday School Offerings	Missions Offerings	Building Fund Offerings	Other Receipts Description	Amount
3/6/96	Weekly Receipts	3,399.36	2,451.24	428.12	150.00	150.00	Benevolence Fd.	40.00
✓							School Project	40.00
✓							Choir Robes	50.00
✓							Youth Trip	70.00
✓							Parking Lot	20.00
3/13/96	Weekly Receipts	3,196.10	2,211.30	410.80	304.00	200.00	School Project	50.00
✓							Youth Trip	20.00
3/20/96	Weekly Receipts	3,686.90	2,680.40	431.50	285.00	180.00	Benevolence Fd.	10.00
✓							Missions Trip	30.00
✓							Choir Robes	25.00
✓							Parking Lot	45.00
3/27/96	Weekly Receipts	3,632.80	2,580.70	485.10	247.00	175.00	School Project	15.00
✓							Choir Robes	25.00
✓							Missions Trip	30.00
✓							Youth Trip	50.00
✓							Parking Lot	25.00
		13,915.16	9,923.64	1,755.52	986.00	705.00		545.00

Example of Computer-Generated Cash Receipts Journal

Date	Reference	Entry Description	Account No.	Account Name	Amount Debit	Amount Credit
6/06/96	CR1	Weekly receipts	301-000	Regular Offerings		2,511.12
			302-000	Sunday School		304.78
			303-000	Missions		484.11
			304-000	Building Fund		241.50
			305-000	Benevolence Fund		148.70
			101-000	Valley View Bank	3,690.21	
6/13/96	CR2	Weekly receipts	301-000	Regular Offerings		2,604.80
			302-000	Sunday School		411.12
			303-000	Missions		389.00
			304-000	Building Fund		211.00
			306-000	Camp Fund		43.00
			307-000	Choir Fund		30.00
			308-000	School Fund		50.00
			101-000	Valley View Bank	3,738.92	
6/20/96	CR3	Weekly receipts	301-000	Regular Offerings		2,383.70
			302-000	Sunday School		391.42
			303-000	Missions		411.00
			304-000	Building Fund		305.00
			305-000	Benevolence Fund		30.00
			308-000	School Fund		25.00
			101-000	Valley View Bank	3,546.12	
6/27/96	CR4	Weekly receipts	301-000	Regular Offerings		2,780.12
			302-000	Sunday School		393.23
			303-000	Missions		305.00
			304-000	Building Fund		283.00
			305-000	Benevolence Fund		45.00
			307-000	Choir Fund		20.00
			308-000	School Fund		45.00
			101-000	Valley View Bank	3,871.35	
					14,846.60	14,846.60

**Example of Computer-Generated General Ledger
with Entries Posted From Cash Receipts Journal**

Source	Acct. No./ Date	Reference	Description	Beginning Balance	Current Entries	Ending Balance
	301-000		**Regular Offerings**	65,211.12-		
CR	6/06/96	CR1	Weekly receipts		2,511.12-	
CR	6/13/96	CR2	Weekly receipts		2,604.80-	
CR	6/20/96	CR3	Weekly receipts		2,383.70-	
CR	6/27/96	CR4	Weekly receipts		2,780.12-	
					10,279.74-	75,490.86-
	302-000		**Sunday School Offerings**	7,511.82-		
CR	6/06/96	CR1	Weekly receipts		304.78-	
CR	6/13/96	CR2	Weekly receipts		411.12-	
CR	6/20/96	CR3	Weekly receipts		391.42-	
CR	6/27/96	CR4	Weekly receipts		393.23-	
					1,500.55-	9,012.37-
	303-000		**Missions Offerings**	10,211.80-		
CR	6/06/96	CR1	Weekly receipts		484.11-	
CR	6/13/96	CR2	Weekly receipts		389.00-	
CR	6/20/96	CR3	Weekly receipts		411.00-	
CR	6/27/96	CR4	Weekly receipts		305.00-	
					1,589.11-	11,800.91-
	304-000		**Building Fund**	5,612.70-		
CR	6/06/96	CR1	Weekly receipts		241.50-	
CR	6/13/96	CR2	Weekly receipts		211.00-	
CR	6/20/96	CR3	Weekly receipts		305.00-	
CR	6/27/96	CR4	Weekly receipts		283.00-	
					1,040.50-	6,653.20-
	305-000		**Benevolence Fund**	1,411.70-		
CR	6/06/96	CR1	Weekly receipts		148.70-	
CR	6/20/96	CR3	Weekly receipts		30.00-	
CR	6/27/96	CR4	Weekly receipts		45.00-	
					223.70-	1,635.40-
	306-000		**Camp Fund**	211.00-		
CR	6/13/96	CR2	Weekly receipts		43.00-	
					43.00-	254.00-

Bank deposits

Bank deposit slips should be prepared in duplicate with the original going to the bank and the copy kept for the organization's records. It is wise to deposit funds daily as funds are received. If the offering reports and other receipts have been properly prepared, it is generally not necessary to list each check on the deposit slips.

The Money Goes Out

Payment of expenses

One of the most important principles of handling funds is to pay virtually all expenses by check. The use of the petty cash fund should be the only exception to payment by check. Cash from a deposit should never be used to pay expenses.

If checks are prepared manually, your checkbook should be the large desk-type checkbook. Such a checkbook usually has three checks to a page and large stubs on which to write a full description of each expenditure. Computer-prepared checks should generally have a stub with adequate space to identify the type of expense and account number(s) charged.

Use preprinted, consecutively numbered checks. All spoiled checks should be marked "void" and kept on file with the cancelled checks.

In some instances, it may be wise to require two signatures on every check or on checks over a certain amount. In other situations, one signature may be appropriate. The level of controls over the funds will help you determine if more than one signature is necessary. Access to a checking account should generally be limited to no more than two or three individuals. A church pastor should not have access to the checking account. Checks should never be signed and delivered to anyone without completing the payee and the amount.

Checks should not be written until near the time there are funds available to cover them. Some organizations write checks when bills are due without regard to available cash. Checks are held for days, weeks or sometimes months until they are released for payment. This is an extremely confusing practice that makes it very difficult to determine the actual checkbook balance.

Every check should have some type of written document to support it—an invoice, petty cash receipt, payroll summary, and so on. If such support is not available for some good reason, a memo should be written stating what the check is for. For example, an honorarium paid to a visiting speaker would not be supported by an invoice but should be documented by indicating the date of the speaking engagement and the event.

Occasionally it may be necessary to advance funds before supporting documentation is available (for example, a travel advance for future travel). In these instances, the treasurer must devise a system to ensure documentation is provided on

Disbursements Flow Chart

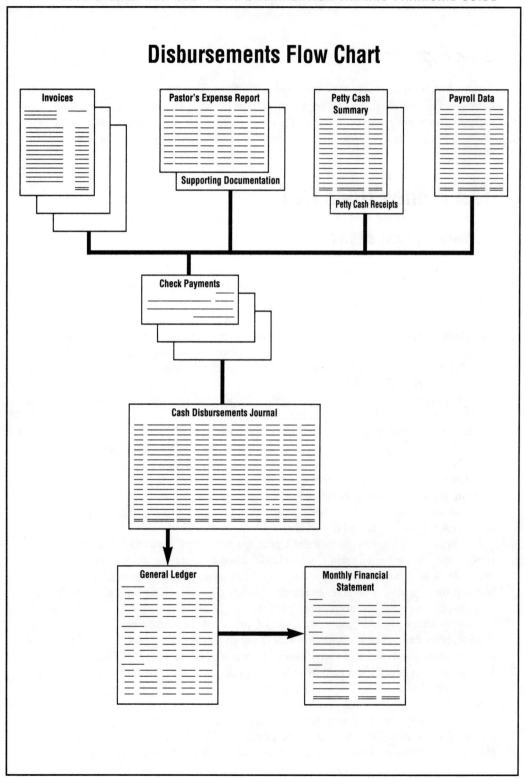

a timely basis and any excess funds are returned.

Payments to venders should be based on *original* copies of invoices. Payments should not be based on month-end statements that do not show the detail of the service or products provided. After payment has been made, all supporting material should be filed in a paid-bills file in alphabetical order by payee.

It is important that a treasurer never mix personal funds with organization funds.

Expense approval

If funds are approved in a church or other organization budget, this is generally sufficient authority for the treasurer to pay the bills. Expenses that exceed the budget may need specific approval.

Although every organization should have a budget, many do not. Even without a budget, routine expenses for utilities, salaries, and mortgage payments normally do not need specific approval before payment by the treasurer.

Recording expenses

All checks should be listed in a cash disbursements journal. The type of expense is reflected in the proper column in a manually prepared journal. Expense account numbers are used to identify the type of expense in a computerized journal. Expenses should be categorized in sufficient detail to provide an adequate breakdown of expenses on the periodic financial statements.

Petty cash system

To avoid having to write many checks for small amounts, it is wise to have a petty-cash fund (with a fixed base amount) from which to make small payments. For example, if the church office needs a roll of stamps, the use of the petty cash fund for the expense is more efficient than writing a check for the minor amount.

A petty cash fund of $50 or $100 is often adequate for small organizations. Large organizations may have multiple petty cash funds in various departments. The amount of the fund may vary based on need.

As funds are disbursed from the petty cash fund, a slip is completed and placed in the petty cash box. If an invoice or receipt is available, it should be attached to the petty cash slip for filing. The petty cash slips are kept with the petty cash. At all times, the total of the unspent petty cash and the petty cash slips should equal the fixed amount of the petty cash fund.

When the cash in the fund is getting low, a check is written payable to "Petty Cash Fund" for an amount equal to the expense slips plus or minus any amounts the fund is out-of-balance. The reimbursement brings the fund up to the fixed balance. Expenses are allocated and recorded based on the purposes reflected on the slips.

PETTY CASH RECONCILIATION

DEPARTMENT __Youth__   DATE __June 30, 1996__

Payments from Petty Cash — Reconciliation Period From __6/1/96__ To __6/30/96__

Cash On Hand	Amount	Account	Date	Amount	Date	Amount	Date	Amount	Date	Amount	Total
$20.00 Bills	100 00	626-010	6/2	3 10	6/16	2 00					5 10
10.00 Bills	10 00	633-021	6/10	5 50							5 50
5.00 Bills	20 00	634-120	6/8	1 30	6/20	4 00	6/29	1 00			6 30
2.00 Bills		636-041	6/18	12 89							12 89
1.00 Bills	10 00	637-910	6/4	6 00							6 00
Checks		644-002	6/21	13 80							13 80
$1.00 Coins		645-001	6/10	2 50	6/12	2 00	6/18	1 50			6 00
.50 Coins		647-102	6/26	11 91							11 91
.25 Coins	3 75	649-023	6/19	5 50							5 50
.10 Coins	2 20	651-101	6/3	8 10							8 10
.05 Coins	80	653-001	6/12	12 40							12 40
.01 Coins	36	655-012	6/14	7 12							7 12
SUMMARY		660-001	6/2	1 02	6/8	2 04	6/12	3 11	6/20	4 00	10 17
		663-004	6/8	7 00	6/21	4 00					11 00
1. Total Cash	147 11	665-012	6/29	16 40							16 40
2. Total Petty Cash Slips	150 89	670-080	6/12	4 70	6/20	8 00					12 70
3. Subtotal (1+2)	298 00										
4. Petty Cash Fund	300 00										
5. Overage (3-4)											
6. Shortage (4-3)	2 00										
7. To be reimbursed (2+6 or 2-5)	152 89										
									TOTAL PETTY CASH SLIPS		150 89

__7/2/96__   _Dave Mason_
Date   Signature of Person Reconciling

When the cash in the petty cash fund is about used up, the custodian summarizes the petty cash receipts on a form like the one illustrated above. A check is then written to replenish the fund.

PETTY CASH RECEIPT

Date __June 7, 1996__

DESCRIPTION OF ITEM / SERVICE PURCHASED	AMOUNT
Office Supplies:	
Pens (1 doz.)	4 90
Envelopes 9x12 (2 doz.)	8 40
Receipt from Complete	
Office Supply is attached	
CHARGE TO ACCOUNT 652-001 **TOTAL**	13 30

Mary Moore   _Dave Mason_
Money Received By   Approved By

CASH EXPENSE REPORT

Name: Pastor Frank Morris

Address: 3801 North Florida Avenue

Miami, Florida 33168

Period Covered: From: 6/1/96 To: 6/15/96

DATE	City	Purpose of Travel	Brkfast	Lunch	Dinner	Snack	Lodging	Trans.	Description	Amount	ACCOUNT TO BE CHARGED
									OTHER *		
6/6/96	Atlanta, GA	Continuing Ed Seminar		10.80	13.40	2.10	90.50	281.00	Tips	8.00	641-002
6/7/96	✓	✓	6.40								641-002
									Entertainment expense from P. 2	42.11	644-010
TOTAL CASH EXPENSES			6.40	10.80	13.40	2.10	90.50	281.00		50.11	

*If this is entertainment, please use the entertainment worksheet on the back of this form.

Frank Morris 6/16/96
Signature (person requesting reimbursement)   Date

Jdf Davis 6/17/96
Approved by   Date

Total cash expenses 454.31

Personal auto business mileage
(Complete worksheet on the back of this form.)

221 miles X 30 per mile 66.30

Less travel advance ⟨300.00⟩

Balance due 220.61

Refund due organization

PERSONAL AUTO BUSINESS MILEAGE

Date	Purpose/Destination	Miles	Account to be charged
6/1/96	Calls/Valley View Rest Home	23	638-000
6/2/96	Funeral Home / Harold Boone Brown	18	✓
6/3/96	Calls / Various Homes	20	✓
6/4/96	Calls / Memorial Hospital	15	✓
6/5/96	Kiwanis Speaker/Pot's Cafeteria	25	✓
6/7/96	Calls /Various Homes	10	✓
6/8/96	Calls /St. Luke's Hospital	17	✓
6/9/96	Calls /Cannon Nursing Home	12	✓
6/10/96	Calls /Various Homes	8	✓
6/12/96	Calls / Memorial Hospital	15	✓
6/15/96	Ministerial Convention /Webb City	58	✓
TOTAL MILES TRAVELED		221	

To mileage summary on page one

ENTERTAINMENT WORKSHEET
(Expenses paid in behalf of individual(s) other than the person filing this expense report.)

Date	Persons Entertained	Purpose of Entertainment	Place	Amount
6/2/96	M/M Bob Cox	Prospective Members	Olive Garden	18.21
6/8/96	Frank Lane	Discuss church bldg. plans	Chi Chi's	12.80
6/14/96	Sam Lee	church goals w/board chair.	Damon's	11.10
TOTAL AMOUNT SPENT				42.11

To "other" expense column on page one

CASH DISBURSEMENTS JOURNAL

Date	Payee	Check No.	Check Amount	Pastor's Salary & Housing	Pastor's Fringe Benefits	Pastor's Expense Reimb.	Office Supplies	Repairs & Maint.	Utilities	Insurance	Other Description	Other Amount
6/1/96	Pastor Mike Cox	1203	1,200.00	1,200.00								
6/1/96	" "	1204	311.12			311.12						
6/3/96	Blue Cross	1205	380.00		380.00							
6/4/96	Jones Insur.	1206	541.00							541.00		
6/7/96	Gas Service	1207	41.50						41.50			
6/8/96	Power & Light	1208	212.00						212.00			
6/10/96	Bell Tele.	1209	181.50						181.50			
6/11/96	Church Supply	1210	248.00								Sunday School Lit.	248.00
6/13/96	Postmaster	1211	150.00				150.00					
6/15/96	Ames Office	1212	31.12				31.12					
6/16/96	Pastor Mike Cox	1213	1,200.00	1,200.00								
6/16/96	" "	1214	361.12			361.12						
6/18/96	Bob's Plumbing	1215	180.70					180.70				
6/20/96	Mary Mason	1216	100.00								Benevolence	100.00
6/22/96	Boone Flooring	1217	82.00					82.00				
6/26/96	Al's Lock Repair	1218	29.80					29.80				
6/30/96	NDA Bank	1219	1,412.00								Loan Prin.	312.00
											Loan Int.	1,100.00
				2,400.00	380.00	672.24	181.12	292.50	435.00	541.00		1,760.00

Example of Computer-Generated Cash Disbursement Journal

Date	Reference	Entry Description	Account No.	Account Name	Amount Debit	Credit
6/01/96	1025	Rev. Glenn Phillips	501-000	Pastor Salary	1,500.00	
			211-000	Income Tax W/H		200.00
6/01/96	1026	Mary Brown	505-000	Secretary Salary	750.00	
			211-000	Income Tax W/H		50.00
			212-000	FICA W/H		57.37
6/03/96	1027	Postmaster	649-000	Postage	29.00	
6/04/96	1028	Bell Telephone	663-000	Telephone	83.92	
6/04/96	1029	City Power & Light	664-000	Utilities	173.12	
6/06/96	1030	Gas Service Co.	664-000	Utilities	20.11	
6/09/96	1031	Harold Reynolds	810-000	Benevolence Expense	50.00	
6/11/96	1032	Blair Insurance	690-000	Insurance Expense	342.00	
6/13/96	1033	Franklin Printing	651-000	Literature & Prtg.	83.29	
6/14/96	1034	Postmaster	649-000	Postage	142.00	
6/15/96	1035	Rev. Glenn Phillips	501-000	Pastor Salary	1,500.00	
			211-000	Income Tax W/H		200.00
6/15/96	1036	Mary Brown	505-000	Secretary Salary	750.00	
			211-000	Income Tax W/H		50.00
			212-000	FICA W/H		57.37
6/20/96	1037	Valley View Bank	505-000	Income Tax W/H	500.00	
			211-000	FICA W/H	114.74	
			212-000	FICA Expense	114.74	
6/20/96	1038	ABC Church Supply	651-000	Literature & Prtg.	200.00	
6/30/96			101-000	Valley View Bank		5,738.18
					6,352.92	6,352.92

Example of Computer-Generated General Ledger
with Entries Posted From Cash Disbursements Journal

Source	Acct. No./ Date	Reference	Description	Beginning Balance	Current Entries	Ending Balance
	649-000		**Postage**	316.61		
CD	6/07/96	1027	Postmaster		29.00	
CD	6/14/96	1034	Postmaster		142.00	
					171.00	487.61
	651-000		**Literature & Printing**	702.58		
CD	6/13/96	1033	Franklin Printing		83.29	
CD	6/20/96	1038	ABC Church Supply		200.00	
					283.29	985.87
	653-000		**Kitchen Supplies**	53.72		53.72
	663-000		**Telephone**	648.12		
CD	6/14/96	1028	Bell Telephone		83.92	
					83.92	732.04
	664-000		**Utilities**	1,401.43		
CD	6/04/96	1029	City Power & Light		173.12	
CD	6/06/96	1030	Gas Service Co.		20.11	
					193.23	1,594.66
	810-000		**Benevolence Expense**	200.00		
CD	6/09/96	1031	Harold Reynolds		50.00	
					50.00	250.00
	850-000		**Missions Expense**	2,411.80		2,411.80
	865-000		**Camp Expense**	1,012.80		1,012.80

Bank reconciliation

A written bank reconciliation should be prepared monthly. A sample reconciliation form follows:

BANK STATEMENT RECONCILIATION
As of ___March 31___, 199_6_

Balance per bank statement		2,481.40
Add: Deposits recorded on books but not credited on bank statement		1,012.80

Subtract:
Outstanding checks

Check No.	Amount	
1312	50.00	
1314	17.80	
1318	411.72	
1321	108.14	
1324	791.12	1,378.78

Adjusted balance per bank statement		2,115.42
Balance per check book		2,365.74

Add:
Interest recorded on bank statement but not reflected in books — 10.42

Corrections of checks or deposits:
Check #1250 written for $80.00/ recorded in books as $90.00 — 10.00 — 10.00

Other:
6/18 deposit not recorded in books — 175.00 — 175.00

Subtract:

Bank service charges	29.80	
Automatic checks paid by bank	311.12	
Nonsufficient fund checks:		
Mike Brown	20.00	
Alex Smith	40.00	

Corrections of checks or deposits:
6/25 deposit recorded on books as $511.80/should be $501.98 — 9.82

Other:
Check printing — 35.00

		445.74
Adjusted balance per checkbook		2,115.42

These items should be recorded in the checkbook and the cash receipts or disbursements journals after the reconciliation is completed.

Accounting Records

Accounting systems differ in shape, size, complexity, and efficiency. The objectives of the system should be to measure and control financial activities and to provide financial information to the church governing body, the congregation, and donors.

In choosing the accounting records for your organization, the most important consideration is the ability of the individual(s) keeping the records. Many organizations do not have personnel with expertise to maintain an ideal accounting system.

Single entry vs. double entry

Double-entry bookkeeping is necessary for most organizations. It shows a twofold effect by recording every transaction twice—as a debit entry in one account and as a credit entry in another. Either or both of the entries may be broken down into several items, but the total of the amounts entered as debits must equal the total of the amounts entered as credits.

As the following table shows, when you pay an expense, the amount paid is entered as a debit to expense and as a credit to your cash account (an asset). When you receive a gift, an asset is debited (cash) and an income account is credited.

Type of account	If the transaction will decrease the account, enter it as a —	If the transaction will increase the account, enter it as a —	Typical balance
Asset	credit	debit	debit
Liability	debit	credit	credit
Capital	debit	credit	credit
Income	debit	credit	credit
Expense	credit	debit	debit

Record-keeping methods

A few organizations still maintain their accounting records on standard loose-leaf forms that can be purchased from an office-supply store. But the accounting records for most organizations are maintained on computers.

Even many small churches have a personal computer that is primarily used for word processing. This computer can be used to run software to process church financial data. Many accounting software packages designed for small businesses can be easily adapted for nonprofit use. Most of these packages include the double-entry process. There are a growing number of software packages designed specifically for churches. Two good resources for church software information are:

Christian Computing Magazine (P.O. Box 200544, Arlington, TX 76006)

Church Bytes (562 Brightleaf Square #9, 905 West Main St., Durham, NC 27701)

Cash and accrual methods

Most small churches and nonprofit organizations use the cash basis of accounting. Other organizations frequently use the accrual method. A common rule of thumb is that organizations with annual revenue of $250,000 and larger probably need to use the accrual method of accounting.

Advantages of cash method

Under this method, revenue is recorded only when cash is received, and expenses are recorded when they are paid. For example, office supplies expense is shown in the month when the bill is paid, even though the supplies were received and used in the previous month.

The primary advantage of the cash method is its simplicity. It is easier for nonaccountants to understand and keep records on this basis. When financial statements are required, the treasurer just summarizes the transactions from the checkbook stubs or runs the computer-prepared financial statements with fewer adjusting entries required. For smaller organizations, the difference between financial results on the cash and on the accrual basis are often not significantly different.

Advantages of accrual method

Many organizations use the accrual method of accounting when the cash basis does not accurately portray the financial picture. Under the accrual method, revenue is recorded when earned. For example, a church charges a fee for the use of the fellowship hall for a wedding.

Under accrual accounting, the revenue is recorded in the month earned even though the cash might not be received until a later month. Under accrual accounting, expenses are recorded when incurred. For example, telephone expense is recorded in the month when the service occurs although the bill may not be paid until the next month.

Generally accepted accounting principles for nonprofit organizations require the use of accrual basis accounting. Organizations that have their books audited by Certified Public Accountants, and want the CPAs to report that the financial statement appear according to "generally accepted accounting principles (GAAP)," must either keep their records on the accrual basis or make the appropriate adjustments at the end of the year to convert to this basis. Financial statements prepared on a cash or other comprehensive basis may qualify under GAAP if the financial statements are not materially different from those prepared on an accrual basis.

Modified cash method

The modified cash method of accounting is a combination of certain features of the cash and accrual methods. For example, accounts payable may be recorded when a bill is received although other payables or receivables are not recorded. The modified cash method portrays the financial picture more accurately than the cash method but not as well as the full accrual method.

Some organizations use the modified cash accounting method during the year and then make sufficient entries at year-end to convert the accounting data to a full accrual basis for audit purposes. This method simplifies the day-to-day bookkeeping process with interim reports focused on cash management.

Fund accounting

Fund accounting (or accounting by classes of net assets) provides an excellent basis for stewardship reporting. It is a system of accounting in which separate records are kept for resources donated to an organization which are restricted by donors or outside parties to certain specified purposes or use.

GAAP requires that net assets be broken down into the following three classes, based on the presence or absence of donor-imposed restrictions and their nature:

✔ **Permanently restricted.** These assets are not available for program expenses, payments to creditors, or other organizational needs. An example is an endowment gift with a stipulation that the principal is permanently not available for spending but the investment income from the principal may be used in current operations.

✔ **Temporarily restricted.** These assets may be restricted by purpose or time, but the restrictions are not permanent. An example of the purpose-restricted gift is a gift for a certain project or for the purchase of some equipment. An example of a time-restricted gift is a contribution in the form of a trust, annuity, or term endowment (principal of the gift is restricted for a certain term of time).

✔ **Unrestricted.** These net assets may be used for any of the organization's purposes. According to accounting standards, "the only limits on unrestricted net assets are broad limits resulting from the nature of the organization and the purposes specified in its articles of incorporation or bylaws."

Donor-imposed restrictions normally apply to the use of net assets and not to the use of specific assets. Only donors or outside parties may "restrict" funds given to a nonprofit organization. The organization's board may not "restrict" monies — they may only "designate" funds. For example, if a donor gives money for a new church organ, the funds should be placed in a restricted fund. If the church board sets funds aside in a debt retirement fund, this is a designated fund.

Fund accounting does not necessarily require multiple bank accounts. One bank account is all that is usually necessary. However, it may be appropriate to place restricted funds into a separate bank account to ensure that the funds are not inadvertently spent for other purposes.

Depreciation

Some organizations charge-off or record land, buildings, and equipment as expense at the time of purchase. Other organizations record land, buildings, and equipment at cost and depreciate them over their estimated useful life. Other organizations capitalize land, buildings, and equipment at cost and do not record depreciation.

For generally accepted accounting principles (GAAP), the Financial Accounting Standards Board requires the recognition of depreciation for nonprofits. The only exception is for certain art or historic treasures. Church and nonprofit property rarely qualifies for this exception. Depreciation is not required for financial statement presentation on any other basis of accounting.

Chart of accounts

The chart of accounts lists all ledger accounts and their account number to facilitate the bookkeeping process. Assets, liabilities, net assets, support and revenue, and expense accounts are listed. For a sample chart of accounts for a church, see page 119.

Account numbers are used to indicate the source of support and revenue or the object of expense. In computerized accounting systems, the account number is used to post an entry to the general ledger. The same concept can be used in a manually-prepared accounting system to avoid writing out the account name each time.

Financial Reports

In preparing financial reports, there is one basic rule: prepare different reports for different audiences. For example, a church board would normally receive a more detailed financial report than the church membership. Department heads in a nonprofit organization might receive reports that only relate to their department.

Financial statements should

✓ be easily comprehensible so that any person taking the time to study them will understand the financial picture;

✓ be concise so that the person studying them will not get lost in detail;

✓ be all-inclusive in scope and should embrace all activities of the organization;

✓ have a focal point for comparison so that the person reading them will have some basis for making a judgment (usually this will be a comparison with a budget or data from the corresponding period of the previous year); and

✓ be prepared on a timely basis (the longer the delay after the end of the period, the longer the time before corrective action can be taken).

SAMPLE CHART OF ACCOUNTS FOR A CHURCH

Assets
  Cash and cash equivalents
  Prepaid expenses
  Short-term investments
  Land, buildings, and equipment:
    Church buildings
    Parsonage
    Furnishings
  Long-term investments

Liabilities
  Accounts payable
  Notes payable
  Long-term debt

Revenues and Support
  Contributions
    Regular offerings
    Sunday school offerings
    Missions offerings
    Building fund offerings
    Other offerings
  Investment income
    Interest income
    Rental income
  Other income
    Tape sales
    Other sales
    Other income

Expenses
  Salaries and wages
    Salary including cash housing allowance
    Tax deferred payments (TSA/IRA)
  Benefits
    Pension
    Social security (SECA) reimbursement
    Social Security (FICA)
    Medical expense reimbursement
    Insurance premiums

Supplies
  Postage
  Literature and printing
  Office supplies
  Maintenance supplies
  Food
  Kitchen supplies
  Flowers
  Other supplies
Travel and entertainment
  Auto expense reimbursements
  Vehicle rental
  Other travel expense
Continuing education
Insurance
  Workers' Compensation
  Health insurance
  Property insurance
  Other insurance
Benevolences
  Denominational budgets
  Other benevolences
Services and professional fees
  Speaking honoraria
  Custodial services
  Legal and audit fees
  Other fees
Office and occupancy
  Rent
  Telephone
  Utilities
  Property taxes
  Other office and occupancy
Depreciation
Interest expense
Other
  Banquets
  Advertising

Suffix digits may be used to indicate the functional expense category such as

- 10	Program expenses		- 16		Youth
- 11	Pastoral		- 17		Singles
- 12	Education		- 18		Seniors
- 121	Sunday school		- 20		Management and general
- 122	Vacation Bible school		- 21		Church plant
- 123	Camps and retreats		- 22		Parsonages
- 13	Music and worship		- 23		Office
- 14	Missions		- 30		Fund raising
- 15	Membership and evangelism				

For additional reading on this topic, see the *Accounting and Financial Reporting Guide for Christian Ministries* (published by the Evangelical Joint Accounting Committee and available from the Christian Management Association 800-727-4CMA) and *Financial and Accounting Guide for Not-for-Profit Organizations* by Melvin J. Gross, Jr., and Richard F. Larkin (John Wiley & Sons).

Statement of activity

The statement of activity (also referred to as a statement of revenues and expenses) reflects an organization's support and revenue, expenses, and changes in net assets for a certain period of time. It shows the sources of an organization's income and how the resources were used. The form of the statement will depend on the type of organization and accounting method used. But the statement must present the change in unrestricted, temporarily restricted, permanently restricted, and total net assets.

Many smaller organizations will have several lines for support and revenue such as contributions, sales of products, investment income and so on. Expenses are often listed by natural classification such as salaries, fringe benefits, supplies, and so on.

Larger organizations and those desiring to meet GAAP accounting standards must reflect functional expenses (for example, by program, management and general, fund raising, and membership development) in the statement of activity or footnotes. Smaller organizations will tend to show expenses by natural classification in the statement of activity and functional expenses in the footnotes. The reverse approach will generally be true of larger organizations. While the reporting of expenses by natural classification is not generally required under GAAP, readers of the financial statements will often find the additional reporting very helpful.

Statement of financial position

A statement of financial position shows assets, liabilities, and net assets as of the end-of-period date. This statement is also called a balance sheet because it shows how the two sides of the accounting equation (assets minus liabilities equal net assets) "balance" in your organization.

Anything an organization owns that has a money value is an asset. Cash, land, buildings, furniture, and fixtures are examples of assets.

Anything the organization owes is a liability. Liabilities might include amounts owed to supplies (accounts payable) or to the bank (notes payable, and other amounts due).

Statement of cash flows

The statement of cash flows provides information about the cash receipts and disbursements of your organization and the extent to which resources were obtained from, or used in, operating, investing, or financing activities. The direct method of

Fall Creek Church
Statement of Activity
Year Ended June 30, 1996

	Unrestricted	Temporarily Restricted	Permanently Restricted	Total
Support and revenues				
Contributions				
Regular offerings	$260,000			$260,000
Sunday school offerings	45,000			45,000
Missions offerings	50,000			50,000
Other offerings	25,000	$10,000		35,000
Investment income				
Interest income	1,000		$2,000	3,000
Rental income	3,000			3,000
Total revenues	384,000	10,000	2,000	396,000
Expenses				
Program expenses				
Worship	25,000	9,000		34,000
Sunday school	35,000			35,000
Youth	30,000			30,000
Management and general	296,000			296,000
Fund raising	5,000			5,000
Total expenses	391,000	9,000		400,000
Change in net assets	(7,000)	1,000	2,000	(4,000)
Net assets at beginning of year	645,000	4,000	18,000	667,000
Net assets at end of year	$ 638,000	$ 5,000	$ 20,000	$ 663,000

Expenses incurred were for:

	Total	Worship	Sunday School	Youth	Mgt. & Gen.	Fund Raising
Salaries, wages, and benefits	$142,000	$5,000	$6,000		$131,000	
Supplies	73,000	25,000	24,000	$24,000		
Travel	16,000			1,000	10,000	$5,000
Insurance		20,000				20,000
Benevolences						
Denominational budgets	20,000				20,000	
Other benevolences	50,000				50,000	
Services and professional fees	14,000	4,000	5,000	5,000		
Office and occupancy	30,000				30,000	
Depreciation		10,000				10,000
Interest		25,000				25,000
	$400,000	$ 34,000	$ 35,000	$ 30,000	$296,000	$ 5,000

Note: This is a multi-column presentation of a statement of activity. Reporting of expenses by natural classification (at bottom of page), though often useful, is not required.

Castle Creek Church
Statement of Activity
Year Ended June 30, 1996

Changes in unrestricted net assets:
Revenues:

Contributions	$ 141,000
Fees	6,250
Income on long-term investments	5,400
Other	20,100
Total unrestricted revenues	172,500

Expenses (Note A)

Salaries, wages, and benefits	90,500
Supplies	3,000
Travel	5,000
Insurance	7,500
Benevolences	
Denominational budgets	10,000
Other benevolences	20,000
Services and professional fees	8,000
Office and occupancy	7,000
Depreciation	5,000
Interest	20,000
Total expenses	176,000

Net assets released from restrictions:	
Satisfaction of program restrictions	2,000
Expiration of time restrictions	3,000
Total net assets released from restrictions	5,000
Increase in unrestricted net assets	2,500
Changes in temporarily restricted net assets:	
Contributions	23,000
Net assets released from restrictions	(5,000)
Increase in temporarily restricted net assets	19,500
Changes in permanently restricted net assets:	
Contributions	5,000
Increase in permanently restricted net assets	7,000
Increase in net assets	29,000
Net assets at beginning of year	910,000
Net assets at end of year	$941,000

Note A:
Functional expense breakdown:

Program expenses:	
Worship	$16,000
Sunday school	7,000
Youth	5,000
Management and general	145,500
Fund raising	2,500
Total expenses	$176,000

Note: This is an alternate, single-column, presentation of a statement of activity. If the natural classification of expenses is shown in the body of the statement, the functional expenses must be reflected in a footnote to meet accounting standards.

Fall Creek Church
Statement of Financial Position
June 30, 1996 and 1995

	1995	1994
Assets:		
Cash and cash equivalents	$20,000	$15,000
Prepaid expenses	5,000	4,000
Short-term investments	10,000	8,000
Land, buildings, and equipment:		
Church buildings	525,000	525,000
Parsonage	110,000	110,000
Furnishings	175,000	160,000
Long-term investments	30,000	25,000
Total assets	875,000	847,000
Liabilities and net assets:		
Accounts payable	$8,000	$7,000
Notes payable	9,000	10,000
Long-term debt	195,000	205,000
Total liabilities	212,000	222,000
Net assets:		
Unrestricted	638,000	601,000
Temporarily restricted (Note 1)	5,000	4,000
Permanently restricted (Note 2)	20,000	20,000
Total net assets	663,000	625,000
Total liabilities and net assets	$875,000	$847,000

Note 1: Restricted net assets result when a donor has imposed a stipulation to use the funds or assets contributed in a manner which is more limited than the broad purpose for which tax-exempt status is granted for an organization. For example, a church may receive a contribution to establish a scholarship fund with the principal and earnings available for scholarship payments. This gift is a temporarily restricted contribution. If the scholarship funds were all expended in the church's fiscal year when the gift was received, the contribution would be unrestricted.

Note 2: Permanently restricted contributions are those which contain a stipulation which will always be present. For example, if a scholarship gift is made with the stipulation that only the earnings from the fund may be spent for scholarships, this is a permanently restricted net asset.

The financial statements illustrated on pages 121-123 are presented based on Statement No. 117 issued in 1994 by the Financial Accounting Standards Board of the American Institute of Certified Public Accountants.

presenting a cash flow statement starts by listing all sources of cash from operations during the period and deducts all operating outflows of cash to arrive at the net cash flow. The indirect method begins with the change in net assets and adjusts backwards to reconcile the change in net assets to net cash flows. The financial Accounting Standards Board encourages the use of the direct presentation method.

Audit Guidelines

An annual audit of the organization's records is a must. External audits are performed by an independent auditor that has no impairing relationship to the organization and can review the data procedures with maximum objectivity. Internal audits are generally performed by members or those closely associated with the organization.

External audits

The ideal is to have an annual audit performed by independent CPAs. However, only medium to large nonprofits generally can afford this extra expense. External audits of smaller organizations are often done on a non-GAAP basis—-the statements do not conform to the full accrual method with depreciation recognized. Non-GAAP audits of smaller organizations are often acceptable to banks and other agencies that require audited financial statements.

Internal audits

Members of the organization may form an audit committee to perform an internal audit to determine the validity of the financial statements. (Sample internal audit guidelines for churches are shown on pages 125-128.) If the committee takes its task seriously, the result may be significant improvements in internal control and accounting procedures. Too often, the internal audit committee only conducts a cursory review, commends the treasurer for a job well done, and provides the organization with a false sense of security.

Key Concepts

■ Good accounting records and good stewardship go hand in hand.

■ Your organization is the trustee of the money it receives—handle it carefully.

■ Tailor meaningful financial statements for your organization.

■ Prepare timely financial reports covering all of your funds—not just the operating fund.

■ An annual audit—either external or internal—is a must.

Church Internal Audit Guidelines

Financial statements

✓ Are monthly financial statements prepared on a timely basis and submitted to the organization's board?

✓ Do the financial statements include all funds (unrestricted, temporarily restricted and permanently restricted)?

✓ Do the financial statements include a statement of financial condition and statement of activity?

✓ Are account balances in the financial records reconciled with amounts presented in financial reports?

Cash receipts

✓ **General**

- Are cash handling procedures in writing?

- Has the bank been notified to never cash checks payable to the church?

- Are Sunday school offerings properly recorded and delivered to the money counters?

- Are procedures established to care for offerings and monies delivered or mailed to the church office between Sundays?

✓ **Offering counting**

- Are at least two members of the counting committee present when offerings were counted? (The persons counting the money should not include a pastor of a church or the church treasurer.)

- Do money counters verify that the contents of the offering envelopes are identical to the amounts written on the outside of the envelopes?

- Are all checks stamped with a restrictive endorsement stamp immediately after the offering envelope contents are verified?

- Are money counters rotated so the same people are not handling the funds each week?

- Are donor-restricted funds properly identified during the process of counting offerings?

✓ **Depositing of funds**

- Are two of the people who counted the money in custody of it until it is deposited in the bank, placed in a night depository or the church's safe?

- Are all funds promptly deposited? Compare offering and other receipt records with bank deposits.

- Are all receipts deposited intact? Receipts should not be used to pay cash expenses.

✓ **Restricted funds**

- Are donations for restricted purposes properly recorded in the accounting records?

- Are restricted funds held for the intended purpose(s) and not spent on operating needs?

Donation records/receipting

✓ Are individual donor records kept as a basis to provide donor acknowledgments for all single contributions of $250 or more?

✓ If no goods or services were provided (other than intangible religious benefits) in exchange for a gift, does the receipt include a statement to this effect?

✓ If goods or services (other than intangible religious benefits) were provided in exchange for a gift, does the receipt

- inform the donor that the amount of the contribution that is deductible for federal income tax purposes is limited to the excess of the amount of any money and the value of any property contributed by the donor over the value of the goods and services provided by the organization, and

- provide the donor with a good faith estimate of the value of such goods and services?

✓ Are the donations traced for a selected period of time from the weekly counting sheets to the donor records for audit purposes?

Cash disbursements

✔ Are all disbursements paid by check except for minor expenditures paid through the petty cash fund?

✔ Is written documentation available to support all disbursements?

✔ If a petty cash fund is used, are vouchers prepared for each disbursement from the fund?

✔ Are pre-numbered checks used? Account for all the check numbers including voided checks.

✔ Are blank checks ever signed in advance? This should never be done.

Petty cash funds

✔ Is a petty cash fund used for disbursements of a small amount? If so, is the fund periodically reconciled and replenished based on proper documentation of the cash expenditures?

Bank statement reconciliation

✔ Are written bank reconciliations prepared on a timely basis? Test the reconciliation for the last month in the fiscal year. Trace transactions between the bank and the books for completeness and timeliness.

✔ Are there any checks that have been outstanding over three months?

✔ Are there any unusual transactions in the bank statement immediately following year-end? Obtain the bank statement for the first month after year-end directly from the bank for review by the audit committee. Otherwise, obtain the last bank statement (unopened) from the church treasurer.

Savings and investment accounts

✔ Are all savings and investment accounts recorded in the financial records? Compare monthly statements to the books.

✔ Are earnings or losses from savings and investment accounts recorded in the books?

Land, buildings, and equipment records

✔ Are there detailed records of land, buildings, and equipment including date acquired, description and cost or fair market value at date of acquisition?

✔ Was an equipment physical inventory taken at year-end?

✔ Have the property records been reconciled to the insurance coverages?

Accounts payable

✔ Is there a schedule of unpaid invoices including vendor name, invoice date and due date?

✔ Are any of the accounts payable items significantly past-due?

✔ Are there any disputes with vendors over amounts owed?

Insurance policies

✔ Is there a schedule of insurance coverage in force? Reflect effective and expiration dates, kind and classification of coverages, maximum amounts of each coverage, premiums and terms of payment.

✔ Is Workers' Compensation insurance being carried as provided by law in most states? Are all employees (and perhaps some independent contractors) covered under the Workers' Compensation policy?

Amortization of debt

✔ Is there a schedule of debt such as mortgages and notes?

✔ Have the balances owed to all lenders been confirmed directly in writing?

✔ Have the balances owed to all lenders been compared to the obligations recorded on the balance sheet?

Securities and other negotiable documents

✔ Does the church own any marketable securities or bonds? If so, are they kept in a safety deposit box, and are two signatures (excluding a pastor) required for access?

✔ Have the contents of the safety deposit box been examined and recorded?

CHAPTER SEVEN

Charitable Gifts

In This Chapter

- Percentage limitations
- Gift options
- What gifts are not tax-deductible?
- When is a gift tax-deductible?
- Gift reporting requirements
- Receipting charitable contributions
- Special charitable contribution issues

There are right and wrong ways to give. While most donors care more about the reason for giving than they do about the tax implications, the spirit of giving should never be reduced by unexpected tax results.

A gift is the voluntary transfer of cash or property motivated by something other than "consideration." Consideration is something being received in return for a payment. The mere transfer of funds to a church or charitable nonprofit is not necessarily a gift. Thus, when a parent pays the college tuition for a child, there is no gift or charitable deduction.

If payments are made to a church or other nonprofit organization to receive something in exchange, the transaction is more in the nature of a purchase. The tax law states that a transfer to a nonprofit is not a contribution when made "with a reasonable expectation of financial return commensurate with the amount of the transfer." When one transfer comprises both a gift and a purchase, only the gift portion is deductible.

The two broad categories of charitable gifts are *outright* gifts and *deferred* gifts. Outright gifts require that the donor immediately transfer possession and use of the gift property to the donee. In deferred giving, the donor also makes a current gift, but the gift is of a future interest. Accordingly, actual possession and use of the gift property by the donee is deferred until the future.

According to U.S. tax laws, charitable contributions are deductible if given "to and for the use" of a "qualified" tax-exempt organization to be used under its control to accomplish its exempt purposes. ("Qualified" organizations are churches and other domestic 501(c)(3) organizations). To be deductible, contributions must be unconditional and without personal benefit to the donor.

Three types of gifts commonly given to a church or other nonprofit organization are

✓ **Gifts without donor stipulations.** Contributions received without donor restriction are generally tax-deductible.

✓ **Donor restricted gifts.** Contributions may be designated (*also referred to as restricted*) by the donor for a specific exempt purpose of the organization rather than being given without donor stipulation. If the gifts are in support of the organization's exempt program activities and not designated or restricted for an individual, they are generally tax deductible.

   If gifts are designated or earmarked for a specific individual, no tax deduction is generally allowed unless the church or nonprofit organization exercises full administrative control over the funds and they are spent for program activities of the organization.

✓ **Personal gifts.** Gifts made through an organization to an individual, where the donor has specified, by name, the identity of the person who is to receive the gift, are generally non-tax-deductible. Processing of personal gifts through a church or nonprofit organization should generally be discouraged by the organization unless it is done as a convenience to donors and the ultimate recipients where communication between the two parties might otherwise be difficult.

Tax-deduction receipts should not be issued to a donor for personal gifts and the organization should affirmatively advise donors that the gifts are not tax-deductible.

Percentage Limitations

Charitable deductions for a particular tax year are limited by certain percentages of an individual's adjusted gross income (AGI). These are the limitations:

✓ Gifts of cash and ordinary income property to public charities and private operating foundations are limited to 50% of AGI. Any excess may generally be carried forward up to five years.

✓ Gifts of long-term capital gain property to public charities and private operating foundations are limited to 30% of AGI. The same five-year carry-forward is possible.

✓ Donors of capital gain property to public charities and private operating foundations may use the 50% limitation, instead of the 30% limitation, where the amount of the contribution is reduced by all the unrealized appreciation (nontaxed gain) in the value of the property.

✓ Gifts of cash, short-term capital gain property, and ordinary income property to private foundations and certain other charitable donees (other than public charities and private operating foundations) are generally limited to the item's cost basis and 30% of AGI. The carry-forward rules apply to these gifts.

✓ Gifts of long-term capital gain property to private foundations and other charitable donees (other than public charities and private operating foundations) are generally limited to 20% of AGI.

There is no carry-forward for these gifts. Charitable contribution deductions by corporations in any tax year may not exceed 10% of pretax net income. Excess contributions may be carried forward up to five years.

Gift Options

Irrevocable nontrust gifts

✓ **Outright gifts.** Outright gifts generally involve an immediate transfer, without reservation, of cash or property to or for the use of a qualified charity. Outright gifts are the donees' top preference because the contributions may be used immediately and they are usually simple to administer. Donors may place restrictions on an outright gift.

The amount allowable as a charitable contribution deduction often depends upon the value of the gift property on the date of the gift. For gifts made in cash, the amount of the allowable deduction is readily known. This is not necessarily so for gifts of other property.

✓ **Cash.** A gift of cash is the simplest method of giving. The value of the gift is easily known. A cash gift is deductible within the 50% or 30% of adjusted gross income limitations, depending on the type of the recipient organization. Generally the 50% limit applies.

✓ **Securities.** The contribution deduction for stocks and bonds held long-term, is the mean between the highest and lowest selling prices on the date of the gift where there is a market for listed securities. The contribution deduction is limited to cost for securities held short-term.

Example: An individual taxpayer plans to make a gift of $50,000 to a college. The taxpayer initially intended to make an outright cash contribution. To provide the capital, the taxpayer planned to sell stock that had cost $20,000 some years earlier. Sale of the stock would have yielded long-term capital gain of $30,000. The taxpayer decides to donate the stock itself instead of the proceeds of its sale. The taxpayer receives a contribution deduction of $50,000 and the unrealized gain on the stock is not taxable. By contributing the stock, the taxpayer's taxable income is $30,000 less than if the stock were sold to fund the gift.

✓ **Real estate.** The contribution deduction for a gift of real estate is based on the fair market value on the date of the gift. If there is a mortgage on the property, the value must be reduced by the amount of the debt.

✓ **Life insurance.** The owner of a life insurance policy may choose to give it to a charitable organization. The gift will produce a tax deduction equal to one of several amounts. The deduction may equal the cash surrender value of the policy, its replacement value, its tax basis or its "interpolated terminal reserve" value (a value slightly more than cash surrender value). The deduction cannot exceed the donor's tax basis in the policy.

✓ **Bargain sale.** A bargain sale is part donation and part sale. It is a sale of property in which the amount of the sale proceeds is less than the property's fair market value. The excess of the fair market value of the property over the sale's price represents a charitable contribution to the organization. Generally each part of a bargain sale is a reportable event so the donor reports both a sale and a contribution.

✓ **Remainder interest in a personal residence or life estate.** A charitable contribution of the remainder interest in a personal residence (including a vacation home) or farm creates an income tax deduction equal to the present value of that future interest.

✓ **Charitable gift annuity.** With a charitable gift annuity, the donor purchases an annuity contract from a charitable organization for more than its fair value. This difference in values between what the donor could have obtained and what the donor actually obtained represents a charitable contribution. The contribution is tax-deductible in the year the donor purchases the annuity.

✓ **Deferred charitable gift annuity.** A deferred gift annuity is similar to an immediate payment annuity except that the annuity payments begin at a future date. This date is determined by the donor at the time of the gift.

Irrevocable gifts in trust

✓ **Charitable remainder annuity trust.** With an annuity trust, the donor retains the right to a specified annuity amount for a fixed period or the lifetime of the designated income beneficiary. The donor fixes the amount payable by an annuity trust at the inception of the trust.

✔ **Charitable remainder unitrust.** The unitrust and annuity trust are very similar with an important difference—the determination of the payment amount. The unitrust payout rate is applied to the fair market value of the net trust assets, determined annually, to establish the distributable amount each year.

✔ **Charitable lead trust.** The charitable lead trust is the reverse of the charitable remainder trust. The donor transfers property into a trust, creating an income interest in the property in favor of the charitable organization for a period of years or for the life or lives of an individual or individuals. The remainder interest is either returned to the donor or given to a noncharitable beneficiary (usually a family member).

✔ **Pooled income fund.** A pooled income fund consists of many separate contributions of property from numerous donors. A pooled income fund's payout to its income beneficiaries is not a fixed percentage. The rate of return that the fund earns each year determines the annual payout.

Revocable gifts

✔ **Trust savings accounts.** A trust savings account may be established at a bank, credit union or savings and loan. The account is placed in the name of the depositor "in trust for" a beneficiary, a person, or organization other than the depositor.

   The depositor retains full ownership and control of the account. The beneficiary receives the money in the account either when the depositor dies, or when the depositor turns over the passbook.

✔ **Insurance and retirement plan proceeds.** A nonprofit organization may be named the beneficiary of an insurance policy or retirement plan. The owner of the policy or retirement plan completes a form naming the nonprofit as the beneficiary, and the company accepts the form in writing. The gift may be for part or all the proceeds.

✔ **Bequests.** By a specific bequest, an individual may direct that, at death, a charity shall receive either a specified dollar amount or specific property. Through a residuary bequest, an individual may give to charity the estate portion remaining after the payment of other bequests, debts, taxes, and expenses.

What Gifts Are Not Tax-Deductible?

Some types of gifts do not result in a tax deduction. These gifts include

✓ **Strings Attached.** A gift must generally be complete and irrevocable to qualify for a charitable deduction. There is usually no gift if the donor leaves "strings attached" that can be pulled later to bring the gift back to the donor or remove it from the control of the donee.

Example: A donor makes a "gift" of $10,000 to a charity. The "gift" is followed or preceded by the sale from the charity to the donor of an asset valued at $25,000 for $15,000. In this instance, the $10,000 gift does not qualify as a charitable contribution.

✓ **Services.** No deduction is allowed for the contribution of services to a church or nonprofit.

Example: A carpenter donates two months of labor on the construction of a new facility built by your organization. The carpenter is not eligible for a charitable deduction for the donation of his time. He is entitled to a charitable deduction only for the out-of-pocket expenses for any supplies he donated to the project. His mileage driving to and from the project is deductible at the charitable mileage deduction rate (12 cents per mile for 1995).

✓ **Use of property.** The gift to a nonprofit of the right to use property does not yield a tax deduction to the donor.

Example: A donor provides a church with the rent-free use of an automobile for a year. There is no charitable deduction available to the donor for the value of that use. If the donor paid the taxes, insurance, repairs, gas or oil for the vehicle, these items would be deductible as a charitable contribution based on their cost.

✓ **Individuals.** Gifts made to poor or needy individuals ordinarily do not qualify as charitable contributions. Gifts made personally to ministers are not charitable contributions.

✓ **Foreign organizations.** Donations must be made to domestic organizations to qualify for a charitable deduction.

Example 1: A gift made directly to a missionary group organized and operating in Israel does not qualify for a charitable deduction.

Example 2: A gift to an U.S.-based missionary organization with a designation that the funds be used for mission work in China may qualify for a charitable deduction.

✓ **Contingencies.** If a contribution will not be effective until the occurrence of a certain event, an income tax charitable deduction generally is not allowable until the occurrence of the event.

Example: A donor makes a gift to a college to fund a new education program that the college does not presently offer and is not contemplating. The donation would not be deductible until the college agrees to the conditions of the gift.

When Is a Gift Tax-Deductible?

A charitable contribution can be deducted by an individual for income tax purposes only in the year in which it is paid. A pledge to make a contribution is deductible only upon payment or other satisfaction of the pledge.

Gifts by check

A gift by check is effective when the check is unconditionally delivered or mailed, if the check subsequently clears the donor's bank in due course.

Example 1: Donor mails a check with a postmark of December 31, 1995. The donee organization operates on a calendar year. It does not receive the check until January 7, 1996. The donee organization deposits the check in its bank on January 7 and it clears the donor's bank on January 10. The gift is deductible for the donor in 1995.

Example 2: Donor delivers a check to the donee organization on December 31, 1995. The donor asks that the check be held for three months. Heeding the donor's request, the donee organization deposits the check on March 31, 1996. This gift is deductible for the donor in 1996.

Gifts by credit card

A contribution charged to a bank credit card is deductible by the donor in the year the charge is made, though the donor does not pay the credit card charge until the next year.

Gifts of securities

A gift of stock is effective upon the unconditional delivery of a properly endorsed stock certificate to the donee or the donee's agent. If the certificate is mailed and is received by the charitable organization or its agent in the ordinary course of the mail, the gift is effective on the date of mailing.

Gifts of property

A gift of real estate is generally completed for tax purposes at the time possession of the property and the benefits and burdens of ownership are transferred. A properly executed deed to the property must be delivered by the donor to the donee to effect the charitable deduction.

Gifts of church bonds

Many churches and some nonprofit organizations receive capital or operational financing by issuing bonds. Individuals who purchase bonds often keep the bonds for several years and then donate them back to the church or nonprofit organization.

The charitable tax deduction for a gift of bonds is based on the face of the bond plus any accumulated interest on the date of donation. If the value of the gift is over $500, the donor must file Form 8283 with Form 1040. The donee must file Form 8282 within 125 days of the bonds' being converted to cash.

Gifts of inventory

Assets held by a taxpayer for sale to customers are known as inventory. Ordinary income results from the sale of inventory. Under the basic reduction rule, the value of inventory items contributed to a charitable organization must be reduced by the amount of ordinary income that would have been realized had the items been sold.

If an inventory item is deducted as a charitable contribution, it cannot be deducted again as part of the donor's cost of goods sold. Regulations distinguish between inventory items included in a taxpayer's beginning inventory and those items acquired in the year of contribution. When items are in the beginning inventory, there is a contribution deduction (after applying the basic reduction rule), and the item is excluded from cost of goods sold. For items acquired in the year of contribution, there is no contribution deduction and the cost of the item is deducted as part of cost of goods sold.

Special rules apply when the value of inventory is less than its cost. Other rules apply to inventory gifts of scientific equipment to certain organizations or gifts of inventory for the care of the ill, the needy, and infants.

Gifts of a partial interest

A contribution of less than the donor's entire interest in property is a gift of a partial interest. Generally, there is no charitable deduction for gifts of partial interest in property, including the right to use the property. Gifts of a partial interest which qualify for charitable deductions are

✓ gifts made in qualified trust form (using a so-called "split-interest trust," i.e., pooled income funds, charitable remainder trusts, charitable lead trusts, etc.),

✓ outright gifts of a future remainder interest (also called a life estate) in a personal residence or farm,

✓ gifts of an undivided portion of one's entire interest in property,

✓ gifts of a lease on, option to purchase, or easement with respect to real property granted in perpetuity to a public charity exclusively for conservation purposes, or

✓ a remainder interest in real property granted to a public charity exclusively for conservation purposes.

Gift Reporting Requirements

Gifts of property in excess of $5,000

Most charitable deductions for contributions of property claimed by an individual, a closely held corporation, a personal service corporation, a partnership, or an S (Chapter S of the Internal Revenue Code) corporation must meet certain substantiation requirements.

The requirements apply to contributions of property (other than money and publicly traded securities), if the aggregate claimed or reported value of the property is more than $5,000. For these gifts, the donor must obtain a qualified appraisal and attach an appraisal summary to the return on which the deduction is claimed. There is an exception for nonpublicly traded stock. If the claimed value of the stock does not exceed $10,000 but is greater than $5,000, the donor does not have to obtain an appraisal by a qualified appraiser. A qualified appraisal is performed by one who holds himself or herself out to the public as an appraiser and who is qualified to determine the value of the property.

The appraisal summary must be on Form 8283, signed and dated by the donee and appraiser, and attached to the donor's return on which a deduction is claimed. The signature by the donee does not represent concurrence in the appraised value of the contributed property.

Gifts of property in excess of $500

Gifts of property valued at $500 or more require the completion of certain infor-

Sample Letter to Noncash Donors

Charitable Gift Receipt
RETAIN FOR INCOME TAX PURPOSES

Donor's Name
Address
City

Thank you for your noncash gift as follows:
   Date Received:
   Description of Property:

You may deduct your gift on your income tax return if you itemize. However, you must follow the IRS's reporting rules to assure your charitable deduction. We have enclosed a copy of IRS Form 8283 (Noncash Charitable Contributions) and its instructions.

If your noncash gifts for the year total more than $500, you will have to include Form 8283 with your income tax return. Section A is used to report gifts valued at $5,000 or under. You can complete Section A on your own. When the value is more than $5,000, you will need to have the property appraised. The appraiser's findings are reported in Section B of Form 8283. Those rules also apply if you give "similar items of property" with a total value above $5,000—even if you gave the items to different charities.

You never need an appraisal or an appraisal summary for gifts of publicly traded securities, even if their total value exceeds $5,000. But you must report those gifts (when the value is more than $500) by completing Section A of Form 8283 and attaching it to your return.

For gifts of closely held stock, an appraisal is not required as long as the value is under $10,000, but part of the appraisal summary form must be completed if the value is over $5,000. And if the gift is valued over $10,000, then both an appraisal and an appraisal summary form are required.

The appraisal summary goes on Section B of Form 8283. (We have included a copy of the latest form with this letter). It must be signed by the appraiser. As the donee, we have already signed the form. It is essential to attach the form to your tax return.

You might want an appraisal (even if your gift does not require one) in case you have to convince the IRS of the property's worth. Form 8283 asks how you valued your gifts.

If we receive a gift of property subject to the appraisal summary rules, we must report to both the IRS and you if we dispose of the gift within two years. We do not have to notify the IRS or you if we dispose of a gift that did not require an appraisal summary (e.g., marketable securities). Nor must we report when we use the gift to further our charitable purposes.

Finally, we need not report our disposal of an item that you certify is worth $500 or less. Form 8283 has a section for that purpose (Section B, Part III).

Again, we are grateful for your generous contribution. Please let us know if we can give you and your advisors more information about the IRS's reporting requirements.

Your Nonprofit Organization

Form **8283**
(Rev. November 1992)

Department of the Treasury
Internal Revenue Service

Noncash Charitable Contributions

▶ Attach to your tax return if the total deduction claimed
for all property contributed exceeds $500.

▶ See separate instructions.

OMB No. 1545-0908
Expires 11-30-95

Attachment
Sequence No. **55**

Name(s) shown on your income tax return

Mark A. and Joan E. Murphy

Identifying number

392-83-1982

Note: *Figure the amount of your contribution deduction before completing this form. See your tax return instructions.*

Section A—Include in this section **only** items (or groups of similar items) for which you claimed a deduction of $5,000 or less per item or group, and certain publicly traded securities (see instructions).

| Part I | Information on Donated Property—If you need more space, attach a statement. |

1	(a) Name and address of the donee organization	(b) Description of donated property
A	Endless Mountain Church 561 Maple, Rochester, NY 14623	Used bedroom furniture
B		
C		
D		
E		

Note: *If the amount you claimed as a deduction for an item is $500 or less, you do not have to complete columns (d), (e), and (f).*

	(c) Date of the contribution	(d) Date acquired by donor (mo., yr.)	(e) How acquired by donor	(f) Donor's cost or adjusted basis	(g) Fair market value	(h) Method used to determine the fair market value
A	10/1/96	6/87	Purchased	3,400	750	Sale of comparable
B						used furniture
C						
D						
E						

| Part II | Other Information—If you gave less than an entire interest in property listed in Part I, complete lines 2a–2e. If restrictions were attached to a contribution listed in Part I, complete lines 3a–3c. |

2 If less than the entire interest in the property is contributed during the year, complete the following:

a Enter letter from Part I that identifies the property _____ If Part II applies to more than one property, attach a separate statement.

b Total amount claimed as a deduction for the property listed in Part I: **(1)** For this tax year _____
(2) For any prior tax years _____

c Name and address of each organization to which any such contribution was made in a prior year (complete only if different than the donee organization above).

Name of charitable organization (donee)

Address (number, street, and room or suite no.)

City or town, state, and ZIP code

d For tangible property, enter the place where the property is located or kept _____

e Name of any person, other than the donee organization, having actual possession of the property _____

3 If conditions were attached to any contribution listed in Part I, answer the following questions and attach the required statement (see instructions):

		Yes	No

a Is there a restriction, either temporary or permanent, on the donee's right to use or dispose of the donated property? . . . .

b Did you give to anyone (other than the donee organization or another organization participating with the donee organization in cooperative fundraising) the right to the income from the donated property or to the possession of the property, including the right to vote donated securities, to acquire the property by purchase or otherwise, or to designate the person having such income, possession, or right to acquire? . . . .

c Is there a restriction limiting the donated property for a particular use? . . . .

For Paperwork Reduction Act Notice, see separate instructions.   Cat. No. 62299J   Form **8283** (Rev. 11-92)

Note: This form must be completed and filed with the donee's income tax return for gifts of property valued at $500 or more.

There is no requirement of an appraisal of signature of the donee organization for gifts valued between $500 and $5,000.

Form 8283 (Rev. 11-92)   Page **2**

Name(s) shown on your income tax return	Identifying number
Mark A. and Joan E. Murphy	392-83-1982

Section B—Appraisal Summary—Include in this section only items (or groups of similar items) for which you claimed a deduction of more than $5,000 per item or group. Report contributions of certain publicly traded securities only in Section A.

If you donated art, you may have to attach the complete appraisal. See the **Note** in Part I below.

Part I Information on Donated Property—To be completed by the taxpayer and/or appraiser.

4 Check type of property:

- ☐ Art* (contribution of $20,000 or more)   ☒ Real Estate   ☐ Gems/Jewelry   ☐ Stamp Collections
- ☐ Art* (contribution of less than $20,000)   ☐ Coin Collections   ☐ Books   ☐ Other

*Art includes paintings, sculptures, watercolors, prints, drawings, ceramics, antique furniture, decorative arts, textiles, carpets, silver, rare manuscripts, historical memorabilia, and other similar objects.

Note: If your total art contribution deduction was $20,000 or more, you must attach a complete copy of the signed appraisal. See instructions.

5	(a) Description of donated property (if you need more space, attach a separate statement)	(b) If tangible property was donated, give a brief summary of the overall physical condition at the time of the gift	(c) Appraised fair market value
A	Residence & two lots:	Good repair	42,500
B	2080 Long Pond Road		
C	Syracuse, New York		
D			

	(d) Date acquired by donor (mo., yr.)	(e) How acquired by donor	(f) Donor's cost or adjusted basis	(g) For bargain sales, enter amount received	(h) Amount claimed as a deduction	(i) Average trading price of securities
A	7/20/87	Purchased	36,900		42,500	
B						
C						
D						

Part II Taxpayer (Donor) Statement—List each item included in Part I above that is separately identified in the appraisal as having a value of $500 or less. See instructions.

I declare that the following item(s) included in Part I above has to the best of my knowledge and belief an appraised value of not more than $500 (per item). Enter identifying letter from Part I and describe the specific item: _____

Signature of taxpayer (donor) ▶   Date ▶

Part III Certification of Appraiser

I declare that I am not the donor, the donee, a party to the transaction in which the donor acquired the property, employed by, married to, or related to any of the foregoing persons, or an appraiser regularly used by any of the foregoing persons and who does not perform a majority of appraisals during the taxable year for other persons.

Also, I declare that I hold myself out to the public as an appraiser or perform appraisals on a regular basis; and that because of my qualifications as described in the appraisal, I am qualified to make appraisals of the type of property being valued. I certify that the appraisal fees were not based upon a percentage of the appraised property value. Furthermore, I understand that a false or fraudulent overstatement of the property value as described in the qualified appraisal or this appraisal summary may subject me to the civil penalty under section 6701(a) (aiding and abetting the understatement of tax liability). I affirm that I have not been barred from presenting evidence or testimony by the Director of Practice.

Sign Here Signature ▶ Andrew J. Noble   Title ▶ President   Date of appraisal ▶ 9/15/96

Business address (including room or suite no.) | Identifying number
1100 North Adams Street

City or town, state, and ZIP code
Elmira, NY 14904

Part IV Donee Acknowledgment—To be completed by the charitable organization.

This charitable organization acknowledges that it is a qualified organization under section 170(c) and that it received the donated property as described in Section B, Part I, above on _____9/25/96_____ (Date)

Furthermore, this organization affirms that in the event it sells, exchanges, or otherwise disposes of the property (or any portion thereof) within 2 years after the date of receipt, it will file an information return (**Form 8282**, Donee Information Return) with the IRS and furnish the donor a copy of that return. This acknowledgment does not represent concurrence in the claimed fair market value.

Name of charitable organization (donee)	Employer identification number
Fairlawn Heights Church	35-4029876

Address (number, street, and room or suite no.)	City or town, state, and ZIP code
P. O. Box 829	Oswego, NY 13126

Authorized signature	Title	Date
James A. Black	Executive Pastor	10/31/96

140

Form **8282**	**Donee Information Return**	OMB No. 1545-0908
(Rev. Nov. 1992)	**(Sale, Exchange, or Other Disposition of Donated Property)**	Expires 11-30-95
Department of the Treasury Internal Revenue Service	▶ See instructions on back.	**Give Copy to Donor**

	Name of charitable organization (donee)	Employer identification number
Please Print or Type	Oneonta First Church	35 : 4829942
	Address (number, street, and room or suite no.)	
	292 River Street	
	City or town, state, and ZIP code	
	Oneonta, NY 13820	

Note: *If you are the original donee, **DO NOT** complete Part II or column (c) of Part III.*

Part I Information on ORIGINAL DONOR and DONEE You Gave the Property to

1a Name(s) of the original donor of the property
Keith E. Chapman

1b Identifying number
512-40-8076

Note: *Complete lines 2a–2d only if you gave this property to another charitable organization (successor donee).*

2a Name of charitable organization   **2b** Employer identification number

2c Address (number, street, and room or suite no.)

2d City or town, state, and ZIP code

Part II Information on PREVIOUS DONEES—Complete this part only if you were not the first donee to receive the property. If you were the second donee, leave lines 4a–4d blank. If you were a third or later donee, complete lines 3a–4d. On lines 4a–4d, give information on the preceding donee (the one who gave you the property).

3a Name of original donee   **3b** Employer identification number

3c Address (number, street, and room or suite no.)

3d City or town, state, and ZIP code

4a Name of preceding donee   **4b** Employer identification number

4c Address (number, street, and room or suite no.)

4d City or town, state, and ZIP code

Part III Information on DONATED PROPERTY

(a) Description of donated property sold, exchanged, or otherwise disposed of (if you need more space, attach a separate statement)	(b) Date you received the item(s)	(c) Date the first donee received the item(s) (if you weren't the first)	(d) Date item(s) sold, exchanged, or otherwise disposed of	(e) Amount received upon disposition
Real estate/vacant lot, 82 White Street, Oneonta, New York	9/4/95		11/10/96	3,780

For Paperwork Reduction Act Notice, see instructions on back.   Cat. No. 62307Y   Form **8282** (Rev. 11-92)

Note: The donee must file this form with the IRS if property received as a charitable contribution is sold, exchanged, or otherwise disposed of within two years after the date of its contribution.

mation on page one of Form 8283. For gifts between $500 and $5,000 in value, there is not a requirement of an appraisal or signature of the donee organization.

Donee reporting for contributed property

If property received as a charitable contribution requiring an appraisal summary on Form 8283 is sold, exchanged, or otherwise disposed of by the donee within two years after the date of its contribution, the donee must file Form 8282 with the IRS within 125 days of the disposition.

This form provides detailed information on the gift and the disposal of the property. A copy of this information return must be provided to the donor and retained by the donee.

A donee organization that receives a charitable contribution valued at more than $5,000 from a corporation generally does not have to file a donee information return.

A letter or other written communication from a donee charitable organization acknowledging receipt of the property and showing the name of the donor, the date and location of the contribution, and a detailed description of the property is an acceptable contribution receipt for a gift of property.

There is no requirement to include the value of contributed property on the receipt. Most organizations cannot properly value gifts of property. A tension often surrounds a significant gift of property because the donor may request the organization to include an excessively "high" value on the charitable receipt. It is wise for the nonprofit organization to remain impartial in the matter and simply receipt the property by description without the inclusion of a dollar amount.

Example 1: A nonprofit organization receives the gift of an automobile. The charitable contribution receipt should reflect the make, model, vehicle number, options, mileage and condition with no indication of dollar value.

Example 2: A nonprofit organization receives a gift of real estate. The receipt should include the legal description of the real property and a description of the improvements with no indication of dollar value.

Receipting Charitable Contributions

Dramatic changes in the tax rules for acknowledging and substantiating the giving and receiving of charitable contributions took effect in 1994. These changes are a result of provisions included in the Omnibus Budget Reconciliation Act of 1993.

Gifts of $250 or more

Effective January 1, 1994, contributors seeking a federal income tax charitable contribution deduction must produce, if asked, a written receipt from the charity if a single contribution's value is $250 or more.

Strictly speaking, the burden of compliance with the $250 or more rule falls on the donor. In reality, the burden and administrative costs fall on nonprofit organizations, not on the donor.

A donor will no longer be allowed a charitable deduction for donations unless he or she has a receipt from your church or other charity. This law applies to any type of donation. For a donation that is made by check, the cancelled check is not adequate substantiation.

Information to be included in the receipt

The following information must be included in the gift receipt:

✓ if cash, the amount of cash contributed,

✓ if property, a description, but not the value, of the property,

✓ whether the organization provided any goods or services to the donor in exchange for the contribution,

✓ if goods or services were provided, a description and good faith estimate of their value and a statement that the donor's charitable deduction is limited to the amount of the payment in excess of the value of the goods and services provided,

✓ if services were provided consisting solely of intangible religious benefits, a statement to that effect, and

✓ the date the receipt was issued.

When receipts should be issued

Donors must obtain their receipts no later than the earlier of the due date (plus any extensions) of their income tax returns or the date the return is filed. If a donor gets the receipt too late to include with his or her return, it appears that the donor will be unable to claim the contribution on an amended return.

Frequency of issuing receipts

The receipts or acknowledgements can be issued gift-by-gift, monthly, quarterly, annually, or at any other frequency. For ease of administration, many churches and other nonprofit organizations are providing a receipt for all gifts, whether over or under $250.

If your organization is issuing receipts annually, they should be provided to

Sample Charitable Gift Receipt

Received from: Jackie J. Burns

Cash received as an absolute gift:
Received on March 6, 1995 $300.00

Property received described as follows:
(*Note:* If property was given instead of cash or check, the property would have been described here. No value would have been shown for the property.)

Any goods or services you may have received in connection with this gift were solely intangible religious benefits. (*Note:* It is very important for a religious organization to use wording of this nature when no goods or services were given in exchange for the gift.)

This document is necessary for any available federal income tax deduction for your contribution. Please retain it for your records.

Receipt issued on: January 31, 1996
Receipt issued by: Harold Morrison, Treasurer
                        Castleview Church
                        1008 High Drive
                        Dover, DE 19901

Note: This sample receipt is based on the following assumptions:
1. No goods or services were provided in exchange for the gift(s).
2. The receipt is issued for a single gift (versus one receipt for multiple gifts).

Sample Charitable Gift Receipt

Received from: Howard K. Auburn

Cash received as an absolute gift:

Date Cash Received	Amount Received
1/2/95	$250.00
1/16/95	50.00
3/13/95	300.00
3/27/95	100.00
6/12/95	500.00
7/10/95	150.00
8/21/95	200.00
10/16/95	400.00
11/20/95	350.00
	$2,300.00

Property received described as follows:
Received on May 1, 1995, one 1992 Honda Civic, 4-door sedan LX, automatic transmission, 64,231 miles, vehicle ID# IBfHP53L2NH440968.

Any goods or services you may have received in connection with this gift were solely intangible religious benefits. (*Note:* It is very important for a religious organization to use wording of this nature when no goods or services were given in exchange for the gift.)

This document is necessary for any available federal income tax deduction for your contribution. Please retain it for your records.

Receipt issued on: January 10, 1996
Receipt issued by: Harold Morrison, Treasurer
Castleview Church
1008 High Drive
Dover, DE 19901

Note: This sample receipt is based on the following assumptions:
1. No goods or services were provided in exchange for the gifts.
2. The receipt is issued on a periodic or annual basis for all gifts whether over or under $250.

your donors by at least January 31 each year and earlier in January if possible. This will assist your donors in gathering the necessary data for tax return preparation.

Form of receipts

No specific form design is required. The government has not issued any sample receipts and it probably will not.

The receipt can be a letter, a postcard or a computer-generated form. It does not have to include the donor's social security number (or other taxpayer identification number).

Separate gifts of less than $250

If a donor makes separate gifts during a calendar year of less than $250, there is no receipting requirement since each gift is a separate contribution. The donor's cancelled check will provide sufficient substantiation.

> **Example 1:** A donor makes two separate gifts of $200 on different dates in a calendar year. Since neither gift was $250 or more, you do not have to provide the donor a receipt.

> **Example 2:** A donor gives $350 every two weeks. She will need a receipt for all gifts. One receipt, acknowledging each gift by date and amount, will be sufficient.

> **Example 3:** A donor writes multiple checks on the same day, each less than $250, but which total over $250. The IRS regulations will likely require gifts made on the same day to be combined for purposes of the $250 or more test.

Donations payable to another charity

A church member may place a check in the offering plate of $250 or more payable to a mission organization designated for the support of a particular missionary serving with the mission. In this instance, no reporting is required by your church. Since the check was payable to the mission agency, that entity will need to issue the acknowledgment to entitle the donor to claim the gift as a charitable contribution.

Additional guidance from the IRS

Many of these questions and answers were prepared by the IRS for use in training its agents. They cannot be cited as official legal authority. However, they do provide an indication of how the IRS will enforce the new requirements.

✓ **Responsibility for acknowledgments for gifts of $250 or more**

Question: Does a church or nonprofit organization have to provide receipts for single gifts of $250 or more?

Answer: No. It is up to donors to make sure they have the receipts before they file their tax returns. But the law's practical effect is that many nonprofits will routinely provide the receipts to keep their donors happy.

✓ **Penalties for receipting in general**

Question: Can the government punish an organization for failing to provide receipts to donors?

Answer: No. But the IRS can fine a charity that deliberately issues a false acknowledgment to a contributor. The fine is up to $1,000 if the donor is an individual and $10,000 if the donor is a corporation.

✓ **Gift under $250 but no receipt**

Question: A donor makes a $249.99 gift to a charity and does not get a receipt. Is the gift deductible?

Answer: Yes. The donor must be prepared to prove the contribution was made but a receipt is not necessary to claim the deduction.

✓ **Gift over $250 but no receipt**

Question: A donor makes a $500 gift to a charity and does not get a receipt. Can the donor still deduct $249.99?

Answer: No. A receipt is necessary to deduct a gift of $250 or more.

✓ **Charity provides a delayed receipt**

Question: In 1995, a taxpayer presents a charity with a contribution in the form of a check of $1,000 for which the taxpayer neglected to claim a charitable deduction on his Form 1040 for 1995, which he filed on April 15, 1996, because he did not get a receipt from the charity until July 15, 1996. In 1997, the taxpayer filed an amended return for 1995. Will the 1996 receipt obtained by the taxpayer satisfy the substantiation requirement since it was obtained prior to the date of filing the amended return?

Answer: The acknowledgment must be obtained by the due date (including extensions) of a return. Unlike the IRS's granting of an extension of time to file, the IRS's acceptance of amended returns for a tax year after the due date does not require the IRS to recognize the gift acknowledgment obtained after the due date as being timely.

✓ Notation of donation on check

Question: A taxpayer wrote a check to a charity of $500 and notes "donation" on the check. The taxpayer does not receive a receipt from the charity. The taxpayer takes a charitable deduction for the gift on Form 1040. Is this proper?

Answer: No, the deduction is not allowed. The check alone is not sufficient substantiation of the contribution.

Quid pro quo disclosure requirements

Another section of the new charitable substantiation rules applies to "quid pro quo contributions." This term is defined as a payment made partly as a contribution and partly in consideration for goods or services provided to the payor by the donee organization.

The charity is required to provide a receipt for all transactions where the donor makes a payment of more than $75 to the charity and receives goods or services (other than intangible religious benefits or items of token value).

Form of the receipt

The receipt must

✓ inform the donor that the amount of the contribution that is deductible for federal income tax purposes is limited to the excess of the amount of any money and the value of any property other than money contributed by the donor over the value of the goods or services provided by the organization, and

✓ provide the donor with a good faith estimate of the value of such goods or services.

Only single payments of more than $75 are subject to the rules. Payments are not cumulative.

Note that it is not a difference of $75 between the amount given by the donor and the value of the object received by the donor that counts, but the amount actually paid by the donor.

Charitable Contribution Substantiation Requirements

	Not more than $75	Over $75 and under $250	At least $250 and under $500	At least $500 and under $5,000	$5,000 and over
Canceled check acceptable for donor's deduction?	Yes	Yes	No	No	No
Contribution receipt required for deduction?	No	No	Yes	Yes	Yes
Charity's statement on donor's receipt of goods or services required?	No	Yes*	Yes*	Yes*	Yes*

*May be avoided if the charity meets the low-cost items or de minimis benefits exceptions described below.

Calculating the gift portion

It is not a requirement for the donee organization to actually complete the subtraction of the benefit from the payment, showing the net charitable deduction. However, providing the net amount available for a charitable deduction is a good approach for clear communication with your donors.

Where to make the required disclosures

The disclosure of the value of goods or services provided to a donor may be made in the donor solicitation as well as in the subsequent receipt. However, sufficient information will generally not be available to make proper disclosure upon solicitation. For example, the value of a dinner may not be known at the time the solicitation is made.

Low-cost items or de minimis benefits provided to donors

A charitable contribution must be reduced by the fair market value of any premium, incentive, or other benefit received by the donor in exchange for the contribution. Common examples of premiums are books, tapes, and Bibles. Organizations must advise the donor of the fair market value of the premium or incentive and that the value is not deductible for tax purposes.

Sample Charitable Gift Receipt

Received from: Nancy L. Wilson

Cash received:
Received on April 1, 1995 $100.00

Property received described as follows:
(*Note:* If property was given instead of cash or check, the property would have been described here. No value would have been shown for the property.)

In return for your gift described above, we provided you with a study Bible *(Note: Insert the description of goods and/or services provided in exchange for the gift)* which we estimate has a value of $30.00. You may have also received goods or services consisting solely of intangible benefits, but these benefits do not need to be valued for tax purposes.

The deductible portion of your contribution for Federal income tax purposes is limited to the excess of your contribution over the value of goods and services we provided to you. Your cash payment of $100.00 less the $30.00 value of benefits received makes a net charitable contribution of $70.00. *(Note: For receipting purposes, do not calculate the net contribution for gifts of property to the church because the church does not place a value on the property received.)*

This document is necessary for any available federal income tax deduction for your contribution. Please retain it for your records.

Receipt issued on: January 10, 1996
Receipt issued by: Harold Morrison, Treasurer
                                 Castleview Church
                                 1008 High Drive
                                 Dover, DE 19901

Note: This sample receipt is based on the following assumptions:
1. Goods or services were provided in exchange for the gift(s).
2. The receipt is issued for a single gift (versus one receipt for multiple gifts).

Sample Charitable Gift Receipt

Received from: Charles K. Vandell

Cash received as an absolute gift:

Date Cash Received	Gross Amount Received	Value of Goods or Services	Net Charitable Contribution
1/23/95	$80.00	$25.00 [1]	$ 55.00
3/20/95	300.00		300.00
4/24/95	60.00		60.00
6/19/95	500.00	100.00 [2]	400.00
9/04/95	275.00		275.00
10/30/95	200.00		200.00
12/18/95	1,000.00		1,000.00
			$2,900.00

Property received described as follows:
Received on October 22, 1995, 12 brown Samsonite folding chairs.

In return for certain gifts listed above, we provided you with the following goods or services:

(1) Christian music tapes $25.00
(2) Limited edition art print $100.00

You may have also received goods or services consisting solely of intangible religious benefits, but these benefits do not need to be valued for tax purposes.

The deductible portion of your contribution for Federal income tax purposes is limited to the excess of your contribution over the value of goods and services we provided to you.

This document is necessary for any available federal income tax deduction for your contribution. Please retain it for your records.

Receipt issued on: January 15, 1996
Receipt issued by: Harold Morrison, Treasurer
                      Castleview Church
                      1008 High Drive
                      Dover, DE 19901

Note: This sample receipt is based on the following assumptions:
  1. Goods or services were provided in exchange for the gifts.
  2. The receipt is issued on a periodic or annual basis for all gifts whether over or under $250.

If donors receive low-cost items, or the value of benefits they receive is small, they are allowed a full tax deduction for the donation:

✓ **Low-cost items.** If an item has a cost (not retail value) of less than $6.60 and an item that bears the name or logo of your organization is given in return for a donation of more than $33.00 (1995 inflation-adjusted amount), the donor may claim a charitable deduction for the full amount of the donation. Examples of items that often qualify as tokens are coffee mugs, key chains, bookmarks, and calendars.

✓ **De minimis benefits.** A donor can take a full deduction if the fair market value of the benefits received in connection with a gift does not exceed 2% of the donation or $66.00 (1995 inflation-adjusted amount), whichever is less.

Application of the quid pro quo rules

Here are various examples of how the quid pro quo rules apply:

✓ **Admission to events.** Many organizations sponsor banquets, concerts, or other events to which donors and prospective donors are invited in exchange for a contribution or other payment. Often, the donor receives a benefit equivalent to the payment and there is no charitable deduction available.

But if the amount paid is more than the value received, the amount in excess of the fair market value is deductible if there was intent to make a contribution.

✓ **Auctions.** The IRS generally takes the position that the fair market value of an item purchased at a charity auction is set by the bidders. The winning bidder, therefore, cannot pay more than the item is worth. That means there is no charitable contribution in the IRS's eyes, no deduction, and no need for the charity to provide any charitable gift substantiation document to the bidder. The IRS is currently reviewing this policy.

However, many tax professionals take the position that when the payment (the purchase price) exceeds the fair market value of the items, the amount that exceeds the fair market value is deductible as a charitable contribution. This position also creates a reporting requirement under the quid pro quo rules. Most charities have assumed that their auctions were covered by the new law, and have taken steps to set the value of every object sold and to provide receipts to buyers.

Example: Your church youth group auctions goods to raise funds for a mission trip. An individual bought a quilt for $200. The church takes the position that the quilt had a fair market value of $50 even though the bidder paid $200. Since the payment of $200 exceeded the $75 limit, the church is required to provide a written statement indicating that only $150 of the $200 payment is eligible for a charitable contribution.

✓ **Bazaars.** Payments for items sold a bazaars and bake sales are not tax deductible to donors since the purchase price generally equals the fair market value of the item.

✓ **Banquets.** Whether your organization incurs reporting requirements in connection with banquets where funds are raised depends on the specifics of each event.

Example 1: Your church sponsors a banquet for missions charging $50 per person. The meal costs the church $15 per person. There is no disclosure requirement since the amount charged was less than $75. However, the amount deductible for each donor is only $35.

Example 2: Your church may invite individuals to attend a missions banquet without charge. Attenders are invited to make contributions or pledges at the end of the banquet. These payments probably do not require disclosure even if the amount given is $75 or more because there is only an indirect relationship between the meal and the gift.

✓ **Sale of products or a service at fair market value.** When an individual purchases products or receives services at fair market value, no part of the payment is a gift.

Example 1: An individual purchases tapes of a series of Sunday morning worship services for $80. The sales price represents fair market value. Even though the amount paid exceeds the $75 threshold, the church is not required to provide a disclosure statement to the purchaser.

Example 2: The Brown family uses the fellowship hall of the church for a family reunion. The normal rental fee is $300. The Browns give a check to the church for $300 marked "Contribution." No receipt should be given because no charitable contribution was made.

Example 3: The Brown family uses the church sanctuary and fellowship hall for a wedding and the reception. The church does not have a stated use fee but asks for a donation from those who use the facility. The comparable fee to rent similar facilities is $250. The Browns give a check to the church for $250 marked "Contribution." No receipt should be given because no charitable contribution was made.

Example 4: Your church operates a Christian school. The parent of a student at the school writes a check payable to the church for his child's tuition. No receipt should be given because no charitable contribution was made.

Additional guidance from the IRS

Many of the following questions and answers were prepared by the IRS for use in training its agents. They cannot be cited as official legal authority. However, they do provide an indication of how the IRS will enforce the new requirements.

✓ Disclosure statement safe harbors

Question: Can a nonprofit ever skip making a disclosure statement when it provides goods or services in exchange for a gift?

Answer: Yes, if:
- It provides donors with token goods or services of little value, such as a key chain.
- Services to donors are religious in nature and, therefore, their value cannot be measured.

✓ Multiple payments by donor totalling more than $75

Question: What happens when donors make several small payments throughout the year that total more than $75?

Answer: Receipts do not have to be provided for the separate payments. However, it is not permissible to ask donors to write several small checks for the same event or transaction to avoid the over $75 threshold.

✓ Penalties for failure to make disclosure statements

Question: Can the government punish a charity for failing to provide disclosure statements (when goods or services are provided in exchange for gifts)?

Answer: Yes, the IRS can fine an organization $10 for each contribution received without providing donors the proper information. The penalty cannot exceed $5,000 for any one event or mailing.

✓ Gift over $250/responsibility of charity to furnish statement

Question: The law states that it is the responsibility of the donor to secure the substantiation from the charity regarding any contributions of cash or property of $250 or more. The law goes on to state that if goods or services are provided by the charity in consideration for the contribution, the substantiation document must include a good faith estimate of the value of these goods or services. Presumably, as a $250-or-more contribution, the responsibility for obtaining the documentation is on the donor. However, the law pertaining to disclosure of $75-plus quid pro quo contributions stipulates that the charity receiving such contribution is obligated to furnish a statement. Does this mean that if the quid pro quo donation is $250 or more, the charity is no longer obliged to furnish a statement?

Answer: No. The $250 rule pertains only to the requirement of the *donor* to document the contribution by obtaining the stipulated information.

The $75 rule relates only to the requirement of the *charity* to provide a breakdown of the value of the component parts of the quid pro quo contribution.

The charity's disclosure for the quid pro quo contribution does not have to be individualized in the form of a "receipt" issued to each donor. It simply has to inform donor(s), whether in an individualized or a generic format, that the item (or service/event) made available to each donor/purchaser will carry a value of $X and a charitable donation component of $Y.

Example: A flyer advising purchasers of $75 tickets to a concert that the tickets have a value of $45 and that the remaining $30 cost of a ticket will thus be deductible to the donor as a charitable contribution will not suffice to substantiate a $300 deduction claimed by the purchaser of a block of ten tickets. That person will have to secure an acknowledgment from the charity that the $750 check received made out to the charity represents payment for ten tickets valued at $450, of which $300 represents a charitable contribution. The flyer sent to promote ticket sales will not suffice for purposes of substantiating that patron's claimed charitable deduction of $300.

✓ Donor purchases tickets but does not attend events

Question: What is the proper tax treatment of a donor who has purchased from a charity at a premium a subscription series ticket to an entire run of performances? If the donor does not attend, but gives no advance indication of this intention, is there a mechanism through which the donor can take the entire amount paid or value of the ticket as a charitable deduction?

Answer: The determining factor is not whether or not the donor has an *intention* of exercising the right to admission but whether or not the tickets are accepted by the *donor*. If the ticket holder wants to support the charity and forgo the right of admission, the donor can simply pay the charity the face value of the ticket and refuse to accept it or the admission entitlement.

The charity might consider advising any such persons in advance that it is their right to refuse the tickets and claim the entire amount of payment.

The donor who earns the right of admission through giving a prescribed dollar amount, rather than by outright purchase of the ticket, is also entitled to deduct the full amount of the payment if the donor relinquishes the prerogative of attending the events.

✓ Gift of clothing/donor received proper acknowledgment

Question: A taxpayer donates ten old suits and ten of his used shirts to a charity, which resells them at its thrift store. The taxpayer left these items on his doorstep. The charity picked them up and left a receipt stating the number and nature of the items collected and that nothing was provided to the taxpayer in return for the donated goods. Is the substantiation requirement met?

Answer: Yes. The receipt properly describes the property donated, and it states whether or not the charity provided any goods or services in consideration, in whole or in part, for the property donated. It is important to remember that the quid pro quo aspect has to be addressed in the substantiation document one way or the other; that is, if no goods or services were furnished to the donor, then this fact must be noted. Also note that the charity is not remiss in failing to include a dollar amount since the charity has no obligation to place a value on the donation.

✓ Gift of clothing/donor receives improper acknowledgment

Question: The same charity that received the box of clothing noted in the previous question leaves the donor a receipt which consists entirely of the following statement:

"Thank you for your kind donation. We intend to use the proceeds of any sale of the property to provide disaster relief to the victims of the recent flood in Tasmania. Any unsold items will be furnished directly to these victims for their use. Your contribution will assist us in our mission of demonstrating to the unfortunate victims of disasters throughout the world that Americans are a generous and caring people. You might note your estimated value of the contributed goods on the line at the bottom of this receipt."

Is the substantiation requirement met?

Answer: No. The notice fails to provide a description of the contributed property. It also neglects to mention whether any goods or services were furnished to the donor in return.

Pending regulations

On May 27, 1994, the IRS issued temporary regulations for substantiation of charitable contributions. The regulation provided little additional information to the material in the 1993 tax bill. Nonprofit organizations have asked the IRS to clarify the following issues when the final regulations are issued:

✓ **Substantiating expenses of volunteers.** The out-of-pocket expenses for volunteers may be $250 or more per activity. How does the nonprofit handle this? One organization suggested that substantiation could be completed with an expense receipt and proof of participation in the charitable activity at the meet without causing the nonprofit to issue a gift receipt. Another organization suggested that the volunteer obtain from the nonprofit an acknowledgment that (1) the taxpayer attended or participated in the charitable activity giving rise to the expenses; (2) the expenses were incurred in the activity; and (3) the taxpayer received no reimbursement from the nonprofit for the expenses.

Under the proposed regulations issued in 1995, donors should receive an abbreviated written acknowledgment. See page 8 for more details on the form of the receipt.

✓ **Contributions in return for which a donor receives services that have a clear cost.** For example, a $250 charge is made for a religious retreat that includes room and board valued at $125. What is the proper treatment? (1) no part of the $250 is deductible because it presents "a classic" quid pro quo transaction; (2) the entire payment is deductible because the seclusion and duration of the retreat is an integral part of the religious experience; or (3) this is a quid pro contribution as defined in section 6115(b), and $125 is deductible.

✓ **Pledges.** Would a pledge of $1,000 paid in four equal installments of $250 require substantiation for each payment as it is made, but a $1,000 pledge paid in five equal installments of $200 not trigger the substantiation rules?

✓ **Advertising.** For example, a business's advertisement for $250 in a school yearbook is not unrelated business income to the school (because the activity is not regularly carried on) but, for the business, it could be either a business expense or a charitable contribution. If it is a business expense, do the charitable substantiation rules come into play?

✓ **Valuation of celebrity status.** If a celebrity appears at an event, is the fair market value of the event limited to the actual retail cost of the tickets? Or, is the ticket value increased based on the celebrity status of one of the speakers, singers, and so on?

✓ **Charitable trusts.** Nonprofits are often unaware of charitable trusts that have been created for their benefit. In such instances, how can a charity receipt a gift at the time the property is transferred to the trust?

The proposed regulations issued in 1995 indicate that transfers of property to charitable trusts are exempt from the substantiation rules.

Special Charitable Contribution Issues

Membership fees

Sometimes a membership fee may be partially or fully deductible. If the member receives benefits from the membership, a monetary value must be assigned to the benefits as the nondeductible portion of the payment.

Example 1: An individual pays a $100 membership fee to a nonprofit organization. In exchange, the individual receives publications and admission privileges to certain events. The value of the benefits received approximates the membership amount. Therefore, the membership fee is nondeductible as a charitable contribution.

Example 2: A nonprofit organization solicits funds for a particular program based on membership in a fund-raising "club." The donors do not receive any benefits from the membership. In this instance, membership fees are fully deductible as contributions.

Payments to private schools

Tuition payments to private schools are generally nondeductible since they correspond to value received. The IRS has ruled that payments to private schools are not deductible as charitable contributions

✓ if there is the existence of a contract under which a parent agrees to make a "contribution" and that contains provisions ensuring the admission of the child;

✓ if there is a plan allowing a parent either to pay tuition or to make "contributions" in exchange for schooling;

✓ if there is the earmarking of a contribution for the direct benefit of a particular individual; or

✓ if there is the otherwise unexplained denial of admission or readmission to a school for children of individuals who are financially able, but who do not contribute.

The IRS also will take into consideration other factors to decide deductibility such as

✓ no significant tuition charge;

✓ the parents of children attending a school receive substantial or unusual pressure to contribute;

✓ contribution appeals made as part of the admissions or enrollment process;

✓ no significant potential sources of revenue for operating the school other than contributions by parents or children attending the school; and

✓ other factors suggesting that a contribution policy was created to avoid the characterization of payments as tuition.

Payments to a church that operates a private school

Some churches operate related private schools on a "tuition-free" basis. These churches typically request that families with children in the school increase their contributions by the amount that they would otherwise have paid as tuition.

In reviewing "tuition-free" situations, the IRS often questions the deductibility of gifts to the church if

✓ contributions of several families increased or decreased markedly as the number of their children enrolled in the school changed;

✓ the contributions of parents of students drop off significantly in the summer months when the school is not in session; and

✓ the parents are not required to pay tuition out of their pockets.

Generally, contributions by parents are not deductible as charitable contributions to the extent that the church pays the parent's tuition liabilities.

Contributions to organizations that support specific individual workers

Many charitable organizations raise funds to support the ministry of specific individual workers. The individuals may be missionaries, youth workers, or employees of the organization.

Contributions to support the ministry of specific individual workers of a non-profit organization may be deductible if

 ✓ the organization controls and administers the funds following its board-

159

approved policies and procedures, and the work it supports is in the furtherance of its exempt purpose;

✓ the amounts distributed to the recipient missionary/staff members are in salary payments for services rendered for the organization or in payment for business expenses related to the work of the missionary/staff member;

✓ the amounts distributed to the recipient missionary/staff members are properly included for information reporting purposes (such as on Forms W-2, 1099-MISC, etc.); and

✓ the organization clearly distinguishes the funds given to the organization for the support of a missionary/staff member from funds that are nondeductible personal gifts passed on directly to the individual.

Contributions that benefit specific individuals other than staff members and other than the needy

Occasionally individuals give money to a church but request that it be sent to a particular recipient who is not on the staff of the organization, not a missionary related to the organization and does not qualify as a "needy" individual. When told that this "conduit" role is improper, the donor usually responds, "But I can't get a tax deduction otherwise!" The donor is absolutely correct.

The general rule in a conduit situation is that the donor is making a gift to the ultimate beneficiary. The IRS will look to the ultimate beneficiary to decide whether the gift qualifies for a charitable contribution deduction.

There are certain limited circumstances in which an organization may serve as an intermediary with respect to a gift that will be transferred to another organization or to a specific individual. In such circumstances, it is essential that the organization first receiving the monies have the right to control the ultimate destination of the funds.

Example: Frank Lee makes a gift of $5,000 to Shady Lane Church. Mr. Lee stipulates that the gift must go to a particular music group of which his son is a member. The money will be used to purchase sound equipment. The group will go on tour to present religious music in churches. The group is not an approved ministry of Shady Lane Church. This gift would generally be termed a personal gift to the music group and would not be deductible as a charitable contribution. It is best if the church returns the gift to Mr. Lee. If the church accepts the gift and passes the money on to the music group, the church should advise Mr. Lee that the gift is not deductible and would not provide him with a charitable receipt.

Donor intent is also a key factor. If the donor intends for a gift to benefit a specific individual instead of supporting the ministry of the charity, the gift is generally not deductible.

Contributions to needy individuals and benevolence funds

Contributions made directly by a donor to needy individuals are not deductible. To qualify for a charitable deduction, contributions must be made to a qualified organization.

Benevolence should be paid from the general fund of an organization. Contributions to benevolence funds may be claimed as charitable deductions if they are not earmarked for particular recipients.

A gift to a charitable organization involved in helping needy people marked "to aid the unemployed" is generally deductible. Yet if the gift is designated or restricted for the "Brown family" and the organization passes the money on to the Browns, the gift is generally not tax-deductible.

If a donor makes a suggestion about the beneficiary of a benevolent contribution, it may be deductible if the recipient organization exercises proper control over the benevolence fund. The suggestion must only be advisory in nature and the charity may accept or reject the gift. However, if every "suggestion" is honored by the organization, the earmarking could be challenged by the IRS.

A church or nonprofit organization may want to help a particular individual or family that has unusually high medical bills or other valid personal financial needs. To announce that funds will be received for the individual or family and receipt the monies through the church or nonprofit organization makes the gifts personal and not deductible as charitable contributions. A better option would be for the church to set up a trust fund at a local bank. Contributions to the trust fund would not be

Suggested Benevolence Fund Policy

Whereas, New Haven Church has a ministry to needy individuals; and

Whereas, The church desires to establish a Benevolence Fund through which funds for the support of needy individuals may be administered;

Resolved, That New Haven Church establish a Benevolence Fund to help individuals in financial need and will develop written procedures to document the need, establish reasonable limitations of support per person during a specified time period and obtain external verification of the need; and

Resolved, That the church will accept only contributions to the Benevolence Fund that are "to or for the use" of the church and their use must be subject to the control and discretion of the church board. Donors may make suggestions but not designations or restrictions concerning the identity of the needy individuals; and

Resolved, That the church will provide a charitable contribution receipt for gifts that meet the test outlined in the previous resolution. The church reserves the right to return any gifts that do not meet the test.

deductible for tax purposes. Payments from the trust fund would not represent taxable income to a needy individual or family. This method of helping the needy person or family is clearly a legal approach and would represent personal gifts from one individual to another.

Contributions to political candidates

In certain instances, political campaign funds are raised in churches. Collections taken in church do not make the political candidate a charitable organization. In addition, such collections probably violate the political activity restrictions for a church (see page 44-45).

Payments to retirement homes

The IRS generally treats payments to nonprofit retirement homes and communities (often referred to as "founders' gifts" or "sustainers' gifts") as nondeductible transfers when the payment is made at or near the time of entry.

If the benefit provided by the home is out of proportion to the benefit, the payment is part nondeductible purchase and part deductible contribution. The burden is on the donor to prove that the contribution is not the purchase price of the benefit and that part of the payment does qualify as a contribution.

If an individual pays a tax-exempt retirement home for the right to choose an apartment and live there, the payment is not a deductible charitable gift.

Gifts designated for missionaries

Charitable contributions must be made "to or for the use of" a qualified charitable organization. The IRS has interpreted "for the use of" to mean "in trust for," implying the use of a trust or similar legal arrangement for the benefit of the organization.

Generally, gifts made by an individual directly to a missionary are not deductible as charitable contributions. The funds need to be given to a missionary organization designated for the ministry of a particular missionary to be deductible.

Donated travel and out-of-pocket expenses

Unreimbursed out-of-pocket expenses of a volunteer performing services for a charity are generally deductible. The expenses must be directly connected with and solely attributable to the providing of the volunteer services.

The type of expenses that are deductible include transportation; travel, meals, and lodging while away from home if there is no significant element of personal pleasure, recreation, or vacation associated with the travel; postage; phone calls; printing and photocopying; expenses in entertaining prospective donors; and required uniforms without general utility.

It is inappropriate to provide a volunteer with a standard charitable receipt. But a letter of appreciation may be sent to the volunteer thanking the individual for the specific services provided. It may be helpful to remind the volunteer of the guidelines for deducting related expenses as a charitable contribution.

The burden is on the volunteer to prove the amount of the expenses and that they were incurred for the charity. Usually the charity cannot confirm the actual amount of a volunteer's expenses. See page 164 for a sample letter to volunteers.

Gifts to domestic organizations for foreign use

Gifts must be made to recognized U.S. charities to qualify for an income tax deduction. Some taxpayers have attempted to avoid this rule by funnelling gifts for a foreign-organized entity through a U.S. charity.

There are some acceptable situations where a U.S. charity may receive gifts for which a deduction is allowed with the money used abroad:

✓ The money may be used by the U.S. charity directly for projects that it selects to carry out its own exempt purposes. In this instance, the domestic organization would generally have operations in one or more foreign countries functioning directly under the U.S. entity. The responsibility of the donee organization ends when the purpose of the gift is fulfilled. A system of narrative and financial reports is necessary to document what was accomplished by the gift.

✓ It may create a subsidiary organization in a foreign country to facilitate its exempt operations there, with certain of its funds transmitted directly to the subsidiary. In this instance, the foreign organization is merely an administrative arm of the U.S. organization, with the U.S. organization considered the real recipient of the contributions. The responsibility of the U.S. organization ends when the purpose of the gift is fulfilled by the foreign subsidiary.

✓ It may make grants to charities in a foreign country in furtherance of its exempt purposes, following review and approval of the uses to which the funds are to be put. The responsibility of the U.S. organization ends when the purpose of the gift is fulfilled by the foreign organization. A narrative and financial report from the foreign organization will usually be necessary to document the fulfillment of the gift.

✓ It may transfer monies to another domestic entity with the second organization fulfilling the purpose of the gift. The responsibility of the first entity usually ends when the funds are transferred to the second organization.

Charity-sponsored tours

Many religious and charitable organizations sponsor cruises and tours. The location is often a resort or tourist area. Can individuals take a charitable deduction

Sample Letter to Volunteers

Dear Volunteer:

We appreciate the time, energy, and out-of-pocket costs you devote to our cause. Some of your costs are treated as charitable contributions that you can deduct on your income tax return if you itemize.

You may deduct unreimbursed expenses that you incur incidental to your volunteer work. So transportation costs (travel from home to the office or other places where you render services), phone calls, postage stamps, stationery, and similar out-of-pocket costs are deductible.

You can deduct 12 cents per mile in computing the costs of operating your car while doing volunteer work as well as unreimbursed parking and toll costs. Instead of using the 12-cents-per-mile method, you can deduct your actual auto expenses, provided you keep proper records. However insurance and depreciation on your car are not deductible.

If you travel as a volunteer and must be away from home overnight, reasonable payments for meals and lodging as well as your travel costs are deductible. Your out-of-pocket costs at a convention connected with your volunteer work are deductible if you were duly chosen as a representative of your church, group, or alumni body.

You cannot deduct travel expenses as charitable gifts if there's a significant element of personal pleasure, recreation, or vacation in the travel. Here's how Congress explained this rule:

In determining whether travel away from home involves a significant element of personal pleasure, recreation, or vacation, the fact that a taxpayer enjoys providing services to the charitable organization will not lead to denial of the deduction. For example, a . . . leader for a tax-exempt youth group who takes children belonging to the group on a camping trip may qualify for a charitable deduction with respect to his or her own travel expenses if he or she is on duty in a genuine and substantial sense throughout the trip, even if he or she enjoys the trip or enjoys supervising children.

By contrast, a taxpayer who only has nominal duties relating to the performance of services for the charity, who for significant portions of the trip is not required to render services, or who performs activities similar to activities that many individuals perform while on vacations paid out of after-tax dollars, is not allowed any charitable deduction for travel costs. . . . The disallowance rule does not apply where an officer of a charity travels to another city for the organization's annual meeting and spends the day attending meetings, even if the individual's evening is free for sightseeing or entertainment activities.

You cannot deduct the value of your services themselves. If you devote 100 hours during the year to typing for us and the prevailing rate for these services is $8.00 per hour, you can't deduct the $800 value of your services. Although deductions are allowed for property gifts, the IRS doesn't consider your services "property." Nor is the use of your home for meetings a "property contribution."

Finally, you may be required to substantiate your deduction to the IRS. Be prepared to prove your costs with cancelled checks, receipted bills, and diary entries. Also be ready to show the connection between the costs and your volunteer work.

The tax aspects and reporting requirements for gifts to our charity depend on your circumstances. As in all cases, we urge you to consult your own advisors. Again, thank you for furthering our cause with that most precious commodity: your time.

Your Nonprofit Organization

for tour expenses? Should the organization give a charitable receipt to tour partici-pants? If tour expenses cannot be deducted as charitable expenses, what about tak-ing a business or education expense deduction? Are work trips to mission fields deductible as charitable contributions?

Tours sponsored by nonprofit organizations rarely provide a tax deduction to the participant. In instances where a tax deduction is available, the deduction is almost always in the business or education expense category. Even these expense deductions are denied if there is a significant element of personal pleasure, recre-ation, or vacation.

The general rule is that there is no charitable contribution deduction for the cost of a travel or study tour. The only exception is where individuals are actually pay-ing for their expenses and doing work for the organization. Then there is a limited deduction available, subject to a restriction on the amount of pleasure and recreation involved in a particular trip.

Discounts provided charity by a vendor

A business donor may provide a charitable discount for goods or services purchased by a nonprofit organization and denote the discount as a "charitable contribution."

A charitable discount is generally not deductible as a charitable contribution. The donor should not receive a standard receipt, but may receive an appropriately worded acknowledgment.

Interest on restricted gifts

There is often a time period between the receipt of restricted donations and the expenditure of the funds for the specified purpose. If investment income is earned on the monies before their expenditure, do the investment earnings accrue to the gift or may the earnings be used for the general budget of the organization? Unless there are donor or other legal restrictions on the earnings on the funds, state law controls the use of the earnings. Often, the interest earned on restricted funds held for a tem-porary period prior to expenditure are considered to be unrestricted.

Refunding contributions to donors

Charitable contributions generally should not be returned to donors. However, there are a few instances where donors must be given the option of receiving their contributions back and in some cases the refund should actually occur.

Since contributions must be irrevocable to qualify for a charitable deduction, there is no basis to return an undesignated gift to a donor. Requests from donors to return undesignated gifts should be denied under nearly any circumstances. A prac-tice of refunding such gifts would be an extremely dangerous precedent.

Donors often contribute funds based on the anticipation that a certain event will occur. Their intent is to make an irrevocable gift. For example, a church raises money to buy new pews. However, an insufficient amount is raised and the church board abandons the project. What happens to the money that was designated by donors for the pews? If the donors can be identified, they should be asked whether they would like to remove the designation related to their gift. Otherwise, the money should be returned to the donor. If the donors cannot be identified (as in the case of cash contributions), the congregation could re-direct use of the funds.

If contributions are returned to donors, a written communication should accompany the refund advising donors of their responsibility to file amended tax returns if a charitable deduction was claimed. A written notice should be filed with the IRS to document the initial date of the gift, the date of the refund, the amount, and name and address of the taxpayer.

Key Concepts

■ Since 1917, Congress has provided favored tax treatment to charitable contributions by individuals.

■ Most nonprofit organizations qualify to receive tax-deductible contributions.

■ Not all gifts to your organization are tax-deductible such as gifts of services or the use of property.

■ Certain gifts of property may require you to file reports with the IRS.

■ Gifts that are designated for the benefit of individuals may be inappropriate for your organization to receive or at least receipt as a charitable contribution.

Insuring Your Organization

In This Chapter

- Abuse or molestation insurance
- Automobile insurance
- COBRA
- Crime insurance
- Dental insurance
- Director's and officer's liability insurance
- Disability insurance
- General liability insurance
- Group life insurance
- Health insurance
- Key employee insurance
- Long-term care insurance
- Professional liability insurance
- Property insurance
- Travel and accident insurance
- Umbrella liability insurance
- Workers' Compensation

Most nonprofit entities need full insurance coverage similar to for-profit organizations. You will need a frequent review of insurance requirements and a good relationship with an insurance agent or broker to provide a complete insurance program at competitive cost.

Setting deductible limits is a very important decision. Generally, the higher the deductible, the lower the premium will be. If the organization is financially strong enough to assume a certain degree of risk, the choice of high deductibles will often save in overall insurance costs.

Abuse or Molestation Insurance

All churches and many other nonprofit organizations should purchase a general liability policy that includes an abuse or molestation endorsement or separate coverage. This coverage should apply to the actual or threatened abuse or molestation by anyone of any person while in the care, custody, or control of your organization. It would also extend to the negligent employment, investigation, supervision, reporting to the proper authorities or failure to so report, or retention of an individual for whom your organization was legally responsible and who was involved in actual or threatened abuse.

Automobile Insurance

Automobile insurance is required if your organization owns one or more automobiles, buses, or other vehicles. Even if no vehicles are owned by your organization, hired and non-owned automobile insurance is usually needed. If an employee runs an errand for an organization using the employer's car and is in an auto accident, this coverage protects the organization.

A commercial auto policy is generally more narrow in coverage than a personal auto policy. For example, personal auto policy coverage usually transfers to other cars that you may drive. This is generally not true with a commercial auto policy.

Medical payments provide a goodwill type of coverage. If someone is injured in your auto, the person may be treated up to the medical payment limit of the policy. Often this helps avoid a lawsuit.

Typical policy coverages are $100,000/$300,000 bodily injury, $100,000 property damage, $50,000 uninsured motorist, and $2,000 or $5,000 for medical payments. Endorsements may be added for towing or road service and rental car reimbursement. Your liability coverage should be at least $100,000. If you only purchase the minimum required by your state, you may be inadequately insured.

COBRA

The Consolidated Omnibus Budget Reconciliation Act of 1985 (COBRA) requires covered employers to offer 18 months of group health coverage beyond the time the coverage would have ended because of certain "qualifying events." Premiums are reimbursable by the former employee to the former employer.

A "qualifying event" includes any termination of the employer-employee relationship, whether voluntary or involuntary, unless the termination is caused by the employee's gross misconduct. COBRA coverage applies even if the employee retires, quits, is fired, or laid off.

Churches are excluded from the COBRA requirements. Other nonprofits are generally subject to COBRA if they employ 20 or more employees during a typical working day.

Crime Insurance

Employee dishonesty coverage is usually essential for nonprofit organizations because of the handling of donations. The coverage usually relates to employees but may be extended to volunteers such as a church treasurer.

Protection against robbery inside and outside is often a desirable part of the crime insurance coverage. A high deductible will lower premium cost.

Dental Insurance

An insured dental care program is among the most popular of benefit options. It is a benefit that employees want to take advantage of and can use regularly.

In the traditional approach, a dental plan is similar to medical insurance in that the employer pays a premium to an insurer who acts as the administrator. Covered employees submit claims and the insurer pays according to a "usual and customary" schedule. Employees are typically free to select their dentists.

Similar to the HMO concept in medical insurance, "managed care" dental programs usually work with a list of contracted care providers who provide service to members in the covered group.

Reimbursed self-insurance represents an alternative approach for dental benefits. This concept allows covered employees to select their dentists, have all work done without exclusion, pay for services themselves, and file for reimbursement from the employer.

For example, a company might choose to pay 100% of the first $200 per employee family and a decreasing percentage up to a ceiling limit of their determination. Since the plan can be structured flexibly, this allows employers to predetermine their maximum costs for budget purposes.

Director's and Officer's Liability Insurance

Nonprofits should provide protection to board members against individual liability. The two primary options are:

✓ **Insurance.** Director's and officer's (D&O) liability insurance is designed to protect board members and officers against certain liabilities they may incur while acting in their official capacities. D&O policies usually cover legal fees and other expenses involved in defending against a claim.

✓ **State law protection.** More than 30 states have legislation limiting the liability of individuals who serve as volunteer directors or officers on nonprofit boards. Generally, these laws provide that a director or officer can be held liable only for willful or wanton behavior, not just for simple negligence.

Even if protection is provided under state laws, it may be wise for the organization to purchase D&O insurance to cover the acts of negligence not covered under the state law.

Disability Insurance

Disability insurance may be provided for nonprofit organization employees. Coverage is usually limited to 60% to 75% of the annual salary of each individual. Social security and pension benefits are often offset against disability insurance benefits. Disability insurance premiums may be paid through a flexible benefit plan to obtain income tax and social security tax (FICA) savings.

If the organization pays the disability insurance premiums (and the employee is the beneficiary) as a part of the compensation package, any disability policy proceeds are fully taxable to the employee. If the organization pays the premiums, the premiums are excluded from the employee's income.

The benefit waiting period is generally in the 90-to-120-day range. Coverage may be extended to age 65 or even life.

General Liability Insurance

General liability insurance provides for the avoidance of unforeseeable payments and also protects against the catastrophic hazards when large groups of individuals gather under the sponsorship of an organization. Endorsements to the liability policy may cover such additional hazards as product liability, premises medical payments, real property fire legal liability, advertising injury, contractual liability, and personal injury.

Coverage is usually written for at least $500,000 for each occurrence, $500,000 aggregate, $500,000 products and completed operations, $500,000 personal and advertising, $50,000 fire damage, and $5,000 medical.

If an umbrella liability policy is not purchased, the $500,000 limits listed above probably should be raised to $1,000,000. If umbrella liability coverage is purchased, the insurance company may require that the general liability limit be $1,000,000.

General liability insurance may be purchased with limits higher than $1,000,000. It is usually more cost-effective to use a $500,000 or $1,000,000 limit for the general liability policy and then purchase an umbrella policy with higher limits.

Many churches and nonprofits need liability insurance for special events such as summer camps, skiing, beach activities, softball, basketball, and other sports. Coverage for these events should be provided with a specific endorsement under a general liability policy.

Group Life Insurance

Group life insurance may be written to provide a minimum amount of insurance for each employee. The first $50,000 of coverage is a tax-free benefit for employees. Premiums may be paid wholly or partially by the employer.

Health Insurance

Escalating health-care costs continue to cause employers to struggle to provide cost-efficient health care programs for employees.

In recent years there has been a shift to managed care—prepaid health-insurance programs that stress preventive care. But for most churches and other small-to-medium charities, an indemnity plan may be the only avenue available.

Medium-to-larger nonprofits typically offer a group health-insurance plan for the benefit of employees as an important fringe benefit. Very small nonprofits usually help their employees secure individual health policies.

Health insurance purchased through a group policy is usually more expensive than individual policies if the individual can qualify for coverage. Insurers often require that 75% of the full-time employees be enrolled to qualify for a group plan. This enrollment requirement is necessary to avoid adverse selection. Adverse selection occurs when a disproportionate number of employees with very high-cost medical problems are enrolled in a plan.

The basic offerings in employer-provided health-insurance plans include the following:

✓ **Health Maintenance Organization (HMO).** Medical treatment is prepaid and delivered by the HMO provider organization.

✓ **Preferred Provider Organization (PPO).** Medical treatment is supplied through a designated network of physicians and hospitals at discounted rates.

✓ **Indemnity plan.** These plans may include cost containment features such as prehospital authorization and a second opinion before surgery, while also offering incentives for outpatient treatment. Indemnity plans typically feature a per-person, per-year deductible and co-insurance factors and a limit on total lifetime claims covered.

Traditional indemnity plans offer little flexibility of employer design. The partially self-funded concept allows the employer to design the exact coverage and build in customized cost-containment features. The two basic indemnity plan concepts are as follows:

● **Fully insured through a carrier.** This is the traditional approach for health insurance with most of the risk borne by the insurance carrier.

- **Partially self-funded by organization.** This method is a shared-risk approach. This concept may make sense if there are 25 or more employees and the maximum annual liability is only slightly higher than the premium under a fully insured plan.

    An employee group primarily composed of nonsmokers and nondrinkers and without the incidence of AIDS also may provide an incentive to consider the partially self-funded approach. Traditional fully insured plans must factor the possibility of all types of illness into their rates.

    The principles of a partially self-funded plan include payment by the organization of the first-dollar medical costs. The organization buys a high deductible medical plan. For example, the deductible may be $10,000 or $20,000 per person per year. Expenses over the $10,000 or $20,000 are covered by the insurance carrier. This is commonly called a "specific deductible."

    An "aggregate stop-loss" policy is also purchased. This policy will provide that annual medical expenses exceeding a total of a certain amount will be paid by the insurance carrier. This is a type of overall stop-loss for the employer.

✓ **Traditional fully insured plan with HMO option.** Under this concept the employer gives the employee the choice of being covered under a traditional indemnity plan or using an HMO.

    HMOs are typically more expensive than indemnity plans. Therefore, if the employee chooses the HMO plan, the difference between the cost of the HMO and the fully insured plan usually is paid by the employee.

Current trends in health insurance

✓ **Premium cost-shifting.** Many organizations require some contribution for single coverage and even more require employee contributions toward dependent coverage.

✓ **Deductibles.** While a $100 deductible used to be the norm, today deductibles of $500 to $1,000 per person per year are common.

    There is a trend toward setting deductible amounts based on an employee's pay level. For example, a higher paid employee would have a higher deductible than a lower paid employee.

✓ **Co-insurance.** Higher co-insurance limits are common today. An 80%/20% split of the first medical dollar costs after the deductible up to $5,000 or $10,000 per person per year is not unusual.

✓ **Extend the preexisting conditions waiting period.** Some organizations have extended the preexisting waiting period to 18 months. New employees with preexisting conditions are often willing to pay to keep COBRA coverage from their previous employer. However, churches and many small nonprofit organization's employees are exempt from COBRA (see page 168).

✓ **Employee health assessment.** Some insurance companies offer health assessment for a per employee fee. Doctors evaluate employees' present conditions and prescribe a personal health program for them. A healthier employee helps to curb premium hikes.

✓ **Second opinions and precertification.** It is more common today to require second opinions before surgery and to precertify hospital stays.

✓ **Prescriptions.** Medical costs can be reduced by providing generic prescriptions by mail.

Medical plan continuation features

Securing medical coverage while an individual is between jobs is often a concern. Churches and small nonprofit employers are exempt from the coverage continuation requirements of COBRA (see page 168) but they may voluntarily comply. Also, some state laws require continued insurance coverage for spouses and children after a divorce.

Some health plans have a conversion feature that allows conversion of group coverage to an individual policy after employment ends. The conversion policy is usually expensive and the benefits are very limited. Still, conversion may be the best alternative for someone with health problems and unable to obtain other insurance.

Flexible benefit plans

Many employers have shifted to a flexible benefit plan (often referred to as a cafeteria plan) to provide health coverage and to allow employees to choose between taxable and nontaxable benefits. In the simplest plans, employees might be offered an opportunity to choose (and pay for) additional medical benefits or for health benefits to cover family members.

More complex plans offer a full menu of benefits: additional vacation time, disability insurance, child-care allowances or emergency child-care service, life and disability insurance, and legal insurance. Each benefit has a price. Each employee then selects the package of benefits that best meets the employee's needs (and ability to pay).

The expense money employees choose to keep in their flexible benefit plan is deducted before taxes. The money is held in reserve, and the employee is reimbursed for expenses as they are incurred.

Depending on the state of employment, employee savings may apply to both federal and state income taxes and social security taxes. This may amount to a discount of around 40% (28% federal tax, 7.65% FICA, 3%-5% state tax) on what was formerly paid personally for health care insurance or child-care expense.

The flexible benefit plan offers some distinct advantages to employers. The organization does not have to pay social security taxes on money that is being withheld from employees under the plan. In some states, lower Workers' Compensation and unemployment insurance payments also result.

Some potential drawbacks for employees are

✓ employees must use the money they have set aside within the plan year or forfeit that money to their employer, and

✓ there might be a slight reduction in some of their social security benefits.

Key Employee Insurance

Key employee insurance reimburses the organization for financial loss resulting from the death of a key employee of the organization. It may be used to build up a fund to be available upon the individual's retirement should death not be a factor.

Long-Term Care Insurance

Long-term care or nursing home insurance provided by the nonprofit is generally considered to represent additional taxable income to the employee. Although the IRS has not issued a ruling on this matter, informal comments by top IRS officials indicate their position.

Payments of long-term care premiums should not be included in flexible benefit plans.

Professional Liability Insurance

Pastoral counseling is rarely covered in standard policies. Each church should purchase a pastor's professional liability policy to cover any act or omission in the furnishing of pastoral counseling services. The coverage protects both pastor and church. Your pastor will feel more comfortable handling delicate matters because adequate insurance coverage is provided.

Property Insurance

A multi-peril policy provides comprehensive property and general liability insurance tailored to the needs of the insured. Endorsements may be added to provide earthquake, employee dishonesty, and money loss coverages.

A general property policy provides fire insurance coverage for structures and fixtures that are a part of the structures.

Machinery used in building service, air conditioning systems, boilers, and elevators are covered under a boiler policy.

Endorsements may be added to the general property policy to cover replacement cost, loss caused by windstorm, hail, explosion, riot, aircraft, vehicles and smoke, vandalism and malicious mischief, flood, sprinkler leakage, and earthquake. It may be desirable to eliminate the co-insurance provision by using an agreed amount endorsement. Be sure there is coverage on equipment, such as personal computers and video equipment, that you may take off-premises to conventions or other meetings.

Many church policies do not cover the pastor's personal property located on church premises. Even when some coverage is provided, the limit may be too low, considering the value of books, sermons, and computers.

Try to use your property insurance as catastrophic coverage and not a maintenance policy. Your organization should take care of the small property damage losses.

Travel and Accident Insurance

Travel and accident insurance is often purchased for nonprofit organization executives or perhaps all the employees. It covers injury occurring during travel authorized by the employer. The coverage also may be written on a 24-hour basis.

Travel and accident insurance usually does not apply to certain "war zones" unless a special rider is purchased.

Umbrella Liability Insurance

Through an umbrella liability insurance policy, you may purchase liability coverage with higher limits. The particular liabilities covered do not get broader.

Example: If your underlying general liability policy has a $500,000 limit and you purchase an umbrella liability policy with a $2,000,000 limit, your total liability coverage will be $2,500,000.

Umbrella policies are usually more liberal in their coverages but tend to be higher priced than excess liability policies (which are only extensions of policy limits).

Workers' Compensation

Workers' Compensation insurance coverage compensates workers for losses caused by work-related injuries. It also limits the potential liability of the organization for injury to the employee related to his job.

Workers' Compensation insurance is required by law in all states to be carried by the employer. A few states exempt churches from Workers' Compensation coverage, and several states exempt all nonprofit employers. Still, churches and nonprofit organizations are covered in most states. Most states also consider ministers to be employees and therefore they must be covered under Workers' Compensation policy.

Even if a church or nonprofit organization is exempt from Workers' Compensation, the voluntary purchase of the coverage or the securing of additional general liability coverage may be prudent.

Workers' Compensation premiums are based on the payroll of the organization with a minimum premium charge to issue the policy. An audit is done later to determine the actual charge for the policy.

Most Workers' Compensation insurance is purchased through private insurance carriers. A few states provide the coverage and charge the covered organizations.

Key Concepts

■ Your nonprofit organization probably needs a broad range of insurance coverages.

■ Obtaining adequate insurance and competitive prices usually requires working closely with your insurance agent or broker.

■ Providing adequate health insurance for your employees continues to challenge especially smaller organizations.

■ Many organizations overlook the legal requirement to provide Workers' Compensation insurance.

CHAPTER NINE

Laws For Nonprofits

In This Chapter
- Age discrimination
- Americans With Disabilities Act
- Canadian Goods and Services Tax
- Charitable solicitation
- Church-operated child care facilities
- Equal pay
- Environmental issues
- Fair Labor Standards Act
- Family and Medical Leave Act
- Immigration control
- Mailing at third-class rates
- National Child Care Act
- Occupational Safety and Health Act
- Pregnancy discrimination
- Racial discrimination
- Religious discrimination
- Sexual harassment
- State taxes and fees

The non-payroll laws and regulations governing nonprofits, at best, can be confusing, and at worst, downright intimidating. Legal assistance may be required to provide interpretation of the laws and regulations for your organization.

This chapter is designed to provide you a very basic explanation of some key laws that may impact your organization. Complying with these laws will often result in good stewardship. There is generally a financial risk if they are ignored.

Age Discrimination

The Age Discrimination in Employment Act of 1967 (ADEA) applies to employers in any industry affecting commerce with 20 or more employees. Churches with 20 or more employees may be exempt from the ADEA because of a lack of involvement in commercial activities.

The ADEA prohibits employment discrimination on the basis of age against applicants for employment and employees who are age 40 and older. The top age limit for mandatory retirement has generally been eliminated. Compulsory retirement is still permissible for certain executives or tenured college faculty members who have reached age 65. Ministers are subject to compulsory retirement.

Americans with Disabilities Act

The employment provisions of the American With Disabilities Act (ADA) became effective July 26, 1992, covering employers with 25 or more workers in 20 or more weeks a year. Effective July 26, 1994, coverage was expanded to employers with 15 or more workers in 20 or more weeks a year. The public accommodations provisions of the ADA have been effective since January 26, 1992. For ADA questions, you can call a special information line at the Justice Department: (202) 514-0301.

The ADA requirements relate to two areas:

✔ **Employment.** Hiring must be without regard to disabilities and also make reasonable accommodation for disabled individuals.

There are limited exceptions to the employment provisions of the ADA for churches and religious employers. Preferential treatment may be given in hiring individuals of a particular religion. Additionally, churches and religious organizations may require employees to conform to their religious tenets.

Example: Two applicants are members of the United Methodist denomination. A Methodist church or Methodist religious organization cannot refuse to hire the disabled applicant simply because of a disability, but it may give preference to a Methodist applicant over a Baptist.

✔ **Public accommodations.** Facilities open to the public must be accessible to the disabled. The primary focus is on facilities like restaurants, museums, hotels, retail stores, and banks.

Religious organizations or entities controlled by religious organizations (including places of worship) are exempt from the public accommodation requirements of the ADA. Caution: Although a church is exempt under the public accommodations provisions, they may still be covered under similar provisions of local building codes.

Canadian Goods and Services Tax

The Canadian Goods and Services Tax (GST) applies to all goods and services introduced into Canada. The GST applies to imports and may have impact on U.S. nonprofit organizations that have even minimal contact in Canada.

The 7% tax may be assessed on all membership dues, publication sales, magazine subscriptions, group insurance sales, advertising revenues, classified ad sales, seminar and training course revenues, and any other product or service offered by a U.S. nonprofit to a Canadian consumer.

There are certain exemptions for membership dues and educational services. Certain products and services offered by U.S. nonprofits to Canadian consumers may be covered under the GST.

For more information on the GST, write the Canadian Society of Association Executives, 45 Charles Street East, Toronto, Ontario, M4Y 1S2 and request the *Goods and Services Tax Booklet.*

Charitable Solicitation

Federal, state, and local governments have enacted laws regulating the solicitation of contributions by nonprofit organizations. These laws are known as "charitable solicitation acts."

Charitable solicitation laws have resulted from greater interest in accountability on the part of nonprofit organizations. The laws are designed to assure contributors that funds solicited for a specified charitable purpose will be used for the intended purpose. Many states require the filing of annual registration and reports to comply with the solicitation laws (48 states have some form of solicitation laws).

Church-Operated Child Care Facilities

Federal funds are available to low-income families for child care through the Child Care and Development Block Grant Act of 1990. States must use 75% of the grants from the federal government to issue child care certificates to qualified low-income parents. The certificates may be redeemed at eligible facilities for child care services. Churches may be eligible to provide child care under this program even if they engage in religious instruction or display religious symbols.

Through another segment of this program, states may provide funds directly to eligible child care facilities, including churches, to assist them in providing child care to children from low-income families. Churches may receive these direct grants only if the funds are not used for religious worship and instruction.

Equal Pay

The Equal Pay Act of 1963 prohibits employers from paying employees of one sex at a lower rate than employees of the opposite sex for equal work for positions that require the same skill, effort, and responsibility and that are performed under similar working conditions.

Environmental Issues

Environmental risks are a major concern for nonprofit organizations purchasing or receiving charitable gifts of real estate. Nonprofits must exercise "due diligence" in conducting an environmental investigation prior to purchasing or accepting donated real estate. These due diligence investigations are usually called "Preliminary Environmental Site Assessments" or "Phase I Environmental Site Assessments." These assessments are performed by qualified environmental consultants.

Environmental laws that may apply to gifts or the purchase of real estate include

✓ Comprehensive Environmental Response, Compensation, and Liability Act (CERCLA/Superfund, 1980)

✓ Resource Conservation and Recovery Act (RCRA, 1976)

✓ RCRA Underground Storage Tank Regulations (RCRA UST, 1984)

✓ Indoor Radon Abatement Act (IRAA, 1988)

✓ Clean Water Act (CWA, 1977)

✓ Clean Air Act (CAA, 1983)

Fair Labor Standards Act

The Fair Labor Standards Act (FLSA) adopted in 1938 provides protection for employees engaged in interstate commerce concerning minimum wages, equal pay, overtime pay, recordkeeping, and child labor. (Some states even have more restrictive versions of the FSLA.) Commerce is defined by the FLSA as "trade, commerce, transportation, transmission, or communication among the several states or between any state and any place outside thereof."

The employees of nonprofit organizations involved in commerce or in the production of goods for commerce are generally considered covered by the provisions

What the FLSA Does Not Regulate

While the Fair Labor Standards Act does set basic minimum wage and overtime pay standards and regulates the employment of minors, there are a number of employment practices which the Act does not regulate. For example, the Act does not require

✓ vacation, holiday, severance, or sick pay;

✓ meal or rest periods, holidays or vacations off;

✓ premium pay for weekend or holiday work;

✓ pay raises or fringe benefits;

✓ a discharge notice, reason for discharge, or immediate payment of final wages to terminated employees; or

✓ any limit on the number of hours of work for persons 16 years of age and over.

of the FLSA. Conversely, nonprofits that are not engaged in commerce or fall below the $500,000 annual gross sales volume requirement are generally exempt from the Act.

The FLSA clearly applies to schools regardless of whether they are nonprofit entities operated by religious organizations. Church-operated day care centers and elementary and secondary schools are generally considered subject to the FLSA.

Most local churches would not meet the definition of being involved in commerce. However, many churches and nonprofits voluntarily choose to follow the FLSA regulations as an equitable guide and as a precaution against possible litigation.

The overtime compensation requirements of the FLSA do not apply to certain employees in executive, administrative, or professional positions. Ministers are generally exempt under the professional provisions of this exemption. Minors under age 14 generally cannot be hired.

The present FLSA minimum wage is $4.25 per hour. Teenagers may be paid a training wage of 85% of minimum ($3.61) for the first three months of work.

Minimum wages are going up in states. Washington is now at $4.90. Hawaii and Washington D.C. are at $5.25, New Jersey, $5.05, Alaska and Oregon, $4.75, Iowa, $4.65, Rhode Island, $4.45, Connecticut, $4.27 and Vermont, moving to $4.75 in 1996.

Family and Medical Leave Act

The Family and Medical Leave Act of 1993 (FMLA) requires certain employers to provide up to twelve weeks of unpaid leave to eligible employees. The FMLA does not override more generous state entitlements. The new law became effective on August 5, 1993 and only applies to organizations with fifty or more employees. There is no exemption for religious employers.

While only large churches and nonprofit organizations may be subject to the Act, some employers will choose to comply with the provisions of the law in an effort to improve employee morale. Even though an organization is not subject to the Act, they may have legal responsibilities to pregnant or ill employees under other federal laws (see other sections of this chapter).

To be eligible under this law, a person must be employed at least twelve months and have worked at least 1,250 hours during the twelve months. Eligible employees are entitled to a total of twelve weeks of unpaid leave for the birth of a child and certain other reasons.

Immigration Control

The Immigration Reform and Control Act of 1986 (IRCA) prohibits all employers from hiring unauthorized aliens, imposes documentation verification requirements on all employers, and provides an "amnesty" program for certain illegal aliens. The law also prohibits employers with three or more employees from discriminating because of national origin. An I-9 Form (see page 183) must be completed and retained on file by all employers for each employee hired after November 6, 1986. The form must be available for inspection at any time.

Effective September 20, 1994, the Form I-551 Alien Registration Receipt Card issued after August 1, 1989, will be the exclusive registration card issued to lawful permanent residents as definitive evidence of identity and U.S. residence status. Holders of other Alien Registration Receipt cards such as Form I-151, AR-3, and AR-103 are urged to obtain Form I-551 as soon as possible.

Mailing at Third-Class Rates

Churches and other nonprofits may qualify to mail at special bulk third-class rates. The application (Form 3624) is available at the post office where you wish to deposit the mail (see page 184 for a sample of Form 3624). The following documents must be provided (some apply only if the organization is incorporated):

 certified copy of articles of incorporation;

 copy of bylaws;

U.S. Department of Justice
Immigration and Naturalization Service

OMB No. 1115-0136
Employment Eligibility Verification

Please read instructions carefully before completing this form. The instructions must be available during completion of this form. **ANTI-DISCRIMINATION NOTICE.** It is illegal to discriminate against work eligible individuals. Employers CANNOT specify which document(s) they will accept from an employee. The refusal to hire an individual because of a future expiration date may also constitute illegal discrimination.

Section 1. Employee Information and Verification. To be completed and signed by employee at the time employment begins

Print Name: Last	First	Middle Initial	Maiden Name
Hendricks	Fred	W.	

Address (Street Name and Number)	Apt. #	Date of Birth (month/day/year)
406 Forest Avenue		6/12/49

City	State	Zip Code	Social Security #
Cincinnati, OH 45960			514-42-9087

I am aware that federal law provides for imprisonment and/or fines for false statements or use of false documents in connection with the completion of this form.

I attest, under penalty of perjury, that I am (check one of the following):
☐ A citizen or national of the United States
☐ A Lawful Permanent Resident (Alien # A _____
☐ An alien authorized to work until ___/___/___
(Alien # or Admission # _____

Employee's Signature	Date (month/day/year)
Fred W. Hendricks	1/20/96

Preparer and/or Translator Certification. (To be completed and signed if Section 1 is prepared by a person other than the employee.) I attest, under penalty of perjury, that I have assisted in the completion of this form and that to the best of my knowledge the information is true and correct.

Preparer's/Translator's Signature	Print Name

Address (Street Name and Number, City, State, Zip Code)	Date (month/day/year)

Section 2. Employer Review and Verification. To be completed and signed by employer. Examine one document from List A OR examine one document from List B and one from List C as listed on the reverse of this form and record the title, number and expiration date, if any, of the document(s)

List A	OR	List B	AND	List C
Document title: _____		Drivers License		_____
Issuing authority: _____		Ohio		_____
Document #: _____		514-42-9087		_____
Expiration Date (if any): ___/___/___		6/30/97		___/___/___
Document #: _____				
Expiration Date (if any): ___/___/___				

CERTIFICATION - I attest, under penalty of perjury, that I have examined the document(s) presented by the above-named employee, that the above-listed document(s) appear to be genuine and to relate to the employee named, that the employee began employment on (month/day/year) 1/15/96 and that to the best of my knowledge the employee is eligible to work in the United States. (State employment agencies may omit the date the employee began employment).

Signature of Employer or Authorized Representative	Print Name	Title
David L. Brown	David L. Brown	Business Manager

Business or Organization Name	Address (Street Name and Number, City, State, Zip Code)	Date (month/day/year)
Fairfield Church, 110 Harding Avenue Cincinnati, OH 45960		1/31/96

Section 3. Updating and Reverification. To be completed and signed by employer.

A. New Name (if applicable)	B. Date of rehire (month/day/year) (if applicable)

C. If employee's previous grant of work authorization has expired, provide the information below for the document that establishes current employment eligibility.

Document Title:_____ Document #:_____ Expiration Date (if any):___/___/___

I attest, under penalty of perjury, that to the best of my knowledge, this employee is eligible to work in the United States, and if the employee presented document(s), the document(s) I have examined appear to be genuine and to relate to the individual.

Signature of Employer or Authorized Representative	Date (month/day/year)

Form I-9 (Rev. 11-21-91) N

Note: This form must be completed and retained on file by all employers for employees hired after November 6, 1986. (For more information on completing this form, contact the Immigration and Naturalization Service office in your area for a free copy of the Handbook for Employers/Form M-274).

U. S. POSTAL SERVICE
APPLICATION TO MAIL AT SPECIAL BULK THIRD-CLASS RATES

PART 1 - FOR COMPLETION BY APPLICANT	SECTION A - APPLICATION

NOTE: PLEASE READ ALL INFORMATION IN SECTION B ON THE BACK OF THIS APPLICATION BEFORE COMPLETING THE FORM BELOW.

Instructions

A. Be sure that all information entered below is legible so that our records will show the correct information about your organization.

B. Show the complete name of the organization in item 1. The name shown must agree with the name that appears on all documents submitted to support this application.

C. A complete address representing a physical location for the organization must be shown in item 2. When mail is received through a post office box, show your street address first and then the box number.

D. The name of the applicant in item 5 must be the name of the individual submitting the application for the organization. The individual must be an officer of the organization. Printers and mailing agents may not sign for the organization.

E. No additional categories may be added in item 6. You must qualify as one of the types of organizations listed in order to be eligible for special rates.

F. Be sure to sign the application in item 12.

G. The date shown in item 14 must be the date that you submit the application to the post office.

NO APPLICATION FEE IS REQUIRED

Please be sure all information is complete. PLEASE TYPE OR PRINT LEGIBLY

1. Complete Name of Organization

Chapel Hill Charity

2. Address of Organization (Street, Apt./ Suite No.)	3. City, State, ZIP+4 Code
300 S. Hillcrest Avenue	*Athens, OH 45701*

4. (Area Code)/ Telephone No.	5. Name of Applicant (must represent organization that is applying.)
(614) 832-9061	*Lewis E. Foster*

6. Type of Organization (Check only one. See 'E' above.)

- [X] (01) Religious
- [ ] (02) Educational
- [ ] (03) Scientific
- [ ] (04) Philanthropic
- [ ] (05) Agricultural
- [ ] (06) Labor
- [ ] (07) Veterans'
- [ ] (08) Fraternal
- [ ] (09) Qualified Political Committee

7. Check whether this organization is for profit or whether any of the net income inures to the benefit of any private stockholder or individual.
- [ ] YES
- [X] NO

8. Check whether this organization is exempt from Federal income tax. (If 'YES', attach a copy of the exemption issued by the Internal Revenue Service which shows the section of the IRS code under which the organization is exempt. If an application for exempt status is pending with the IRS, you must check the 'NO' box.)
- [X] YES
- [ ] NO

9. POST OFFICE where authorization is requested and bulk mailings will be made (City, State, and ZIP+4 Code of Main Post Office)
NOTE: An authorization may NOT be requested at a station or branch of a post office.

Athens, OH 45701

10. If your organization has previously mailed at the special bulk rates, list the post offices where mailings were most recently deposited at these rates:

N/A

11. Has your organization had special bulk third-class rate mailing privileges denied or revoked? If you answered "YES", please list the post office (city and state) where an application was denied or an authorization was revoked:
- [ ] YES
- [X] NO

I certify that the statements made by me are true and complete. I understand that if this application for authorization is approved, it may only be used for our organization's mail at the post office specified above, and that we may not transfer or extend it to any other mailer. I further understand that if this application is approved, a postage refund for the difference between the regular and special bulk rates may be made for only those regular bulk third-class mailings entered at the post office identified above during the period this application is pending, provided the conditions set forth in Domestic Mail Manual 626.5, are met.

12. SIGNATURE OF APPLICANT	13. TITLE	14. DATE
Lewis E. Foster	*Manager*	*1/20/96*

Willful entry or submission of false, fictitious, or fraudulent statements or representations in this application may result in a fine up to $10,000 or imprisonment up to 5 years or both (18 U.S.C.1001)

PART 2 - POSTMASTER AT ORIGINATING OFFICE

THIS PART SHOULD BE COMPLETED AT THE TIME THE APPLICATION IS FILED WITH YOUR OFFICE

1. Signature of Postmaster (or designated representative)	2. Date application was filed with your office (Round Stamp)

PS Form 3624, April 1990   *(Page 1 of 3)*

Note: This form may be obtained at the post office where you wish to mail at special third-class bulk rates.

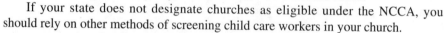

✓ copy of federal (and state) tax exemption determination letter; and

✓ copy of program literature, newsletters, bulletins, and any other promotional materials.

National Child Care Act

The National Child Care Act (NCCA) of 1993 became effective on December 20, 1993. Under the law, states may designate organizations that will be permitted to obtain a nationwide criminal records check on child care workers. If your state designates churches, this will enable you to quickly check on prospective child care workers by asking a state agency to conduct a criminal records check.

If your state does not designate churches as eligible under the NCCA, you should rely on other methods of screening child care workers in your church.

Occupational Safety and Health Act

The Occupational Safety and Health Act (OSHA) was designed to protect workers from unsafe conditions in the workplace. OSHA generally applies to all employers engaged in commerce who have employees.

States are permitted to adopt standards of their own. Some 23 jurisdictions now have an approved state plan in place.

Churches and other nonprofit employers are not specifically exempt from OSHA. A church must employ at least one person in "secular activities" to be covered. A person who performs or participates in religious services is not considered as being involved in secular activities.

Pregnancy Discrimination

Under the Pregnancy Discrimination Act of 1978, women affected by pregnancy, childbirth, or related medical conditions must be treated the same for all employment-related purposes as other workers who have a similar ability or inability to work.

Racial Discrimination

Form 5578, Annual Certification of Racial Nondiscrimination for a Private School Exempt from Federal Income Tax, must be filed by churches that operate, supervise, or control a private school (see page 46). The form must be filed by the 15th day of the fifth month following the end of the organization's fiscal year. For organizations that must file Form 990, there is no requirement to file Form 5578 since the information is included in Part V of Schedule A.

The "private school" definition includes preschools, primary, secondary, preparatory, or high schools, and colleges and universities, whether operated as a separate legal entity or an activity of a church.

Religious Discrimination

Title VII of the Civil Rights Act of 1964 prohibits discrimination in employment with respect to compensation, terms, conditions, or privileges of employment because of an individual's race, color, religion, sex, or national origin. The law applies to organizations with 15 or more employees.

Title VII does permit religious organizations to discriminate on the basis of religion for all positions. However, religious employers may not discriminate on the basis of race, sex, or national origin.

Sexual Harassment

Under Title VII of the Civil Rights Act of 1964 two types of conduct that can constitute unlawful sexual harassment are: harassment in which concrete employment benefits are conditioned upon acquiescence to sexual advances; and harassment that does not affect economic benefits but creates a hostile working environment.

While the standards in this area are not entirely clear, certain basic precautionary steps still serve to reduce the potential for employer liability:

✓ Establish a comprehensive policy against sexual harassment.

✓ Conduct supervisory training on a regular basis.

✓ Implement a meaningful complaint procedure taking into account both the perspective of the aggrieved employee and the rights of the alleged harasser.

✓ Investigate complaints promptly, thoroughly, and tactfully, and document the investigation.

✓ Take appropriate remedial action in cases of proven harassment.

State Taxes and Fees

Exemption from income, franchise, licensing fees, property, sales, use, or other taxes for qualified nonprofit organizations is allowed by many states. Each organization should contact the appropriate state authorities for information on these exemptions.

In a series of decisions in recent years, the Supreme Court has ruled that taxing churches is perfectly legal. A recent Supreme Court decision that permitted sales tax on a religious organization was so broad that many legal experts believe that other church property—like investment income, donation income, and real estate assets—can now be taxed if a state decides to do so.

Property taxes

Church property is generally exempt from property tax. Whether real estate of a nonprofit organization is exempt from property tax usually depends on its use and ownership. Many states restrict the exemption of church property to property used for worship. It is also important to note that not all religious organizations are churches. Call the office of the county tax assessor or collector to determine what property tax exemptions are available.

Parsonages are usually exempt from real estate tax. This is true though there may be several ministers on the staff of one church and therefore multiple parsonages. If the pastor owns the parsonage instead of the church, the parsonage is usually subject to property tax.

Church parking lots are usually exempt if properly recorded. It is often possible to obtain an exemption for vacant land. Property tax exemption of church camps and recreation facilities often comes under attack because of income that may be generated through their use. Property partially used for church use and partially leased to a third-party for-profit entity generally results in the proration of the tax exemption.

An initial (and perhaps annual) registration of the property with the proper state authorities is generally necessary to record exempt property. The initial purchase of real estate with notification of state authorities is usually not sufficient to exempt property from tax.

Sales taxes

There are presently four states with no sales tax law. In most states a nonprofit organization is exempt from sales tax as a purchaser of goods used in ministry. It is generally necessary to obtain recognition of sales tax exemption from the state revenue department. Some states will accept a Federal tax-exemption as sufficient for a state sales tax exemption.

Even if an organization is exempt from paying sales tax, purchases used for the private benefit of the organization's members or employees are not eligible for exemption.

When a nonprofit organization sells goods to others, a sales tax may or may not be applicable. There are some indications that states may begin a stricter enforcement of laws on the books allowing them to impose sales tax on sales by nonprofit organizations. Occasional dinners and sales of goods at bazaars are typically exempt from sales tax.

Sales by a nonprofit within the state where the nonprofit is located are sometimes taxable. Sales to customers located outside of the state, or interstate sales, may not be subject to sales tax. A 1992 Supreme Court case cleared the way for Congress to decide whether states can require organizations to collect state sales taxes on out-of-state mail order purchases. Until Congress acts, nonprofits may continue to ship publications and other taxable materials into states where they have no employees or other significant contacts without having to collect taxes.

When a nonprofit organization operates a conference or convention outside of its home state, it is often possible to obtain sales tax exemption for purchases made within the state where the meeting is held. Sales of products at the convention would generally be covered under sales tax laws without an approved exemption.

Use taxes

Besides sales taxes, many states also have use taxes. A use tax is imposed on the purchaser of a product or service. The use tax is designed to prevent avoidance of a local sales tax by buying property through the mail or in person in another state.

Churches and nonprofit organizations should determine whether they are subject to a use tax on various types of transactions.

Municipal service fees

Several states have recently proposed legislation to permit municipalities to impose "service fees" on property owned by tax-exempt organizations. Cities and counties would be authorized to collect a fee from tax-exempt property to pay for certain municipal services, typically fire and police protection, road construction and maintenance, and snow removal.

While the proposed legislation refers to the amounts to be collected as municipal service charges or fees, the assessments have the characteristics of property taxes. The fees are based on the value of property, not the services consumed. Property owners other than tax-exempt organizations would not be subject to the fees, yet would receive the same services.

Key Concepts

■ The nonprofit organization is subject to many workplace and other laws.

■ Some churches that operate day-care centers, elementary, or secondary schools are unaware that they are generally subject to the Fair Labor Standards Act.

■ The immigration control forms are required to be completed by all nonprofit organizations.

■ Many nonprofits are subject to the payment of sales or use taxes on purchases and the collection of sales taxes on sales.

# Citations

Internal Revenue Code (Code): The Code is the "tax law" as enacted and amended by Congress and is the highest authority in all tax matters.

Federal Tax Regulations (Reg.): These are regulations published by the Department of the Treasury (it oversees the IRS) that seek to explain the sometimes vague language of the Internal Revenue Code. The Regulations give definitions, examples, and more plain-language explanations.

Treasury Decisions (T.D.): These are instructions and interpretations issued by the IRS Commissioner with the approval of the Treasury Secretary.

Private letter rulings (Ltr. Rul.): A private letter ruling is issued by the IRS at the request of a taxpayer. It is requested for the purpose of getting the IRS's opinion on a specific transaction or issue facing a taxpayer. Although it cannot be used as precedent by anyone else, it usually reflects the IRS's current attitude toward a particular tax matter.

Revenue rulings (Rev. Rul.): A revenue ruling is issued by the IRS and is similar to a letter ruling, but it is not directed to a specific taxpayer. It is designed to give the public the IRS's opinion concerning how the tax law applies to some type of transaction, giving examples and explanations. It also gives the tax consequences of specific transactions.

Revenue procedures (Rev. Proc.): A revenue procedure is similar to a revenue ruling, but it gives more general guidelines and procedural information. It usually does not give tax consequences of specific transactions.

Technical Advice Memoranda (T.A.M.): These consist of written counsel or guidance furnished by the IRS National Office on the interpretation and proper application of the tax law to a specific set of facts.

Court cases: Taxpayer disputes with the IRS may end up in court if a taxpayer is issued an unfavorable ruling by the IRS and is hit with back taxes. There are two routes to take if the taxpayer wants to take the IRS to court. The taxpayer can elect not to pay the back taxes and petition the Tax Court to find that the proposed back tax assessment is incorrect. Or, the taxpayer can pay the disputed amount and sue the IRS for a refund in a district court. A taxpayer can appeal an adverse court decision in an appellate court, and if unsuccessful, can take it to the U.S. Supreme Court.

The IRS is bound by decisions of the Supreme Court for all taxpayers. It is bound by the decisions of the other courts only for the particular taxpayer involved and only for the years involved in the litigation.

Chapter 2, Tax-Exemption

- Criteria for qualifying as a church
  Spiritual Outreach Society v. Commissioner,
  T.C.M. 41 (1990)

  Joseph Edward Hardy v. Commissioner,
  T.C.M. 557 (1990)

- Exemption from filing Form 990 for certain missions organizations
  Treas. Reg. 1.6033-2(g)(1)(iv)

- General
  501(c)(3) organization established for religious purposes

  Treas. Reg. 1.511-2(a)(3)(ii)

- Private benefit/private inurement
  Treas. Reg. 1.501(a)-1(c)

  G.C.M. 37789

- Public Disclosure of Information Returns
  P.L. 100-203

- Tax-exempt status revoked for excessive UBI
  United Missionary Aviation, Inc. v.
  Commissioner, T.C.M. 566 (1990)

  Frazee v. Illinois Department of
  Employment, 57 U.S.L.W. 4397, 108 S. Ct.
  1514 (1989)

  Hernandez v. Commissioner, 819 F.2d 1212,
  109 S. Ct. 2136 (1989)

- Unrelated business income: general
  Code Sec. 511-13

- Unrelated business income: jeopardy to exempt status
  Ltr. Rul. 7849003

- Unrelated business income: organization's tour programs
  Ltr. Rul. 9027003

- Unrelated business income: affinity card programs
  Ltr. Rul. 9029047

  G.C.M. 39827, July 27, 1990

- Unrelated business income: mailing list profits
  Disabled American Veterans v. U.S., 94 TC
  No. 6 (1990)

  American Bar Endowment v. U.S., 477 U.S.
  105 (1986)

- Unrelated business income: other
  Hope School v. U.S., 612 F.2d 298, (7th Cir.
  1980)

  Rev. Rul. 64-182

Chapter 3, Compensation Planning

- Accountable expense reimbursement plans
  Treas. Reg. 1.62-2

  Treas. Reg. 1.274-5(e)

  Ltr. Rul. 9317003

- Medical expense reimbursement plans
  Code Sec. 105, 106

- Moving expense exclusion
  Code Sec. 132(g)

- Tax-sheltered annuities
  Code Sec. 403(b)

  Code Sec. 1402(a)

  Code Sec. 3121(a)(5)(D)

  Rev. Rul. 78-6

  Rev. Rul. 68-395

  Azad v. Commissioner, 388 F.2d 74(8th Cir.
  1968)

  Rev. Rul. 66-274

Chapter 4, Employer Reporting

- Classification of workers
  Rev. Proc. 85-18

  Sec. 530 of the Revenue Act of 1978

- Employee v. self-employed for income tax purposes
  Rev. Rul. 87-41

- Moving expenses
  Code Sec. 82

  Code Sec. 3401(a)(15)

- Noncash remuneration
  Code Sec. 3401(a)

- Payment of payroll taxes
  Triplett 115 B.R. 955 (N.D. Ill. 1990)

  Carter v. U.S., 717 F. Supp. 188 (S.D. N.Y. 1989)

- Per diem allowances
  Rev. Proc. 92-17

- Personal use of employer-provided auto
  Temp. Reg. Sec. 1.61-2T

  IRS Notice 91-41

- Rabbi trusts
  Rev. Proc. 92-64

- Reasonable compensation
  Truth Tabernacle, Inc. v. Commissioner of Internal Revenue, T.C.M. 451 (1989)

  Heritage Village Church and Missionary Fellowship, Inc., 92 B.R. 1000 (D.S.C. 1988)

- Taxability of benefits paid under cafeteria plans
  Ltr. Rul. 8839072

  Ltr. Rul. 8839085

- Temporary travel

Rev. Rul. 93-86

Comprehensive National Energy Policy Act of 1992

- Unemployment taxes
  Code Sec. 3309(b)

  St. Martin Evangelical Lutheran Church v. South Dakota, 451 U.S. 772 (1981)

  Employment Division v. Rogue Valley Youth for Christ, 770 F.2d 588 (Ore. 1989)

- Voluntary withholding for ministers
  Rev. Rul. 68-507

Chapter 5, Information Reporting Requirements

- Backup withholding
  Code Sec. 3406

- Cash reporting rules for charities
  T.D. 8373

  G.C.M. 39840

- Issuing Form 1099-MISCs
  Rev. Rul. 84-151

  Rev. Rul. 81-232

- Medical expense reimbursements to employees
  Ltr. Rul. 9112022

- Moving expense reporting
  IRS Announcement 94-2

- Nonresident alien payments
  Code Sec. 1441

  Code Sec. 7701(b)

- Volunteer fringe benefits
  Prop. Reg. 1.132-5(r)
- Withholding of tax on nonresident aliens
  Pub. 515

Chapter 7, Charitable Gifts

- Church school gifts

Rev. Rul. 83-104

- Contributions denied/indirectly related school
  Ltr. Rul. 9004030

- Contributions earmarked for a specific individual
  Ltr. Rul. 9405003

  IRS Announcement 92-128

  Ltr. Rul. 8752031

  Rev. Rul. 79-81

- Contributions sent to children who are missionaries
  Davis v. U.S., 110 S. Ct. 2014 (1990)

- Contribution of church bonds
  Rev. Rul. 58-262

- Contribution of promissory note
  Allen v. Commissioner, U.S. of Appeals, 89-70252, (9th Cir. 1991)

- Contributions designated for specific missionaries
  Hubert v. Commissioner, T.C.M. 482 (1993)

- Contribution of unreimbursed travel expenses
  Vahan Tafralian v. Commissioner, T.C.M. 33 (1991)

  Rev. Rul. 84-61

  Rev. Rul. 76-89

- Contributions of services
  Rev. Rul 67-236

  Grant v. Commissioner, 84 T.C.M. 809 (1986)

- Contributions to needy individuals
  Stjernholm v. Commissioner, T.C.M. 563 (1989)

  Ltr. Rul. 8752031

  Rev. Rul. 62-113

- Contributions that refer to donor's name
  IR-92-4

- Criteria used to determine deductibility of payments to private schools
  Rev. Rul. 83-104

  Rev. Rul. 79-99

- Deduction of out-of-pocket transportation expenses
  Treas. Reg. 1.170A-1(g)

  Rev. Rul. 76-89

- Deductibility of membership fees as contributions
  Rev. Rul. 70-47

  Rev. Rul. 68-432

- Deductibility of payments relating to fund-raising events
  Pub. 1391

  Rev. Rul. 74-348

- Deductibility of gifts to domestic organizations for foreign use
  Ltr. Rul. 9211002

  Ltr. Rul. 9131052

  Ltr. Rul. 9129040

  Rev. Rul. 75-65

  Rev. Rul. 63-252

- Determining the value of donated property
  IRS Pub. 561

  Rochin v. Commissioner, T.C.M. 262 (1992)

- Gifts of inventory
  Code Sec. 170(e)

  Reg. 1.161-1

  Reg. 1.170A-1(c)(2), (3), (4)

Reg. 1.170A-4A(c)(3)

Rev. Rul. 85-8, superseding

- Gifts of life insurance
  Ltr. Rul. 9147040

  Ltr. Rul. 9110016

- Incentives and premiums
  IRS. Pub. 1391

  Rev. Proc. 92-102

  Rev. Proc. 92-58

  Rev. Proc. 92-49

  Rev. Proc. 90-64

  Rev. Proc. 90-12

  Rev. Proc. 90-7

- Payments in connection with use of ministry services
  Rev. Rul. 76-232

- Payments to a retirement home
  T.A.M. 9423001

  U.S. v. American Bar Endowment, 477 U.S.105 (S. Ct. 1986)

  Rev. Rul. 72-506

  Rev. Rul. 67-246

- Scholarship gifts
  Ltr. Rul. 9338014

  Rev. Rul. 83-104

  Rev. Rul. 62-113

- Substantiation rules
  Omnibus Budget Reconciliation Act of 1993

- Travel tours
  Ltr. Rul. 9027003

- Unitrusts
  IRS Notice 94-78

Chapter 9, Laws for Nonprofits

- Americans With Disabilities Act
  Public Law 101-336, 42 U.S.C. 12101 et sec.

- Child care and Development Block Grant Act of 1990, 42 U.S.C. 9801

- Equal Pay Act
  EEOC v. First Baptist Church of Mishawaka, N.D. Ind., S91-179M (1991)

  EEOC v. First Baptist Church N.D. Ind., S89-338 (1990)

- Fair Labor Standards Act
  DeArment v. Harvey, No. 90-2346, (8th Cir. 1991)

  U.S. Department of Labor v. Shenandoah Baptist Church, 899 F.2d 1389 (4th Cir.) cert. denied, 111 S. Ct. 131 (1990)

- Local sales taxes
  Thayer v. South Carolina Tax Commission, 413 S.E. 2d 810 (S.C. 1992)

  Quill Corp. v. North Dakota, S. Ct. No. 91-194

  Jimmy Swaggart Ministries v. Board of Equalization of California, 110 S. Ct. 688 (1990)

- Political activity
  Treas. Reg. 1.501(c)(3)-1(c)(1)(iii)

  IR-92-57

- Property taxes
  Trinity Episcopal Church v. County of Sherburne, 1991 WL 95745 (Minn. Tax 1991)

Index

A

Abatements, *86*
Abuse insurance, *168*
Accountability to donors, *20*
Accountable expense reimbursement plans, *61-63*
Accounting method,
    Change in methods, *42*
    Methods, *116-17*
Accounting records, *115-18*
Accrual method of accounting, *116*
Age discrimination, *178*
Aliens, nonresident, *93*
Allowances, *60*
Americans With Disabilities Act, *178-79*
Annual returns, *41*
Annuitants,
    Payments to, *92-93*
Annuity trust, *9-10, 132-33*
Application for recognition of tax-exempt status, *29, 31-32*
Assignment of ministers, *69-70*
Auctions, *152-53*
Audits, *124-28*
Autos, *(see vehicles)*

B

Backup withholding, *91*
Balance sheet, *120, 123*
Bank,
    Deposits, *101-2, 107*
    Reconciliation, *114*
Bargain sale, *132*
Benevolence fund, *161-62*
Board,
    Compensation of, *19-20*
    Conflicts of interest, *16-19*
    Governance, *14*
    Resolutions, *(see resolutions)*
    Selecting, *16*
Budgeting, *16, 99-100*
Bulk mailing, *182, 184-85*

C

Cafeteria plans, *173-74*
Canadian Goods and Services Tax, *179*
Cash,
    Disbursements, *107-13*
    Method of accounting, *116-17*
    Receipt of large amounts, *90*
    Receipts, *100-6*
CBBB, *14*

Charitable contributions,
    Annuity trust, *132-33*
    Auctions, *152-53*
    Bargain sale, *132*
    Benevolence fund, *161-62*
    Bonds, *136*
    Foreign use, *134-35*
    Gift annuity, *92-93, 132*
    Gifts-in-kind, *23, 162-63, 164*
    Incentives/premiums, *2, 22, 149, 152*
    Insurance, *132, 133*
    Inventory, *136*
    Lead trust, *133*
    Membership fees, *158*
    Missionaries, *162*
    Needy individuals, *161-62*
    Nondeductible, *134-35*
    Overfunding of projects, *21, 165-66*
    Partial interest, *136-37*
    Percentage limitations, *130-31*
    Pledges, *157*
    Pooled income fund, *133*
    Private schools, *158-59*
    Property, *132, 136, 137-42*
    Qualified donees, *130*
    Quid pro quo disclosures, *148-56*
    Receipting, *142-156*
    Refunding, *165-66*
    Reporting requirements, *137-42*
    Restricted, *21, 165*
    Retirement homes, *162*
    Securities, *131-32, 135-36*
    Services, *134*
    Solicitation laws, *179*
    Substantiation, *7-8, 142-58*
    Supporting specific individuals, *159-61*
    Tax deductible, *131-33*
    Tours, *165*
    Travel expense, *163*
    Unitrust, *133*
    Volunteers, *163, 164*
Chart of accounts, *118, 119*
Child care assistance plan, *55*
Child care facilities, *179*
Churches,
    Exempt from FICA, *71*
    Exempt from filing Form 990, *29*
    IRS Tax Guide, *5-6*
    Tax-exempt status, *26-27, 29, 31-32*
Church bonds, *136*
Club dues, *5*
COBRA, *168*

Common-law rules, *66-68*
Compensation, *47-64*
    Board, *19-20*
    Gift planners, *23*
    Reasonable, *47*
    Review, *15-16*
Conflicts of interest, *16-20, 23*
Consumer's Price Index, *47*
Counting money, *100, 102-3*
Crime insurance, *169*

D

Dental insurance, *169*
Dependent care assistance plan, *55*
Depreciation, *118*
Determination letter request, *31*
Director's and officer's liability insurance, *169-70*
Disabilities law, *178-79*
Disability insurance, *170*
Discrimination,
    Age, *178*
    Disabilities, *178-79*
    Fringe benefits, *60-61*
    Immigration, *182, 183*
    Pay, *180*
    Pregnancy, *185*
    Racial, *185-86*
    Religious, *186*
    Sexual, *186*
Donor,
    Communication, *20-21*
    Intent, *21*
    Reporting to, *7-8, 22-23, 142-58*
Dues, club, *5*

E

Earmarked gifts, *159-62*
ECFA, *14*
EFMA, *14*
EFICOM, *14*
Employee vs. independent contractor,
    Classification of,
        Ministers, *69-70*
        Workers, *65-68*
    Common law rules, *66-68*
Employer identification number, *29, 30, 88-89*
Employer-provided vehicles, *51-53*
Environmental law, *180*
Equal pay, *180*
Evangelists, *49*

F

Fair Labor Standards Act, *180-81*
Federal income tax, *71-73*
Federal unemployment tax, *85-86*

FICA, *70-71*
Finances,
    Accounting records, *115-18*
    Bank deposits, *102. 107*
    Budgeting, *16, 99-100*
    Counting money, *100, 102-3*
    Disbursements, *107-13*
    Petty cash, *109-10*
    Receipts, *100-6*
    Reports, *15, 118-24*
Financial accountability, 13-24
Financial advice, *24*
Financial reports, *15, 118-24*
Fiscal year change, *43*
Flexible benefits plan, *173-74*
Forms (explained and/or reproduced)
    I-9, *182, 183*
    SS-4, *29, 30*
    W-2, *78-83*
    W-2c, *83, 84*
    W-3, *83, 84*
    W-3c, *85*
    W-4, *71-73*
    W-4P, *92-93*
    W-5, *72, 73*
    W-9, *88-89*
    843, *86*
    940, *85-86*
    941, *75, 76*
    941c, *75, 77*
    990, *34, 41*
    990-EZ, *41*
    990-T, *36, 41*
    1023, *29, 30-32*
    1042, *93*
    1042-S, *93*
    1096, *87, 88*
    1098, *89*
    1099-INT, *91-92*
    1099-MISC, *93-95*
    1099-R, *92*
    1099-S, *90*
    1120, *41*
    1128, *43*
    3115, *42*
    3624, *182, 184-85*
    4782, *96*
    5500, *41, 57*
    5578, *43, 46*
    8109, *74*
    8109-B, *74*
    8282, *43, 137, 141-42*
    8283, *137-40, 142*
    8300, *90*
    8717, *43*

8718, *43*
Fringe benefits,
    Dependent care, *55*
    Medical expense reimbursement, *56-57*
    Social security tax reimbursement, *58*
Fund accounting, *117*
Fund-raisers,
    Compensation, *23*

G

General ledger, *106, 113, 119*
General liability insurance, *170*
Gift annuity, *4-5, 92-93, 132*
Gift planners, *23*
Gifts to employees, *60*
Gifts-in-kind, *23, 162-63, 164*
Group exemption, *29, 32*
Group term life insurance, *171*

H

Health insurance, *171-74*
Highly compensated employees, *61*
Housing,
    Allowance, *48-51*
    Resolutions, *49*

I

IFMA, *14*
Immigration control, *182, 183*
Incentives, *22, 149, 152*
Incorporation, *28*
Independent contractors, *66-68*
Insurance,
    Abuse or molestation, *168*
    Automobile, *168*
    COBRA, *168*
    Crime, *169*
    Dental, *169*
    Director's and officer's liability, *169-70*
    Disability, *170*
    Flexible benefit, *173-74*
    Health, *171-74*
    Key employee, *174*
    Liability, *170*
    Life, *132, 171*
    Long-term care, *174*
    Medical, *171-74*
    Professional liability, *174*
    Property, *174-75*
    Travel and accident, *175*
    Umbrella, *175*
    Workers' Compensation, *175-76*
Interest,
    Paid, *91-92*
    Received, *89*

Inurement *(see private inurement)*
Inventory, *136*

K

Key employee insurance, *174*

L

Lead trust, *133*
Lease value, autos, *52-53*
Life insurance, *132, 171*
Loans to employees, *57-58*
Lodging *(see housing)*
Long-term care insurance, *174*

M

Magnetic media reporting, *87*
Mailing rates, *182, 184-85*
Medical insurance plans,
    Flexible benefits, *173-74*
    Self-funded, *172*
Medical expense reimbursement plan, *56-57*
Membership fees, *158*
Minimum wage, *180-81*
Ministers,
    Assignment, *69-70*
    Classification, *69-70*
    Housing allowance, *48-51*
    Special tax provisions, *68*
Missionaries, gifts designated for, *162*
Molestation insurance, *168*
Mortgage, interest received, *89*
Moving expenses, *59-60, 95-97*
Municipal service fees, *188*

N

National Child Care Act, *185*
NCIB, *14*
Nonaccountable expense-reimbursement plans, *63*
Nondiscrimination rules, *60-61*
Nonresident aliens, *93*

O

Occupational Safety and Health Act, *185*
Offering envelopes, *102*
Organizational change, *42*
Overfunding of projects, *21, 165-66*
Overtime,
    Payment of, *180-81*

P

Payroll taxes,
    Depositing withheld taxes, *73-74*
    Filing annual returns, *78-86*
    Filing quarterly returns, *74-78*
    Personal liability, *73*
    Unemployment taxes, *85-86*

Withholding, *70-73*
Per diem allowance, *64*
Petty cash, *109-10*
Political activity, *2, 44-45, 162*
Pooled income fund, *133*
Pregnancy discrimination, *185*
Premiums, *(see incentives)*
Private benefit/inurement, *39-41*
Private schools, *158-59*
Professional liability insurance, *174*
Property insurance, *174-75*
Property taxes, *187*
Property transferred to employees, *59*
Public inspection of information returns, *41-42*

Q

Quid pro quo disclosures, *148-56*

R

Racial discrimination, *185-86*
Real estate, *90, 132, 137-42*
Reasonable compensation, *47*
Refunds, abatements, *86*
Reimbursement,
    Expenses, *61-64*
    Social security tax, *58*
Related party transactions, *16-19*
Religious purposes, *26-27*
Religious discrimination, *186*
Resolutions,
    Accountable expense reimbursement, *62*
    Assignment of a minister, *69*
    Benevolence fund, *161*
    Conflict of interest, *17-18*
    Dependent care assistance plan, *55*
    Housing allowance, *49*
    Medical expense reimbursement plan, *57*
    Tax-shelter annuity agreement, *54*
Restricted contributions, *21, 23, 159-62, 165*
Retirement home payments, *162*
Royalties,
    Paid to employees or directors, *23*
    Reporting of payments, *93-95*

S

Sales tax, *187-88*
Securities, *131-32, 135-36*
Self-employment tax, *58, 73*
Sexual harassment, *186*
Social security tax, FICA, *7, 70-71*
Social security tax reimbursement, *58*
Specified contributions *(see restricted contributions)*
Spousal/children travel, *3-4*
Start-up of a nonprofit, *28-32*
State filing requirements, *43-44*

Statement of activity, *120, 121-22*
Statement of financial position, *120, 123*

T

Taxes, state,
    Exemption, *10-12, 186-87*
    Municipal service fees, *188*
    Property, *10-12, 187*
    Sales, *12, 187-88*
    Use, *10, 12, 188*
Tax-exempt status,
    Advantages, *27-28*
    Application, *29-32*
    Churches, *26-27, 29, 31-32*
    Granting, *31-32*
    Group, *29, 32*
    Limitations, *28*
Taxpayer identification number, *29, 30, 88-89*
Tax-sheltered annuities, *54*
Token limitations, *2, 22, 149, 152*
Travel and accident insurance, *175*
Travel expense,
    Spousal/children, *3-4*
Tours, *163, 164*

U

Umbrella liability insurance, *175*
Unitrust, *9-10, 133*
Unrelated business income,
    Debt-financed income, *37*
    Exceptions, *37-38*
    General, *32-39*
    Rental income, *35, 37*
    Reporting and filing requirements, *32-33*
    Tax liability, *38*
Unemployment taxes, *85-86*
Unreasonable compensation, *47*
Use tax, *10-12, 188*

V

Vehicles,
    Expense substantiation, *61-64*
    Insurance, *168*
    Personal use of employer-provided, *51-53*
Voluntary income tax withholding, *71*
Volunteers, *8, 95, 157, 164*

W

Withholding, *70-73*
Worker classification, *65-70*
Workers' Compensation, *175-76*

10 Biggest Tax Mistakes Made By Churches And Nonprofit Organizations

- -

1. Not setting up a accountable expense reimbursement plan for employees (receiving Forms W-2). Chapter 6.

2. Providing or adjusting housing allowances for ministers on a retroactive basis. Chapter 6.

3. Improperly classifying employees as self-employed. Chapter 7.

4. Failure to report taxable fringe benefits paid for self-employed workers. Chapter 7.

5. Deducting FICA tax from the salary of qualified ministers. Chapter 7.

6. Not reporting taxable fringe benefits, reimbursements for moving expenses, and social security as additional compensation to employees. Chapter 7.

7. Failing to file Forms W-2 and 1099-MISC for workers. Chapters 7 & 8.

8. Providing receipts for the donation of services, rent-free use of property and valuing noncash gifts. Receipting contributions designated for individuals without proper control by the board of the donee organization. Chapter 9.

9. Not providing Workers' Compensation coverage where required by law and not coordinating Workers' Compensation with health insurance coverages. Chapter 9.

10. Failure to comply with the Fair Labor Standards Act for church-operated schools, including day-cares, pre-school, elementary and secondary. Chapter 11.